An Approach to the Theory
of Income Distribution

An Approach to the Theory of Income Distribution

SIDNEY WEINTRAUB

Professor of Economics
University of Pennsylvania

CHILTON COMPANY

Publishers   *Philadelphia*

In Memory

Hal (1923–1954)

COE (Bingen), AUS (1942–1946)
Ph.D. (Harvard, 1952)
Assistant Professor of Mathematics,
Tufts College (1953–1954)

Preface

In the following pages I have tried to bring the theory of distribution abreast of modern knowledge of the theory of the firm and the current macroeconomic theory of income and employment determination. To do so has at times involved a restatement of the latter theory in a fashion which, though not an uncommon explanation, is still not the most usual version; ordinarily, the theory is expressed primarily in terms of real output, of production corrected for price-level movements. Yet for the theory of wages, interest, and profits I think that there are distinct advantages in an approach which at all times runs in money terms.

While there has been rapid development over the last twenty-five years in the theory of the firm, and great strides in the theory of income determination in the twenty-odd years since Keynes wrote, the theory of distribution, the other head of the traditional study of value and distribution, has languished. It is not too inaccurate to say that, apart from the theory of interest, the usual presentation is not vastly different from the form it achieved at the hands of Marshall. As a result, dissatisfaction with it, compared with the other areas of analysis and their advances over the last generation, is widespread. Its development has been impeded by the gulf that has appeared to separate income determination and varying activity levels from the Marshallian-type studies predicated in substantial measure on the hypothesis of a given income level. The following pages attempt to indicate one way of crossing this divide. It may serve some purpose if I indicate wherein, in my view, this volume departs from the more usual treatment. Even if individual pieces are not wholly new, it may be that the sum total accomplishes a synthesis which is somewhat more novel. Enumerating the specific ideas, almost in reverse order from the manner in which they are developed, the following points may be noted:

1. Profits are described as a result not only of uncertainty but also of the existence of contracts; the analysis builds on the work of Knight and parallels a more recent contribution by Weston.

Recognition of the part played by contracts is, of course, not new, but it is amazing to learn how often this simple idea has been overlooked and not even mentioned by competent writers.

2. While the remarks on rent are fairly conventional, there is a more consistent emphasis on the difference between rent as an imputed income, an assigned ex post economic value, as against rent payments in fact—the fixed incomes established by negotiation and inscribed in contracts.

3. Though I have embraced a liquidity-preference theory of interest for what seem to me to be good reasons, I think my treatment brings the analysis closer to the facts through two new aspects: a redefinition of the money concept and the inclusion of commercial-bank demand into the liquidity function. Unless these are introduced, the liquidity-preference theory cannot handle certain commonplace, and important, phenomena. Similar modifications are called for in a loanable funds approach, though an exposition of how this might be accomplished is not offered here.

4. Chapter 6 shows how a theory of money wages may be constructed. I think it is well to focus attention once again on this topic so that economists can handle the problem of wage determination systematically and draw the appropriate implications of market wage changes and collective-bargaining agreements. As the latter are always in money terms, it is preferable, I think, to use techniques which keep the monetary aspects always in the foreground rather than, as older analysis tended to do, stress the determination of real wages. I have also attempted to appraise the effects of particular wage changes when the heterogeneity of the labor supply is recognized; this topic has rarely been worked out and would lend itself to more extended study.

5. Relations between distribution and income determination are discussed; I have shied away from those views which stress that the division of income is a phenomenon of aggregate demand rather than productivity. In my view, this is an incomplete version of the economic process and omits the vital part played by the entrepreneur and the firm in organizing the use of resources. If demand alone determines distribution, productivity phenomena are irrelevant. And yet, down at the level of the firm where factors are hired and the income payments are made, so that the distributive pattern is shaped, productivity does enter into the scheme. Though more might be done by way of reconciling the different views on

this subject, I have indicated my own attitude at the close of Chapter 5.

6. The relation of productivity and monopoly in income division occupies most of Chapters 3 and 4. Several reasonably new propositions emerge from this study, not least being the importance of the ratio of marginal to average product in determining labor's *relative* share. In a way, these chapters go back to the classical problem, reiterated but rarely analyzed, of the forces determining relative shares rather than the real wage or the factor's income. These pages show how it is possible to aggregate phenomena important at the firm's level into meaningful totals applicable to the entire economy, the aggregation of firms.

7. Chapter 2 contains the statement of the theory of income determination on which the analysis is built, with an attempt to erect a firm microeconomic foundation for the macroeconomic concepts. Analysis in real terms using "the 45-degree line" and the aggregate demand "cross" have not been very careful in spelling out the price-level implications of nonequilibrium output points; this is but one advantage of the approach suggested. As a by-product, the concept of "forced savings," which *is* meaningful in these times of inflation, has been restored even in a Keynesian-type analysis.

These, then, are the ideas I have sought to develop, with the aim of stimulating argument and eliciting alternate statements of distribution theory compatible with mid-century ideas in other areas of economic conjecture. I should like to acknowledge with thanks the encouragement of Professors Almarin Phillips, Irving Kravis, and Raymond T. Bowman, all members of the faculty of the University of Pennsylvania over the period during which this book was written. Dr. Phillips particularly was subjected to a reading of the manuscript at a very early stage; he has my apologies and my warm gratitude. It ought to be unnecessary to add that responsibility is mine alone.

My wife Sheila has helped in manifold ways in this partnership that began many years ago to absorb some of her energies and test her patience. Too, I should like to mention the aid given by my late brother on what was for me a difficult hurdle in the chapter on wage theory. Though their aid goes deep and I am keenly aware of their contribution, the customary expression of appreciation must always appear perfunctory.

SIDNEY WEINTRAUB

Contents

ix

Chapter 1

Introduction:
Marginal-Productivity Theory

The position taken throughout this work is that the theory of income distribution cannot be separated from a theory of income determination. Rather than developing and defending this proposition immediately, it will be useful to examine the main elements of what is still the dominant distribution theory; namely, the marginal-productivity doctrine.[1] This will serve a dual purpose, in providing a basis for criticism along with a more constructive use in that many of its features inevitably will have to be incorporated in any subsequent elaboration of distribution theory. By and large, only by an examination of the existing theory and its shortcomings will we be able to see the reason for, and the way out, toward a new and reconstructed set of concepts.

MARGINAL-PRODUCTIVITY THEORY

Existing distribution theory, despite all its refinements, has come to be almost purely a theory of factor prices applicable in principle to all agents, with the tone modulated according to short- or long-run accents and the functional responsiveness of factors to their market prices. We shall examine briefly the "own-product" formulation, and thereafter consider the firm, industry, and economy demand and supply of factors in an exchange economy. After this is completed, a short criticism of the doctrine will be offered.

---

[1] Opening a recent article, William Fellner declares: "By contemporary distribution theory we presumably mean a qualified marginal productivity theory; that is to say, a combination of the marginal productivity theory with other analytical elements." See his "Significance and Limitations of Contemporary Distribution Theory," Proceedings, *American Economic Association* (May 1953), p. 484.

THE "OWN-PRODUCT" FORMULATION. The "own-product" approach of W. S. Jevons and J. B. Clark is the most direct exposition of the marginal-productivity theory, devoid as it is of exchange-process subtleties. For simplicity, assume only two factors, and, as is customary, suppose that labor is the variable agent while land is fixed in amount. In Fig. 1, the M_L-curve traces out the course of the marginal product of labor in terms of "bushels" of output (measured vertically) as more units of variable labor (measured

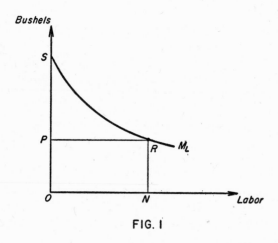

FIG. I

horizontally) are applied to the fixed land expanse. If ON labor is to be engaged—if this represents all of the labor force—then the wage per employee must settle at NR "bushels." The total wage bill amounts to $OPRN$, with the output (and income) total being $OSRN$ and with SPR constituting "rent." Further, the diagram also purports to show that, if labor stipulates a given wage, the level of employment is determined automatically.[2] For example, if OP denotes the rate of pay on which labor is insistent, then ON men would be hired; from analysis of this nature it was commonly deduced that unemployment results from labor's pertinacity in pressing for exorbitant wage scales. The argument frequently was extended to the entire economic system, and in some versions the economy was envisioned as a huge farm, hiring labor on the allotted

[2] The prototype of this diagram goes back to W. S. Jevons, *The Theory of Political Economy* (London, Macmillan, 1888, 3rd ed.), p. 219.

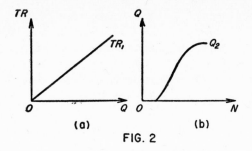

FIG. 2

land area so that aggregate output and income were limited by the labor supply and its productivity.

Manifestly, the transition from a firm (or farm) to the economy in a multi-commodity exchange system using money requires a host of supporting assumptions and hypotheses. It will be our task to show this in subsequent analyses. Yet one truth of this simpler "own-product" approach will remain; namely, that if the marginal product of a factor diminishes, as is true of labor in Fig. 1, then the further hire of the factor must mean a fall in its real income.

THE FIRM AND THE LABOR-DEMAND FUNCTION: PURE COMPETITION. Let us examine now the modern theory of distribution—or factor prices—in its most rigid form, as it is built up from the theory of the firm under pure competition and with all factors of production being fixed while only one factor is variable.

Under pure competition, where the firm is confronted with an externally determined product price, P, its total revenue, TR, function will appear as TR_1 in Fig. 2. Implicit is a product price of, say, P_1. If product price rose to $P_2 > P_1$, the TR-curve would swing leftward. Of course, $TR = PQ$, where Q (quantity) denotes the output volume and P is the price-parameter, which is constant to the firm under pure competition so that the firm's choice extends only to its output volume, Q.

To ascertain how much of sales proceeds are available to compensate any one factor, payments to the other factors would have to be deducted from TR at each output amount, and the sum so obtained would be linked to the amount of factor hire: the resulting function is termed the total *net* revenue-product function, $TNRP$.[3]

---

[3] Analytically, while $TR = PQ = f(Q)$, then $TNRP = PNA - F = \phi(N)$, where N refers to the amount of the variable factor and A is its average product

The relations between Q and N are given in a total-product curve as in Fig. 2 (b). It is the Q-curve that provides the connecting link between revenue and revenue-product conceptions.

Just as average revenue is obtained by dividing TR/Q, the average net revenue-product curve is derived from $TNRP/N$. Thus:

$$ANRP = PA - \frac{F}{N} \tag{1}$$

As F/N approaches zero as N expands and A decreases, this leads $ANRP$ to fall continuously.[4] But if A, the average product of labor, mounts, the average revenue-product curve may rise: this is most likely when "increasing physical returns" (a rising marginal physical product of labor) prevails.

Marginal revenue, MR—the change in sales proceeds as output increases—is denoted by the slope of TR. Marginal revenue *product*, MRP, refers to the slope of $TNRP$ or the change in revenue product as a result of the hire of another unit of the variable factor.[5] Under pure competition, with product price constant, then $MRP = P \cdot MP$, where MP refers to the marginal physical product. Thus, a marginal revenue-product curve can rise under pure competition only if the marginal product of the variable factor is rising. Also, as $MRP = P \cdot MP$ under pure competition, then the MRP-function is identical with the marginal physical-product curve (such as that shown in Fig. 1), except that the marginal physical products are corrected by the price scalar, P: if $P = \$1$, the identity is

---

$(A = Q/N)$, while F denotes the total sum of fixed costs. Clearly, if $F = O$ and $N = Q$, then $TR = TNRP$. Otherwise, if $F > O$ and $N > Q$, the effect is to flatten $TNRP$ relative to TR.

[4] When the deduction of F/N is not made, the reference is to the average *gross* revenue-product function. For causal analysis it is the net revenue-product function that matters, so that this distinction will not be made hereafter.

[5] Thus:

$$MR \equiv \frac{d(TR)}{dQ} = P + Q\frac{dP}{dQ} \tag{2}$$

$$MRP = \frac{d(TRP)}{dN} = \left(P + Q\frac{dP}{dQ}\right)\frac{dQ}{dN} = MR \cdot MP \tag{3}$$

where dQ/dN ($= MP$) denotes the marginal product of labor, and dP/dQ, the change in product price as sales increase.

complete.[6] For the competitive case we will often find it convenient to describe MRP as the marginal *value* product.

An ARP- and MRP-curve set appears in Fig. 3. So long as the marginal physical product exceeds the average product, then $MRP > ARP$. Even when the two are equal, $MRP > ARP$ in view of the presence of F/N; they intersect when $MP < AP$ in amount F/N.

Once the MRP-function is derived, we are possessed simultaneously of the demand curve for the variable factor: *the firm's*

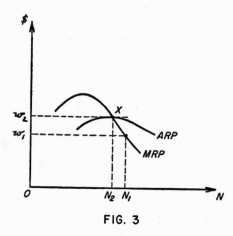

FIG. 3

factor-demand curve is simply MRP. Given the price of the factor, say the wage, w, of labor, from the conditions of profit maximization, it is well known that this requires, in equilibrium, $w = MRP \leqq ARP$. Whenever $w \leqq MRP$, net proceeds can be increased by hiring more labor ($w < MRP$) or releasing some labor ($w > MRP$), with their equality required as a necessary condition for profit maximization. In Fig. 3 this occurs at labor hire ON_1 when the money wage is w_1. According to the diagram, the firm could stay in business and produce output only if the wage were w_2, or less. For at a wage in excess of w_2 (and $ARP < MRP$), hiring factors in amount necessary to equate $w = MRP$ would entail total factor payments in excess of the total revenue product so that output activity could be conducted only at a loss.[7] Only as the wage fell

[6] The same would not hold true for ARP unless $F = O$.
[7] As wage payments equal wN ($= N \cdot MRP$), and as $TRP = N \cdot ARP$, then when $MRP > ARP$ the factor outlays would exceed available revenues.

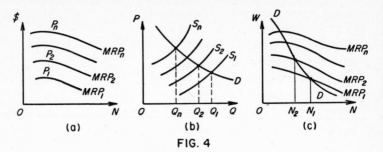

FIG. 4

would profits appear. Hence it is only the course of MRP *after* the intersection with ARP (denoted by the X in Fig. 3) that describes the firm's demand curve for labor.

Summarizing, to derive the firm's demand curve for a variable factor under pure competition: (1) the volume of fixed factors and their compensation must be stipulated, (2) the productivity of the factor, or its total, average, and marginal-product functions must be known, (3) the price of the product must be given. Pondering the implications of (3), it seems that, whenever the price of the product changes, the firm's demand curve for the factor will change. There is, then, a family of factor-demand curves for the firm under pure competition, each attached to a different product price. This is shown in Fig. 4 (a), where $P_1 < P_2 < \cdots < P_n$.

THE INDUSTRY-DEMAND CURVE FOR A FACTOR. Deriving the industry-demand curve for a factor under pure competition is only slightly more intricate. Given the product-demand curve, as D in Fig. 4 (b), at each wage rate the product-supply curve is determinate in that in pursuit of maximum profits each firm will equate price, P, to marginal cost, C'.[8] Thus:

$$P = C' \equiv \frac{w}{MP} \tag{4}$$

Given the wage, w, and the marginal physical-product curves, the requisite amount of labor hire for the firm and, by extension, for every firm, can be extracted at each given product price, P. Varying P along the course of the product-supply curve, while holding w constant, the additional output and labor hire necessary for profit maximization in each firm can be obtained. Given the product-

[8] See for example my *Price Theory* (New York, Pitman, 1949), pp. 109–114.

demand curve, the wage rate, and factor productivity, then output and factor hire will be pushed to such a level as to equate product supply and demand. The implicit labor hire at this equilibrium output is thus also the equilibrium labor demand of the industry *at the given wage*. Varying the wage rate, the full industry product-supply curve moves parametrically, with a higher money wage, from w_1 to w_2, say, lifting the product-supply curve from S_1 to S_2 in Fig. 4 (b). Higher money wages thus entail a lessened labor-demand quantity so long as the product-demand curve slopes downward to the right.

Returning to the family of MRP-curves for the firm, one related to each product price, given the product price and the wage rate, the relevant factor-demand quantity can be extracted from the appropriate curve. Ultimately, therefore, the firm's factor-demand curve is thus an effective cross-cut curve, such as DD in Fig. 4 (c). To illustrate: at a wage of w_2, in view of industry supply and demand phenomena, the product price will be P_2, so that MRP_2 will be the pertinent curve of the family; labor hire will be ON_2. At a wage of w_1, product price will be P_1 and MRP_1 will be revealed as the pertinent curve; labor hire will go to ON_1. Connecting the latter co-ordinates on the respective MRP-curves, the firm's "demand path" will be elicited.

While for our immediate purposes there is no need to pursue this analysis further, it becomes clear that, for deriving the industry-demand curve for a variable factor, then (1) the quantity of fixed factors used in each firm must be specified, (2) the productivity (A- and M-functions) of the variable factor in each firm must be known, (3) the product-demand curve must be posited. Hypothesis (3) is really a compound supposition, for product-demand curves themselves generally are drawn on the premise of (1) given tastes of the consuming body, (2) given prices of other goods, (3) given (money? real?) income of the community, (4) given numbers of income recipients (or households) in the economy. The third hypothesis, we shall argue, must occasion much soul-searching, for it cannot be applied without a precise statement of the underlying theory of income determination.

THE MARKET-DEMAND CURVE FOR A FACTOR. Although the climb from the theory of the firm's demand for a factor to the theory of the industry's factor demand led to the new complication by way of the product-demand curve, curiously enough in moving from the industry to the economy new difficulties have, as a rule, seldom been admitted.[9] Typically, all that is done is to aver that in each industry at each wage (or factor price), the factor-demand quantity is determinate. Summating these, the market-demand quantity of the factor is derived. Varying the wage, the new factor-demand quantity appears, growing larger in the usual case as the wage level falls.

Implicit, then, is the apparent belief that demand curves for each industry can be drawn simultaneously despite the usual acknowledgment (in product-price theory) that each such demand curve rests on the premise of a given price configuration through the economy. Further, it entails the even more anachronistic view that income in the community is constant regardless of the price paid to the particular factor, even one so important as labor: this involves the preconception that product-demand curves remain rigid despite variations of factor prices, as if interdependence between demand and supply phenomena is prima facie implausible—despite its recognition in economic phenomena since the earliest days and its embodiment in Say's Law.

THE FACTOR-DEMAND CURVE: MONOPOLY. Under monopoly hypotheses, the derivation of a factor-demand curve, in the one variable input case, is simpler than even under pure competition; the reason is that there is no separation of firm and industry, so that the principle of profit maximization can be applied directly to the product-demand curve. Let us consider the monopoly analysis.

Recalling the definitions of ARP and MRP, these will now alter not only because A and M ($= MP$) change, signifying movements in physical products, but also because product price changes with every output and sales increase. If A is already falling, then ARP is given a fresh shove downward by the concomitant fall in product price. If M is decreasing, MRP likewise is pressed even lower because of the inroads of lower price phenomena. Thus in the area

---

[9] An examination of so-called elementary, intermediate, and advanced textbooks will confirm this. Generally, the market-demand curve for a factor is brushed off in a few sentences even in the rare instances where the industry-demand curve has been derived with reasonable rigor. This is particularly curious and unfathomable considering the remarks and the influence of Keynes. See Chapter 6.

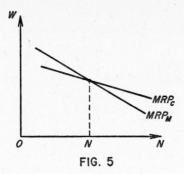

FIG. 5

where $A > M$, the monopoly MRP-curve falls faster than one drawn on a constant product-price hypothesis, so that the effect of monopoly is to pinch-in the ARP- and MRP-curves, to limit their rise in the left extremity where M and A are mounting, and to force them down more rapidly in the region beyond which M starts to decline.[10]

Given the monopoly firm's MRP-curve, particularly the portion to the right of the intersection with ARP, and summating the labor hire by each monopoly firm at each wage (when equated to MRP), the market factor-demand function is held to be at hand. As before, it thus hinges at a minimum on given factor-productivity and product-demand hypotheses.

THE N-VARIABLE-FACTOR CASE. Although the marginal-productivity theory is developed most fully for the one variable-factor case, where all other agents are held constant in amount, through the use of constant product curves and the expansion path it is possible to

[10] To compare the descent of MRP under competition with that under monopoly, it is necessary to specify what we mean by a competitive price for a monopolized product. Naming a particular price as the "competitive" price, then for factor amounts to the left of the "competitive" hire quantity the MRP under monopoly lies above that under competition, while to the right the relations are reversed. This is shown by both MRP_c and MRP_m in Fig. 5. Thus it is incorrect to aver that the "competitive" MRP-curve lies everywhere above the monopoly MRP. But this conclusion is of little importance, for with each new factor price the "competitive-type" price would be compelled to change to reflect the new cost experience. What would be needed under pure competition is a family of MRP-curves, each pertinent to a given wage and price adaptation. There is much confusion on these matters in the usual textbook in the haste to conclude that monopoly is the root of all evil. The problem is as one with all monopoly-competitive comparisons. See Chapter 4.

determine the amount of two factors hired, given the product price (or demand curve), relative factor prices, and their productivity.[11] For more than two (or three) factors, only the mathematical equations of general equilibrium can be utilized. Considering our purposes, there is little point in outlining them: we would find that they, too, rest on the same hypotheses as heretofore—mainly that product-demand functions remain rigid and unaffected regardless of factor prices. As we shall argue in a moment, this constitutes the major shortcoming of the existing theory inasmuch as changes in factor prices not only are capable of modifying product demands but also are probably major factors in causing their shifts.

FACTOR SUPPLY. Once equipped with a factor-demand curve, then, merely by being handed a factor-supply curve, plus the usual provisos concerning the structure of the factor market, the price and the employment of the factor are regarded as determinate, according to marginal-productivity doctrine. Maintaining the laconic tradition whereby the premises of the factor-supply curve are treated only casually, we can by-pass this study as having little relevance to our immediate quest. Usually, once the demand curve is drawn, the supply curve is ordered hastily. By including some details on market conduct, the theory of factor prices has been locked in, with the marginal productivity-demand analysis securing the results.[12]

THE ADDING-UP THEOREM. Generally, in the n-factor case of marginal-productivity theory, there is the added task of demonstrating that, if all factors are paid according to their marginal physical or marginal revenue products, the aggregate proceeds are ample to reimburse each factor, with neither surplus nor deficit remaining.[13]

[11] See, for example, my *Price Theory*, Chapter 3.

[12] That the theory of factor supply has lived a shadier existence than that of factor demand has been noted from time to time. See the remarks of William Fellner and Benjamin F. Haley, editors, in *Readings in the Theory of Income Distribution* (Philadelphia, Blakiston, 1946), p. viii.

[13] This point was at the bottom of the famous dispute between Marshall and Hobson, where the latter insisted that compensation must follow average rather than marginal productivity; otherwise, he argued, the total product would be inadequate. The original, imaginative step toward resolving the issue, which has since been dubbed the "adding-up" theorem, was taken by Wicksteed in his invigorating *Essay on the Coordination of the Laws of Distribution* (1894). See Marshall's lengthy footnote, *Principles of Economics*

This is generally termed the "adding-up" theorem. We can look briefly at the main elements of the proof.

For n-productive factors, the production function stressing the dependence of output on factor hire is written as $Q = Q(A, B, C \cdots N)$, where Q denotes output and $A, B, C \cdots N$ are the productive agents. With each factor finely divisible, and with continuous output changes, the partial derivatives representing marginal physical productivity exist so that:

$$\frac{\partial Q}{\partial A} > 0 < \frac{\partial Q}{\partial B}, \text{ etc.} \tag{5}$$

With constant returns to scale, where a proportionate change in all factors leads to the same proportionate output change, then the production function is described as homogeneous of the first degree, and such functions are subject to *Euler's Theorem:*[14]

$$Q = A\frac{\partial Q}{\partial A} + B\frac{\partial Q}{\partial B} + C\frac{\partial Q}{\partial C} + \cdots + N\frac{\partial Q}{\partial N} \tag{6}$$

In economic jargon, the mathematical expression means simply that total output is equal to the sum of the marginal products multiplied by the respective factor amounts. Hence, when factors are compensated according to their marginal physical products, the aggregate production is precisely sufficient to insure the exhaustion of the output total, without residue or deficit.

While eq. 6 is suitable for an "own-product" formulation of the distributive process, in a monetary framework with competitive product and factor markets, an obvious corrective is suggested: the various terms need only be multiplied through by the product price, P, yielding:

(London, Macmillan, 1920, 8th ed.), pp. 515–517n; also John A. Hobson, *The Industrial System* (London, Macmillan, 1910, 2nd ed.), p. 114. Hobson's argument involves, in part, increasing marginal products. Besides Wicksteed, the modern discussion of the problem appears in Knut Wicksell, *Lectures on Political Economy* (New York, Routledge, 1934), Volume I, pp. 127–131; J. R. Hicks, *Theory of Wages* (London, Macmillan, 1932), Appendix; Joan Robinson, "Euler's Theorem and the Problem of Distribution," *Economic Journal* (September 1934), and George J. Stigler, *Production and Distribution Theories* (New York, Macmillan, 1941), Chapter XII.

[14] See R. G. D. Allen, *Mathematical Analysis for Economists* (London, Macmillan, 1938), pp. 315–319.

$$PQ = A \left(P \frac{\partial Q}{\partial A} \right) + B \left(P \frac{\partial Q}{\partial B} \right) + \cdots + N \left(P \frac{\partial Q}{\partial N} \right) \tag{7}$$

Total proceeds are proved thereby to be just ample to cover factor disbursements according to marginal-value product criteria for homogeneous, first-degree production functions.[15]

Total proceeds will also be fully exhausted with production functions of higher degree if factors are reimbursed according to their marginal-value products in competitive product and factor markets if the following conditions are met: (1) average costs are equal to selling price and (2) average total cost is at a minimum.[16] To secure this result, the firm's perfectly elastic demand curve would have to be tangent to a U-shaped average-cost curve; this must necessarily occur at the minimum point on the latter.[17]

A U-shaped average total-cost curve usually is ascribed to the presence of a lumpy, fixed factor invariant with respect to output, though it has been argued also that even with full divisibility economies and diseconomies of scale will appear.[18]

[15] Nonhomogeneous functions involve a constant term and they imply some output even with zero inputs of variable factors $A, B \cdots N$; generally they appear economically meaningless. Homogeneity of degree greater than, or less than, unity involves increasing and decreasing returns to scale, respectively. Marginal-productivity allocations fail in the first case and are responsible for residuals in the second instance.

[16] For development of the proof see Hicks, *op. cit.*, p. 237. Under monopoly, eq. 7 becomes:

$$PQ = A \left(P \frac{\partial Q}{\partial A} + Q \frac{\partial P}{\partial A} \right) + B \left(P \frac{\partial Q}{\partial B} + Q \frac{\partial P}{\partial B} \right) + \cdots \tag{8}$$

The parenthetical quantities denote what we recognize as marginal revenue rather than price. Note that the tacit premises for the exhaustion of proceeds are again factor divisibility and thus, variation, and that average cost is equal to price. The solution thus involves the tangency of the average cost curve to the monopolist's demand curve. [See Chamberlin, *op. cit.*, p. 99, or Joan Robinson, *Economics of Imperfect Competition* (London, 1933), p. 95.] Clearly, if factors were paid according to marginal-value products, in this case, then, total proceeds would *not* be ample to cover their compensation so that a loss would occur.

[17] At the minimum point the U-shaped AC-curve is tangent to a linear and homogeneous function.

[18] Chamberlin is a strong proponent of the "law of size"; *The Theory of Monopolistic Competition* (Cambridge, Harvard, 1948, 6th ed.), Appendix B. See also Harvey Leibenstein, "The Proportionality Controversy and the

Once the divisibility hypothesis is abandoned, the generality of marginal-productivity theory is altered substantially, for withdrawing an indivisible factor, as the entrepreneur or the equipment mass, might plunge output to zero, while adding a new batch of equipment or new entrepreneurial agents when their existing services are not wholly exploited might fail to enlarge output or even reduce it, implying a zero or negative marginal product. The typical resolution for nonlinear functions is to attribute marginal-value products to the fully variable factors, with the residual proceeds assigned to the fixed factors. This involves adding a catch-all term of either "profits" or "losses" to eq. 7.

Where indivisibilities preponderate and more than one factor remains fixed, other principles dictate the income arbitrament of the income residual. Actually, the "adding-up" theorem becomes an elegant superfluity whenever there is one factor, such as the entrepreneur, ready to amass the residue or withstand the deficit, although the equational exhibit depicts concisely the nature of the income parcels meted out by the firm throughout the economy, when factors are hired according to marginal-productivity criteria. One aspect of the "adding-up" theorem that we ought to note, however, is that it is couched almost independently of price: whatever the product price, it will remain valid so long as the production function is of the particular form specified by it and average cost is equated to the price.

Theory of Production," *Quarterly Journal of Economics* (November 1955). See also the earlier comments (1949) in the same journal by A. W. McLeod and F. H. Hahn.

Full divisibility would suggest that the entrepreneur, too, is a variable factor like other agents. On some interpretations, as entrepreneurial earnings exceed the marginal-value product of labor, there is a new influx into the entrepreneurial ranks with a simultaneous exodus from the labor force; entrepreneurs are envisioned as laborers masquerading at times in managerial capacities which require only common skills.

Sometimes it is argued that the marginal-value product of entrepreneurs can be evaluated in terms of their productivity to the industry. But this introduces new dimensions beyond the productivity aspects within the firms. The proposal would have more merit in a welfare analysis of marginal *social* products, in the fashion of Professor Pigou's *Economics of Welfare*; it would not reveal the actual income division but some optimal pattern. See Joan Robinson, "Euler's Theorem . . . ," *op. cit.*, p. 409.

THE CRITICAL MARGINAL-PRODUCTIVITY
HYPOTHESIS: DERIVED DEMAND

Almost buried amid its less controversial features, the really crucial hypothesis of marginal-productivity analysis is its supposition that, regardless of the price paid for a particular class of productive factors, the demand curve for the products in which the factors are used remains rigid and unaffected: independence of product demand and factor prices is thus the cardinal proviso. As product-demand curves are drawn ordinarily on the premise that the money income of consumers is fixed, at the bottom of marginal-productivity analysis is the somewhat perverse proposition that the income level is a datum despite variations in factor prices and factor incomes.

It was this constant-income obsession which provoked some spirited treatment by Keynes in his reconsideration of the effects of wage changes.[19] The unresolved issue, since he wrote, centers about whether a demand curve for a factor can be posited legitimately if every change in the factor's price alters the demand curve for products and, hence, the income level and, through it, the demand for the factor. Ordinarily, the supply-demand apparatus is rooted in the belief that the forces emanating from the buyer's side are independent of those reared in sellers' positions; when changes in factor prices compel changes in product demand, and thence in factor prices once again, the independence postulate is violated and, instead, interdependence reigns. Conventional theory might be relevant in the case of a single firm or even a single (small) industry hiring productive factors; it is palpably mistaken when it is extended to the multitudinous firms comprising the economy. Thus, since Keynes wrote, the traditional theory of factor prices seems less useful today than it was prior to his attack.[20] A theory of factor prices henceforth will have to build on a demand curve mixed out of varying, rather than constant, income ingredients; to do so will be part of the task of subsequent chapters.

[19] See J. M. Keynes: *The General Theory of Employment, Interest and Money* (New York, Harcourt, Brace, 1936), Chapter 19.
[20] Compare Keynes's pointed argument, pp. 258–259.

DERIVED DEMAND. The argument has some implications for the concept of derived demand which has figured so prominently in the literature in affirming that the demand for factors was a resultant of the demand for products, so that the former could not rise unless there was a prior uplift in the latter, barring productivity changes or variations in other factor prices. Although it involves a momentary digression, we might scrutinize the concept of derived demand, in the strong form given it by Marshall for the case of complementary factors used in fixed proportions, before assessing its vulnerable features.

Marshall's celebrated illustration of the principle of derived demand is one of genuine simplicity, running as it does in terms of the demand for knives, k, blades, b, and handles, h.[21] The interpretative appeal of the case comes from the fact that the quantity used of each agent is equal to the output: $Q_k = Q_b = Q_h$. Further, the increments in the quantities required are also identical: $\Delta Q_k = \Delta Q_h = \Delta Q_b$. In this instance, it can be proved that the elasticity of demand, E, for a factor, such as handles, is always smaller than that for knives, the final product. The relation is given by[22]

$$\frac{E_h}{E_k} = \frac{P_h}{P_k} \frac{\Delta P_k}{\Delta P_h} \tag{9}$$

where P refers to prices and ΔP to the price change. Where $\Delta P_h = \Delta P_k$, then for this case, the relative-demand elasticity of the factor

[21] Alfred Marshall, *Principles,* Mathematical Appendix, p. 853. On derived demand, see his discussion on pp. 383 ff.

[22] Marshall's formula is needlessly obscure, for his second term leads to interpretative difficulties in extreme cases. For proof of eq. 9, remembering that all Q's and ΔQ's are equal, write

$$E_h = \frac{(P_k - P_b{}^s)}{Q} \frac{\Delta Q}{\Delta(P_k - P_b{}^s)} \tag{1a}$$

$$E_k = \frac{P_k}{Q} \frac{\Delta Q}{\Delta P_k} \tag{1b}$$

The term $P_b{}^s$ refers to the supply price of blades; $\Delta P_b{}^s/\Delta Q$ can be zero, with constant supply price; or positive, with increasing supply price. (Decreasing supply price can be ignored under pure competition.) Cancelling $\Delta Q/Q$ and writing E_h/E_k in ratio form, then eq. 9 follows directly for $P_h = P_k - P_b{}^s$ and $\Delta P_h = \Delta(P_k - P_b{}^s)$.

depends on the factor-product price ratio. If $\Delta P_h > \Delta P_k$, as it will be if the supply price of blades is rising, the ratio of elasticities tends to be reduced. To illustrate, in Fig. 6 the product-demand curve is DD. If blades are offered at a constant-supply price, then

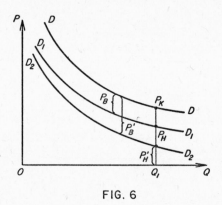

FIG. 6

$D_1 D_1$ is the derived-demand curve for handles; if the supply price of blades rises as more are bought, then $D_2 D_2$ will represent the derived demand for handles.[23] From these diagrammatics successive generations of students have inferred that the demand for a factor is derived from that for the product, a doctrine which ante-

[23] Some realistic problems of factor variation are related to this case of fixed proportions. Under automation, in mass-production industry it is often necessary to hire a team of employees, in the sense of a group, to operate additional equipment; to utilize an additional machine might require a dozen men; the marginal physical product of one man might be nil. Clearly, in this case the appropriate marginal physical-product concept is that of the "average-marginal" product where the added output of the team is divided by the number of participants. So derived, the "average-marginal" revenue product can be calculated and compared to the going wage. Further, in these cases it is also necessary to provide for a flow of materials as a complementary input, for otherwise even the "average-marginal" revenue product will be trifling. Thus, before deducing the true "average-marginal" revenue product, the associated average-material cost per man would have to be deducted, yielding an "average-marginal" net revenue product. Through a redefinition of the key concepts in such fashion, traditional ideas probably could be retained; it will still, even in the group problem, generally be open to the firm to appraise whether additional individuals would repay their hire as a sort of versatile utility man to the production team.

dates Marshall but which was given its sharp, clear features at his hands.[24]

A CRITICISM. Once it is admitted that higher factor prices (when the factor is an agent widely used through all industry) can elevate product-demand curves, as is implied in the wage-price spiral, then the luster of derived demand is somewhat tarnished, for, contrary to its postulates, product demand may grow as a *result* of higher factor prices. Conceivably, if the wage movement, say, does not necessarily enlarge either aggregate output or labor's employment, the heart of the proposition may be preserved when cast in real terms. Still, it cannot be averred, as has been done sometimes, that product demand (in a monetary economy) will be inflexible in the face of factor-price movements, or that the latter must be settled as an effect of the former and never serve as an initiating cause.

These last remarks illuminate some puzzling and confusing features in traditional, and still conventional, distribution theory, and help explain the wide gap between its high promises and meager fulfillment. A former generation of economists would have accepted marginal-productivity theory with substantial unanimity as an explanation of factor prices and factor employment. In the preliminaries to the subject, it was common to assert that distributive theory was merely an extension of price theory, encompassing factor rather than product markets. With the addendum that all factors who sought work at prevailing or lower real earning would secure employment through the forces of competition in a framework of flexible factor prices, then the aggregate income of the factor group would be developed as a simple piece of arithmetic as factor prices multiplied by factor employment, with both magnitudes shown simultaneously in the usual graphics. Focusing on each productive factor in isolation, the analysis generally neglected the broader problem of the determination of aggregate income which was merely

[24] The same doctrine provides the backbone of the Austrian School approach to the value problem. Compare Carl Menger, *Principles of Economics* (Glencoe, Ill., Free Press, 1950), James Dingwall and Bert F. Hoselitz, translators, pp. 63–67, 162–165. Leon Walras also held to the same view, declaring that ". . . the prices of productive services are determined by the prices of their products and not the other way round." See his *Elements of Pure Economics* (London, Clarendon, 1954), William Jaffé, translator, Preface to the 4th edition, p. 45.

assumed as a datum, and embodied in the product-demand curves generating the derived-factor demand.

What particularly strikes the jaundiced eye of a post-Keynesian observer is the confident belief that whole factor classes would secure employment, with its inference that unemployment is always voluntary and due solely to the temerity of factor owners in withholding their services at low real earnings despite the obvious depression experience testifying that this is a distortion of the facts.[25] An even more spurious aspect of the theory, which should have given its proponents pause, was its frequent iteration that the distributive focus was on the pricing of three (or four) factor categories rather than a myriad of prices as found in product markets. In dealing with an infinitely dense product universe, with any one good dwarfed in insignificance in the totality of outputs, it is not unwarranted to invoke supply-demand independence postulates and to envisage a constant income-aggregate and a (fairly) rigid price-output configuration of other products regardless of events in a particular product market. This is the backbone of the particular-equilibrium approach. Conversely, when there are only a few prices to ascertain, especially of a productive agent whose use extends over a vast variety of products, it is singularly myopic to proceed on this basis: for now changes in the factor's price may have significant circular repercussions on product prices, factor employment, and aggregate income. Assessing the fewness of factor groups (with the knowledge of hindsight) ought to have alerted economists to the prospect of substantial interdependence among variables and aroused some apprehension over a technique which ignored such reverberations.

Yet, after all this is said, we too shall regard the distributive story as a projection of price theory, but with important distinguishing features of its own. It would be foolish to deny that distributive ramifications do obtrude in price theory; factor payments comprise the cost elements within the firm and thus provide, from the distributive point of view, the income-content of cost discussions. Implicit in each output quantum are precise magnitudes of factor hire, factor prices, and factor earnings; they constitute the sub-

[25] On all this see Keynes's remarks, which, I think, are incontrovertible. (*Op. cit.*, pp. 8–10.)

stance behind the imposing façade of revenue and cost schedules. To overlook these relations would create an irreparable rift from the modern theory of the firm, depriving us of the information it can impart, and impede the synthesis and the systematization that a distributive theory must achieve.

ASPECTS OF THE DISTRIBUTIVE PROBLEM

This will be as far as we will go in analyzing and criticizing the marginal-productivity theory; perhaps, even, enough has been said already to indicate that the theory of distribution, rather than being concerned with a single problem, involves instead several aspects, so that various distributive problems require to be uncovered. As a chart on progress, the diverse dimensions might be enumerated, each of which must be explored in any investigation that pretends to completeness.

First, it is imperative to develop a theory of factor prices. In the past, this has meant wage, interest, rent, and profit theory, for it was presumed that these represented the exclusive income categories to be imputed to the correlative factor groupings. All of these income types will be analyzed, though factor classes need not be regarded as possessing the distinctive attributes once assigned to them.

Second, a theory of factor hire. Not so long ago, this was thought to be merely the reciprocal image of factor-price determination, with one simultaneously determining the other. This view has been rendered especially suspect by the Keynesian criticism of orthodox wage theory.

Third, an analysis of the aggregate absolute income of the factor class, if broad and homogeneous groupings can be distilled realistically. This total springs naturally from the resolution of the theory of factor prices and employment and deserves mention separately only to underscore the fact that, for some purposes, attention is focused on the absolute earnings of the factor group.

Next, a theory of relative sharing of factor groups, which involves the comparison of the aggregate income of the factor class to total income, though, for some purposes, comparisons of the aggregate income of a factor to earnings of another factor might be more useful. It was this problem, as Keynes was to remind us, that Ricardo felt was the legitimate province of economics when he argued, in a letter to Malthus, that Political Economy

> should be called an enquiry into the laws which determine the division of the produce of industry amongst the classes who concur in its formation. No law can be laid down respecting quantity [of aggregate output], but a tolerably correct one can be laid down respecting proportions. Every day I am more satisfied that the former enquiry is vain and delusive, and the latter only the true objects of the science.[26]

It was to this class of problems that Ricardo's oft-repeated dictum that "a rise in wages must mean a decline in profits" belongs;[27] recently there has been some revival of interest in Ricardo's technique of working in real terms and an "own-product" approach.[28]

Interestingly, surveying what was done rather than professed under the Ricardian system, Edwin Cannan castigated the result as "pseudo-distribution," denouncing it as in "contradistinction to 'Distribution Proper' which I took to be theory about the proportions in which aggregate income is divided between classes and persons."[29] In his own work, Cannan was wont to distinguish between "owners" and "workers," or between property and labor income, viewing the income partition between the two groups as the dominant distributive problem.[30]

This divorcement of analytic practice from substantive precept is worth pondering, for it has created much confusion concerning the matters requiring investigation. Whereas the theory of relative

[26] See the opening passages of J. M. Keynes, *The General Theory of Employment, Interest and Money*, p. 4n. The original letter, dated October 9, 1820, appears in the *Works and Correspondence of David Ricardo*, edited by Piero Sraffa (Cambridge, Cambridge Univ. Press, England, 1952), Volume VIII, pp. 276–280.

A most perceptive though critical appraisal of Ricardo is found in the articles by F. H. Knight, "The Ricardian Theory of Production and Distribution," *Canadian Journal of Economics* (1935).

[27] Compare his *Principles of Political Economy and Taxation*, Sraffa, ed., Volume I, *e.g.*, pp. 35, 50. In his illustrations, Ricardo worked with an absolute income increase for all factors.

[28] See Joan Robinson, *The Accumulation of Capital* (Homewood, Ill., Irwin, 1956), p. vi and passim.

[29] Edwin Cannan, *A Review of Economic Theory* (London, King, 1930), p. 301.

[30] See his eminently readable *Wealth* (London, King, 1938, 3rd ed.), p. 181.

shares was constantly reiterated as the appropriate topic for study, subsequent inquiries were devoted instead to factor-price determination or, as it became fashionable to say, to functional distribution, while relative aspects were effectively suppressed. As one recent writer, in a critical evaluation of Ricardo's contribution, remarked:

> In fact, Ricardo's "principal problem" only received very occasional attention in neo-classical economics. Most of the more forthright exponents of marginal productivity disregarded it. The Ricardian problem was discussed fairly briefly by Wicksell and Bohm-Bawerk, and has been the subject, now and then, of ingenious, if inconclusive abstract formulations, to the effect, largely, that anything may happen. This is not due to any conspiracy of silence or deliberate neglect. It has simply not been found to be a tractable analytical problem—a negative but perfectly sound conclusion.[31]

Despite this adverse judgment, efforts to resolve the problem have not been wholly deterred and, judging from the textbook tendencies, the results have been offered to an ever-widening audience; the work of Michael Kalecki and Kenneth Boulding immediately comes to mind in this connection.[32] Although a different approach will be attempted, one which seeks to weld together some current microeconomics and macroeconomics, part of our study is directed to the same general problem.[33]

[31] T. W. Hutchison, "Some Questions About Ricardo," *Economica* (November 1952), p. 424. The allusion to the "inconclusive abstract formulations" seems to be inspired by the abortive efforts to attack the problem with the concept of the elasticity of substitution in the 1930's.

[32] See M. Kalecki, "The Distribution of the National Income," reprinted in *Readings in the Theory of Income Distribution* (Philadelphia, Blakiston, 1946) and K. Boulding, *A Reconstruction of Economics* (New York, Wiley, 1950), Chapter 14. Besides Joan Robinson's volume on *The Accumulation of Capital*, a most recent contribution is provided by Nicholas Kaldor, "Alternative Theories of Distribution," *Review of Economic Studies* (1955–56).

[33] In recent years, Prof. Milton Friedman also has questioned the stress laid on this problem. Declaring that the sole concern of the theory of distribution was with the pricing of productive factors, he remarked: "I must say I find it hard to see why anybody is interested in the particular figure of the percentage of aggregate income that goes to wages." (*The Impact of the Union* [New York, Harcourt, Brace, 1951], edited by David McCord Wright, p. 306. See also pp. 352–353.)

In view of these doubts, some comment in defense of the study is not amiss. Besides the fact that the resolution of the problem has perplexed competent

Besides these aspects of factor prices, factor hire, absolute shares, and relative shares, the *null* incomes of particular factor groups or of members who are part of a larger group ought to be disclosed: the zero earnings accompanying unemployment tend to be obscured when we concentrate solely on the actual income of employed factors. Considerations of disproportionate impact and income loss through unemployment would alone add novelty to a restatement of distributive theory.

Throughout the analysis, the repercussions of changes in the relative-income partition upon the output configuration as well as the income aggregate must be appraised. For a shift in the income division may affect prices and output, as well as the income aggregate and employment, altering in greater or smaller degree the content and the dimensions of the equilibrium. At a minimum, therefore, distributive matters ought to be studied on the dual hypotheses of constant and variable activity. Although, in delving

---

economists in the past, attention is often focused on the share of labor in the national income, particularly on the matter of whether unionization and the publicized wage boosts have lifted the wage share. Paradoxically, considering his attitude toward relative shares, Friedman has argued that the results of unionization on the structure and the level of wages have been exaggerated. (*Ibid.*, p. 231.) But the answer to this question is one that ought to be reflected in the "wage share." Further, the high constancy of the wage share has been promulgated as an empirical "law"; unless the evidence itself is disputed, it ought to be the task of theory to essay an explanation. Too, Marxists have predicted lopsided imbalance in income division between wage earners and capitalists in the secular growth of the economy. Analysts ought to examine the proposition rather than dismiss its very mention. Business-cycle theories and unemployment totals also have often been alleged to depend in part for amplitude and direction on the income shift. Finally, policy-wise, the question *is* raised by legislators and administrators on the effect of legislative changes on the economic position of major income groupings; economics should provide an answer which, however imperfect, provides a better guide to practical men than unreflective rules-of-thumb.

Though Friedman appears to object to the use of the concept of the wage share, he declares that in analyzing the elasticity of demand for the factor "the most significant of these items for the analysis . . . are the essentiality of the factor and the percentage of total costs accounted for by the factor." (*Ibid.*, p. 207.) This notion of the percentage of total costs which is found significant at the level of the firm is not vastly different from that of the "wage share." It is true that greater homogeneity is assumed in propositions on the latter. But conceptually there is much affinity.

into problems of income division, phenomena associated with the distribution of wealth scarcely can be avoided, nevertheless, our attention span on these matters will be brief, for these questions open up whole new vistas which require, for systematic investigation, analytic techniques somewhat different from those to be utilized in subsequent chapters.

Chapter 2

Aggregate Supply and Demand[1]

The macroeconomic concepts of aggregate demand and aggregate supply, and the theory of income and employment determination, will have to be drawn upon at almost every turn in developing the main themes of relative shares and factor-price determination. For our purposes, it will be necessary to approach the subject of income determination in a manner more suitable for wage theory and a monetary economy than is true of the usual statement of the theory, which runs in real terms and eliminates price phenomena. In a way, then, this chapter constitutes a restatement of a main part of macro-economic theory.[2] Like all such analysis, its origin is to be found in Keynes's *General Theory*.

To facilitate the inquiry, the following assumptions are made: (1) the labor force is a homogeneous class, (2) the stock of equipment is constant, (3) factor prices, particularly the money-wage rate, are given, (4) the production functions or labor-productivity relations for each product are known, (5) each firm is fully integrated, (6) each firm operates in a purely competitive setting and is animated by motives of profit maximization. These assumptions are not uncommon in macroeconomics. All of them will be lifted or relaxed in subsequent chapters.

[1] With some minor changes, this chapter is reproduced from my article, "The Micro-Foundations of Aggregate Demand and Supply," *Economic Journal* (September 1957). Permission to reprint was granted by the Royal Economic Society.

[2] Some relevant articles, concerned mainly with the aggregate supply function, are: F. J. DeJong, "Supply Functions in Keynesian Economics," *Economic Journal* (March 1954); "Comment and Rejoinder," by R. G. Hawtrey and DeJong (December 1954); "Comments," by Sir Dennis Robertson and H. G. Johnson, and "Rejoinder," by DeJong (September 1955); "A Further Note," by Hawtrey, "Two Comments," by Sir Dennis Robertson, and "A Third Rejoinder," by DeJong (September 1956).

AGGREGATE SUPPLY

In Fig. 7 (a), amounts of employment are measured horizontally and sums of money appear vertically. The Z-function, as drawn and lettered Z', relates employment, N, to proceeds, Z, and represents

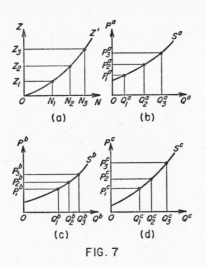

FIG. 7

aggregate supply or aggregate proceeds; it associates amounts of N to expected Z-sums in the sense that each expected-proceeds level generates a particular amount of employment.[3] The impetus for the labor hire comes from the expected-sales receipts, a proposition obviously compatible with a market economy where goods are produced in advance of sale in confident expectation that they will appeal to buyers after completion.

Suppositions identical to those embodied in Z are at the bottom of the industry-supply curve, which connects output and (expected or hypothetical) market price rather than industry proceeds, containing the latter totals implicitly. Whereas the industry-supply curve is confined to a single commodity while the Z-function encompasses the global product mass, still the one proposition correctly extended necessarily embraces the other. At the level of individual industries, each Z-sum is equivalent to the multiple of supply price times the

[3] Symbolically, $N = N(Z)$, with the inverse function $Z = Z(N)$.

associated output quantity, summated over all industries and related to the amount of employment implicit in the particular output totals.[4] In principle, Z will be a unique function if the industry-supply curves are determinate and if the distribution of proceeds, for each expected aggregate volume of proceeds, is determinate.

Diagrammatically, the proceeds function, Z', appears in Fig. 7 (a), while supply curves for industries A, B, and C, as illustrative of all industries, are shown in Fig. 7 (b), (c), and (d), respectively. When aggregate proceeds of Z_1 are expected, in the light of the estimated configuration of demand the output will be distributed among industries in amounts Q_1^a, Q_1^b, and Q_1^c. With proceeds expected to be Z_2, the corresponding outputs will be Q_2^a, Q_2^b, Q_2^c, etc. Expected proceeds in each industry, when Z_1 is expected in the economy, would equal $P_1^a Q_1^a$, $P_1^b Q_1^b$, and $P_1^c Q_1^c$, and totaling Z_1 of course.[5] Thus over n-industries, when proceeds are expected to be Z_r, we have

$$Z_r = \sum_{i=a}^{n} P_r^i Q_r^i$$

Each output volume entails a precise volume of employment within the individual firms comprising the industry, determined by the given factor productivities and the ruling factor prices.

[4] Recalling the hierarchy of national-income concepts, the Z-function is one of anticipated gross product or expenditure. Though sometimes we shall refer to Z as reflecting sales proceeds, this is not wholly correct in view of the deletion of interfirm transactions (except for capital investment). That sales proceeds rather than national income is the vital concept should occasion no dispute: it is comparisons of proceeds versus costs that stir entrepreneurial activity. For similar reasons, Keynes declared that the concept of gross income rather than net income was "the concept relevant to decisions concerning current production . . ." (*op. cit.*, p. 60). Proceeds or sales receipts constitute the least ambiguous link in drawing upon the theory of the firm in a most unequivocal form. Refining the concept to exclude, as in national-income accounting, depreciation and tax sums, etc., would obstruct ready reference to the latter theory; the upshot would be to impede the systematization of these branches of economic inquiry.

[5] Thus the same profit sums which are embodied in the respective supply curves are embedded in the Z-function. If the analysis is interpreted as "short-period," then the implicit profits are "short-period" residual sums rather than "normal" profits. This, the former, is the interpretation given by Sir Dennis Robertson. (Compare "Comment," *Economic Journal* [September 1955], p. 474; also DeJong [March 1954], pp. 17–18.)

Thus the total employment, N_r, accompanying proceeds, Z_r, is determined through the following (inverse) productivity equations:

$$N_r{}^a = f(Q_r{}^a), \quad N_r{}^b = f(Q_r{}^b), \quad \cdots \quad N_r{}^n = f(Q_r{}^n) \qquad (10)$$

$$N_r = \sum_{i=a}^{n} N_r{}^i \qquad (11)$$

Actually, each point on Z is tantamount to the premise of constant gross income; what is presumed, then, is that at each income level, in the light of cost and expected-demand phenomena, the configuration of output is determinate and that thereby the volume of employment can be ascertained. Movement along Z involves varying income phenomena and an accompanying employment displacement, with output changes being implicit. It appears that the chief characteristic of the Z-function is that greater employment awaits an expectation of greater proceeds: the functional connection is positive in nature.[6] Furthermore, when the anticipated proceeds are zero, employment will be nil, so that, in diagrammatic terms, the Z-function will emanate from the zero origin.

Some further aspects of Z ought also to be noted. On a simple distributive scheme, each level of Z-proceeds, either in anticipation or after realization, may be conceived to be allocated as follows:[7]

$$Z = wN + F + R \qquad (12)$$

where w denotes the given wage rate, F the volume of fixed payments (assumed invariant in the light of the fixity of the stock of equipment and the short-period nature of the analysis), and R the residual, a catch-all category termed "profits," though obviously it can be decomposed into depreciation allowances, indirect taxes, variable interest charges, etc., as well as profits proper. It follows

[6] If the Z-curve were flat, it would signify that given proceeds would cover a range of employment; in general, the facts would seem to support the view that more proceeds are required for more employment unless factor prices, or productivity, or the structure of production changes drastically. Likewise, if Z fell, it would mean that with lower sales proceeds more men would be employed; *ceteris paribus* this could occur only if somehow there were a shift to output employing more labor and less equipment in the aggregate as employment expanded. In a mass-production economy this is most unlikely, hence the Z-function can be posited as rising to the right.

[7] See Chapter 3.

that moving along Z, when money wages are constant and employment increases, then

$$\frac{\Delta Z}{\Delta N} = w + \frac{\Delta R}{\Delta N} \tag{13}$$

According to eq. 13, the increment of expected proceeds, when employment rises by one unit, will be divided between the wage payment and the profit increment. Formula 13, which expresses the slope of Z, may be referred to as the *aggregate marginal proceeds or supply price*, for it reveals the necessary increment in proceeds to induce an expansion of employment by one unit.[8]

Equation 12 leads to some further diagrammatic decomposition of the Z-function. For example, the wage bill ($W = wN$) accompanying each N,Z-level can be shown by a curve such as W in Fig. 8. With the money wage constant, then the slope of W is equal to the going money wage.

Firms are also committed to making certain fixed payments, F, over short periods of time. Generally, these are comprised of contractual salaries, rents, and interest charges on indebtedness previously incurred. These payments are shown in Fig. 8 by the dashed line, FF', which is drawn to exceed W by the absolute sum of the

----

[8] It is possible to write this relation in a way which puts greater stress on productivity phenomena. In terms of the elasticity of supply [$E_{si} = (P_i/Q_i)(dQ_i/dP_i)$] and the elasticity of productivity [$E_{qi} = (N_i/Q_i)(dQ_i/dN_i)$], we have

$$\frac{dZ}{dN} = \sum_{i=1}^{n} \left(E_{qi} \frac{Z_i}{N_i} + \frac{w}{E_{si}} \right) \frac{dN_i}{dN} \tag{14}$$

Formula 14 is the form of the aggregate marginal-supply price pertinent under pure competition; a term would have to be added under monopoly to reflect the degree of monopoly power. The increment in proceeds required by entrepreneurs to validate the production advance is dependent positively on the elasticity of productivity and on the reciprocal of the elasticity of supply. An $E_{qi} = 1$ is likely to mean an infinite E_{si}, so that the ΔZ-magnitude is restrained. With diminishing returns, $E_{qi} < 1$, so that the E_{si}-value figures more prominently in the result. As $E_{qi} \to 0$, then $E_{si} \to 0$, so that ΔZ mounts sharply to infinite values. In each particular firm and industry the values of E_q and E_s are weighted by the importance of their employment expansion to the total employment movement (dN_i/dN). Elasticities in large firms are thus likely to dominate the final result.

For the derivation of eq. 14, see the Mathematical Note at the end of this chapter.

fixed charges: the $Z - F$ difference denotes "profits." Until employment, ON_1, rules, losses abound in sum equal to the excess of the FF'-values over the Z-magnitudes. Ordinarily, therefore, output positions below ON_1 can be neglected, for these are veritable whole-

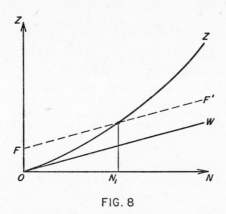

FIG. 8

sale bankruptcy areas; output and employment can settle in this range only temporarily, viewing the economy as a whole, before impelling a write-off and a scaling-down of fixed claims.

An elasticity for Z, written E_z, can be defined in the usual way. From eq. 12 and 13, with money wages constant, it can be shown to equal

$$E_z = \frac{Z}{N} \frac{dN}{dZ} = \frac{w + (F + R)/N}{w + dR/dN} \underset{<}{\overset{>}{=}} 1 \qquad (15)$$

Hence, if dR/dN, which denotes the marginal rate of profits in the case of an expansion of N with w constant, is greater than the average rate of fixed income and profits per unit of employment, then $E_z < 1$. This ought to be the typical pattern after fixed incomes become unimportant relative to the volume of employment.[9]

[9] If an attempt to measure E_z directly in terms of productivity is made, complications arise. Consider the case of $E_z = 1$. Then, *at the industry level*, $Z = PQ$ and $dZ = PdQ + QdP$. So

$$\frac{Q}{N} = \frac{dQ}{dN} + \frac{QdP}{PdQ}\frac{dQ}{dN} \qquad (16)$$

Q/N, of course, is the average product of labor and dQ/dN is the marginal product. Thus, even in the simple case where $E_z = 1$, either the second term on the right

Graphically, E_z can be measured in the same way as the elasticity of supply; a tangent emanating from (positive) values on the vertical axis to a point on Z would denote an $E_z > 1$, while vectors from the (positive) horizontal axis would convey inelastic points. Where the tangent to the curve ran through the origin, E_z would be exactly unity. Elastic values would imply that a 1 per cent rise in proceeds fostered a rise in employment in excess of 1 per cent; this is what we might expect only if increasing returns prevailed generally over industry. With decreasing marginal products, generally the elasticity will be below unity, while with constant returns it will be exactly unity. A zero elasticity, signifying a vertical Z-slope, would suggest perfectly inelastic supply with employment and output unresponsive to a proceeds augmentation. If E_z falls constantly as employment expands, the inference is of continuous diminishing-returns phenomena.[10] A linear Z-function, remembering that Z must stem from the origin, would suggest constant marginal products.[11]

AGGREGATE DEMAND

We now consider the concept of aggregate demand, D, for use in conjunction with the aggregate-supply function. Despite the copious writings on the consumption function, D_c, there is little that is immediately useful for our purposes, inasmuch as we have chosen to work in money terms with price-level changes being an essential component of D_c at each N,Z-position. Practically all

---

can be zero, with marginal and average products equal, or it can be negative, with the marginal product of labor being greater than the average product. The last relation can be eliminated by virtue of the competitive hypothesis, but it indicates an element of murkiness for the cases of $E_z \gtrless 1$.

Writing A for average product of labor, M for marginal product, and E_s for the elasticity of supply, then eq. 16 becomes

$$A = M \left(1 + \frac{1}{E_s}\right) \tag{17}$$

Clearly, A can equal M if $E_s = \infty$ or if $M > A$ and $E_s < 0$, as with falling supply price. For if $E_s = \infty$, supply price will be constant.

[10] In this case, $\dfrac{d^2N}{dZ^2} < 0$.

[11] On the relation between the marginal productivity of labor and the price-level phenomena built into the Z-function, see Chapter 4.

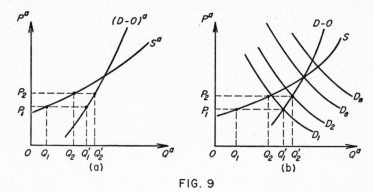

FIG. 9

writings on the consumption function have been conducted in real terms, to the neglect of price changes.[12]

It will facilitate understanding if first we outline the concept of the aggregate-demand price, involving a study of the macroeconomic functions of D_c and investment (D_i) and government (D_g) demand, comprising aggregate demand, D, in a closed economy.

In Fig. 9 (a), the ordinary supply curve for industry A is drawn and lettered S^a. At price P_1 the supply quantity is Q_1, so that the aggregate supply price required by industry A to produce Q_1 and hire labor in amount N_1 is $Z_1 = P_1Q_1$. At P_2, $Z_2 = P_2Q_2$, etc. Although the supply curve for A alone is drawn, the same expectation of proceeds that evoked Q_1^a in A must be conceived to impel output of Q_1^b in B, Q_1^c in C, $\cdots$ etc.

At the supply price P_1, however, the demand quantity may be Q_1': thus the aggregate intended demand outlay at P_1 is $D_1 = P_1Q_1'$. The latter sum will be the *intended*[13] outlay, therefore, when employment is N_1 in A, even though the *expected* or *required* proceeds for A is Z_1. Likewise, at P_2, $D_2 = P_2Q_2'$. In this way, the appropriate *demand-outlay* function for industry A, based on rising output in A and associated outputs in B, C, $\cdots$, together with rising

<hr />

[12] The following pages represent an attempt to describe the average and marginal propensity to consume in money terms as income varies, with the real phenomena implicit. D. H. Robertson has also seemed to be uneasy about the undue concentration on real-income phenomena to the neglect of money amounts. See his *Money* (New York, Pitman, 1948, rev. ed.), p. 211.

[13] Or the actual outlay when employment is N_1, if inventory disinvestment occurs.

factor-income payments through the economy, can be derived. Connecting the desired demand quantities at the respective industry supply prices yields the continuous $(D\text{-}O)^a$-curve. From the latter, *at each supply price, and implicit N,Z-point,* the appropriate aggregate-demand price—the D-points—can be obtained. Over the entire economy, given the expected proceeds and the associated employment and outputs, and selecting the supply prices as (virtually) ruling in the market, the accompanying aggregate-demand outlay that would evolve at the self-same supply prices can then be ascertained.

Essentially, the $D\text{-}O$-curve is extracted from a family of Marshallian industry demand curves, each drawn on the assumption of constant-money income. As output, employment, and aggregate-factor incomes vary—say, when production expands from Q_1 to Q_2 for industry A in Fig. 9 (a)—the industry demand curve moves up from D_1 to D_2 in Fig. 9 (b), so that the particular demand quantity at price P_2 is found on D_2 rather than on D_1. Insofar as $D\text{-}O$ is steeper than S, an ultimate equilibrium is possible; this will be considered shortly. We consider now the factors governing the $D\text{-}O$-curves in individual industries and, by extension, over the entire economy. From what has been said, it should be apparent, however, that embedded in each point on the aggregate-demand function, D, will be the same prices that are found in Z at corresponding $N\text{-}points$. It is the excess or the deficiency of $D - Z$, or aggregate excess (or deficiency) in demand quantity as against supply quantity, that motivates expansory or contractionist behavior on the part of business firms. Technically, too, the $D\text{-}O$-function constitutes the microeconomic basis of the familiar consumption function of macroeconomics. Thus we must consider its underlying components in more detail.

PERSONAL INCOME AND THE CONSUMPTION FUNCTION. While the equation $Z = wN + F + R$ describes the allocation of proceeds among major income categories at each employment position, when we consider consumption, inasmuch as some profits are withheld (which is inevitable, for the R-term contains depreciation allowances as well as profits proper) and as personal income is subject to tax while some individuals receive transfer payments from government, then the personal income available for consumer purchases need not equal Z. A function of disposable personal income, Y_d, such as the following, is thus useful for describing the factor earnings available for consumption outlay:

$$Y_d = wN + F + kR + (T_t - T_x) \tag{18}$$

The T_x-term denotes the reduction of personal incomes through the progressive income-tax structure,[14] while T_t is meant to represent all transfer incomes, such as unemployment relief, old-age pensions, veterans' benefits, charitable aids, government interest payments, etc. The term k is used to denote the fraction of profits actually disbursed as income. Through the presence of wN and R, $Y_d = Y_d(Z)$, where $Z = Z(N)$.

Consumption outlays, D_c, depend primarily on the Y_d-payments. For some individuals, however, consumption outlays exceed their personal income, which may be nil; in their case D_c is linked to dissaving out of their personal wealth or asset holdings, A. Functionally, then[15]

$$D_c = cY_d + \lambda A \tag{19}$$

where c denotes the average propensity to consume out of personal income, while λ is inserted in cognizance of dissaving phenomena. As we shall note, λA depends in part on Y_d so that we could write $D_c = D(Y_d)$, from which we could, if we knew the form of the equation, derive the marginal and the average propensity to consume.

Consider first the consumption outlays of rentiers, D_c', drawing a fixed income (after taxes). In Fig. 10 (a), their earnings are represented by FF'. As employment and proceeds mount and prices go higher, rentier real income and real saving are likely to suffer: in an effort to maintain their real consumption, their consumption outlay presumably rises to an ultimate limit prescribed by the rigid income ceiling. A curve such as D_c', therefore, describes the consumption function, in money terms, of fixed-income recipients.

---

[14] Greater clarity, at the price of more detail, could be obtained by writing separate personal-income-tax terms for wage earners, rentiers, and dividend recipients. With money wages constant, the proportionate tax bite on wage earners will be constant, though the tax bill will rise as N increases. Rentiers will pay a constant tax sum while profit recipients will pay an increasing bill at a higher tax rate.

[15] As in the case of taxes, the D_c-function can be elaborated to contain separate c-terms for wage earners, rentiers, and profit recipients. This approach is implicit in the ensuing diagrammatic analysis.

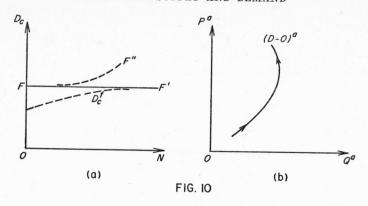

FIG. 10

Analytically, $D_c{}^f = c_f F$, where $c_f = C_f(N)$. Thus, if rentiers save at a maximum one third of their income, c_f will fluctuate between $\frac{2}{3}$ and 1. In Fig. 10 (b), taking the (virtual) rentier expenditure patterns in industry A as typical of rentier outlay over the vast array of goods, the (rentier) D-O-curve for industry A's output at each supply price would taper off to the left, ultimately tending to rise backward to reflect a constant outlay at the higher P^a figures.

Even if fixed payments were conceived to rise slightly, perhaps through the avoidance of bankruptcies as N rose, as shown by FF'' in Fig. 10 (a), the final results would not be vastly different.[16] Presence of fixed incomes, therefore, can explain why aggregate demand exceeds aggregate supply at low employment levels, but certainly not at high levels.

Consider next the transfer incomes, T_t. These are likely to be particularly large at low employment levels when relief payments are substantial, so that T_t is likely to fall off with rising employment. The aggregate consumption outlay, $D_c{}^t$, associated with T_t, will follow the same course, practically merging with T_t, as shown in Fig. 11 (a). The excess, $T_t - D_c{}^t$, denoting some savings, would be attributable primarily to the inclusion of interest payments on

---

[16] It is probably best to treat bonuses to salaried officials at high employment-profit positions as part of "dividends." Otherwise a variable twist is imparted to FF'. In passing, it might be noted that employment, as measured along ON, is not equivalent to the statistical concept of "gainfully employed," for the latter would include salaried officials whose income is regarded here as part of the fixed-income category and whose numbers are not included in N or their earnings in W.

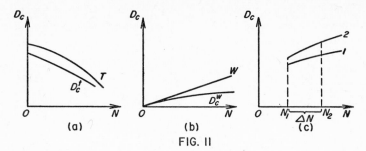

FIG. II

government bonds in T_t, and the occasional fact, sometimes publicized in the press, of individuals saving even on the dole. The $D_c{}^t$-function can also explain the excess of D_c over Z at low N-levels, but points to a decline in D_c at high N-positions. Industry D-O-curves, comparable to $(D$-$O)^a$ in Fig. 10 (b), would thus veer back rather sharply. Hence, $D_c{}^t = c_tT$, where $c_t \approx 1$. As T_t is dependent on the income-employment level, particularly the wage bill, then $T_t = T_t(W)$ and $dT_t/dN < 0$.

The wage bill will climb linearly to the right if the money wage is constant; that is shown by W in Fig. 11 (b). Wage earners, as a class, will save greater absolute amounts as income grows; thus the consumption outlay of this group tends to rise steadily to the right, though probably at a slightly tempered pace. The curve $D_c{}^w$ would thus help explain the *rise* in the aggregate D_c as N advanced. Actually, $D_c{}^w$ is a hybrid function involving some interdependence with $D_c{}^t$, and with the concept of dissaving, λA, which still remains to be developed. Nevertheless, as the consumption outlay of an employed individual exceeds the expenditure of the same person on relief, the rise in $D_c{}^w$ will outweigh the descent in $D_c{}^t$, so that on balance the aggregate D_c will be higher.

Prices ordinarily will rise as N advances, so that those employed and receiving total wages of wN_1 when employment is N_1 will have to expend more to maintain their real consumption pattern when employment advances to N_2. That is, if at N_1 the the virtual $D_c{}^w$-sum is P_1Q_1', where P_1 denotes the price level, then when employment rises to N_2 the N_1-group will tend to spend $P_2Q_2' > P_1Q_1'$, where intended real intake $Q_2' \leqq Q_1'$; where $Q_2' = Q_1'$ the real intended consumption of the N_1-group can be maintained through the prospective diminution of their money savings; where $Q_2' < Q_1'$

their prospective real consumption is decreased. Hence, as the N_1-group strives to maintain its real consumption intake, the total $D_c{}^w$ will be higher at N_2 than at N_1.[17] Graphically, in Fig. 11 (c), if the consumption outlay of the N_1-group is taken as constant despite the price rise, then $D_c{}^w$ is given by curve 1 in the range N_1 to N_2. Allowing for added outlay by the N_1-group because of rising price-level phenomena, as well as the augmented employment and wage bill, then curve 2 is a more apt picture.

As for entrepreneurial income, according to Fig. 8, profits, R, are equal to the $Z - F$ gap, with losses prevailing at low employment levels. An R-function (not drawn) thus can be constructed. Still, as dividends are often paid even with current aggregate losses, inasmuch as some firms have positive profits while others, in the face of losses in period t_1, declare dividends on the basis of t_0 earnings, the appropriate basis for $D_c{}^r$ is the dividend function, kR. As argued later, in the upper regions this is likely to be about $\frac{1}{7}$ of R. In view of the profit rise at a pace in excess of the price rise (for rentier real income and real-wage income both fall as prices rise),[18] consumption outlays out of dividends are likely to keep step with the price movement, despite the inroads of progressive personal-income taxes, so that the real consumption of entrepreneurial groups remains fairly constant. This is likely to entail a $D_c{}^r$-path which rises at about the same pace as Z, so that where Z curls upward to the right, the $D_c{}^r$-curve is likely to do the same.

Finally, dissavings, $D_c{}^s = \lambda A$, are likely to be made by wage earners and entrepreneurial groups when N is low and by older pensioners living partly by asset decumulation; when N rises, dishoarding by the former classes will dwindle to zero. Pensioners, however, are likely to increase their consumption outlays to maintain their real consumption, ultimately limited by their ability to decumulate. As prices continue to advance, their money outlay is

---

[17] Thus, as employment grows, the wage bill is $W = w(N_1 + \Delta N)$, while the incremental consumption outlay of wage earners is $\Delta D_{cw} = W \Delta c_w + c_w \Delta W$. The total D_c-outlay is thus $D_c{}^w + \Delta D_c{}^w = c_w W + W \Delta c_w + c_w w \Delta N$.

[18] Money wages, it will be recalled, have been assumed constant, so that the relative income shift is against labor, as well as rentiers, as N advances to the tune of rising prices. In each firm, as output rises and prices mount, the profit increase will approach $Q \Delta P$, where Q denotes output and ΔP is the price rise accompanying the employment increment, ΔN, and the associated output move, ΔQ. See Chapter 3.

likely to reach a plateau so that their real intake declines. On balance, however, aggregate dissavings are likely to diminish as employment advances.

Thus, it is to $D_c{}^w$ and $D_c{}^r$, chiefly, and in lesser measure to $D_c{}^f$, that we must look for the positive slope of the aggregate D_c-curve. Putting the component D_c parts together into a composite D_c-curve, the results appear as shown in Fig. 12. The widening $D_c{}^w$-band is related to the narrowing $D_c{}^t$- and $D_c{}^s$-components: so long as wage

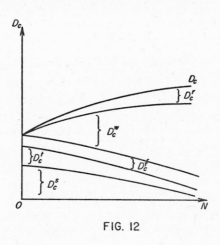

FIG. 12

earners spend more in consumption when employed than when unemployed, these results seem assured.

INVESTMENT DEMAND. In view of the fairly extensive analysis of D_c, the treatment of investment demand, D_i, can be fairly brief.

In general, there are a few main possibilities here. First, it is conceivable that aggregate money-investment outlay is budgeted in money terms and held fixed regardless of the price-level or employment position; this is shown by curve 1 in Fig. 13 (a). Alternatively, entrepreneurial plans for investment may be planned in real terms, so that, as N advances and the price level mounts, the investment outlay manages to keep the price pace. Curve 2 is meant to depict this case. Real investment may also be tethered to aggregate employment and output so that D_i rises even more rapidly than shown in curve 2. Or the D_i-money outlay may rise though real investment falls off, with the appropriate curve occupy-

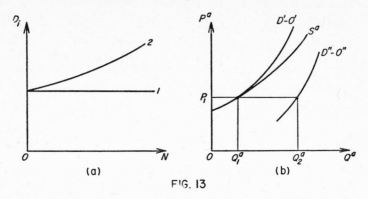

FIG. 13

ing a position intermediate between 1 and 2. The last result is plausible if entrepreneurs tend to defer real-investment plans at high employment, envisaging the position as being at the top of the boom. While for the immediate purposes, on a more formal level, this is all that needs to be said, realistically, it appears reasonable to take D_i as some rising function of N, though much will depend on the anticipations engendered by changes in N and on the implicit monetary policy and interest-rate phenomena as prices and employment go up.

Government outlays may be analyzed in a similar fashion. Most government outlays are budgeted at the start of the year and remain rather stable through the annual period, regardless of price and employment events. If the D- and Z-curves thus refer to the annual period, D_g would appear as a horizontal line. Where this is not the case, the appropriate modifications are fairly obvious.

Taking industry A as illustrative of all *consumer-goods* industries, in Fig. 13 (b) at an output level Q_1 in industries A, B, $C \cdots$ the aggregate intended demand outlay by wage earners, profit recipients, and rentiers receiving income in consumer-goods industries such as A, B, $C \cdots$ is equal, say, to $\Sigma P_1 Q_1$, so that their net savings are zero, with all earnings devoted to consumption outlay. Thereafter, if these groups comprised the only income recipients in the community, as the output of A, B, $C \cdots$ advanced to Q_2, $Q_3 \cdots$ and concomitantly, if they endeavored to save, then the demand outlay forthcoming would be inadequate to sustain a growing output. This is shown by curve D'-O' in the Fig. 13 (b). Hence, it is the presence in the economy of those possessed of transfer in-

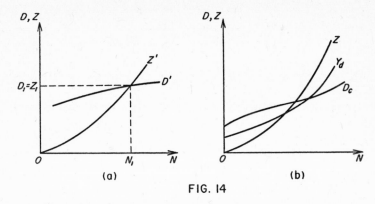

FIG. 14

comes, or of those dissaving, *and of those who receive income in investment-goods industries, and from government,* and who also exercise a demand for consumer goods, who are responsible for shifting the typical D'-O'-curves to the right, to D''-O'', say, in industry A. The latter shift involves the "multiplier" concept of income initially generated in the capital-goods industries leading to an augmented demand for the output of consumer-goods industries. Without investment and the interdependence of consumption demand and investment income, the expansion of consumer-goods industries would tend to be stymied at low-output levels by lack of effective demand.

THE INCOME-EMPLOYMENT EQUILIBRIUM

Having defined the D- and Z-functions, the next step is to illustrate the equilibrium determination. So long as $\Delta D/\Delta N < \Delta Z/\Delta N$, and with $D > Z$ at low employment levels, a determinate and stable equilibrium is possible. This is shown in Fig. 14 (a). Equilibrium employment is at N_1 with proceeds Z_1.

The stability and the determinateness of the income-employment equilibrium deserve further analysis. First, that $\Delta D_c > 0$ seems clear; it remains to show that $\Delta D_c < \Delta Z$.

Using the earlier concept of disposable income, from eq. 18,

$$\frac{\Delta Y_d}{\Delta N} = w + k\frac{\Delta R}{\Delta N} + R\frac{\Delta k}{\Delta R}\frac{\Delta R}{\Delta N} + \frac{\Delta}{\Delta N}(T_t - T_x) \qquad (20)$$

Subtracting this from eq. 13, then

$$\frac{\Delta Z}{\Delta N} - \frac{\Delta Y_d}{\Delta N} = \left(\frac{\Delta R}{\Delta N}(1-k)\right) - \left(R\frac{\Delta k}{\Delta R}\frac{\Delta R}{\Delta N} + \frac{\Delta T_t}{\Delta N} - \frac{\Delta T_x}{\Delta N}\right) \quad (21)$$

As $k < 1$, and by United States data perhaps in the neighborhood of $\frac{1}{7}$, the first bracket on the left will be positive.[19] As N rises, the term $\Delta T_t/\Delta N$ will actually become negative, with the total transfer-income falling off (see Fig. 11 [a]). Likewise, personal-income taxes will mount and, on clearing the bracket on the right in eq. 21, the term will be positive. Thus, whether the rise in Z exceeds that in Y_d hinges on whether the whole second bracket is positive or negative, and thus, whether k rises and whether the rise is ample to offset the first bracket plus the sum of the $\Delta T/\Delta N$ terms. Unless corporations follow dividend policies which become increasingly generous in the percentage of earnings disbursed, Δk is likely to be close to zero, so that $\Delta Z > \Delta Y_d$.[20] This is especially probable if

[19] For example, in 1955 capital-consumption allowances were $31 billion, business taxes were $32 billion, and corporate profits were $40 billion. Taking R as equal to this sum ($103 billion), dividends amounted to $11 billion, so that, on this crude global basis, k equaled about $\frac{1}{10}$. In earlier years it was somewhat higher.

[20] Considering tendencies toward higher corporate taxes and the withholding of earnings to protect stockholders from excessive progressive personal-income taxes while permitting capital gains to be revealed in the stock market, and the penchant for internal-investment financing, it is doubtful that k will rise. Actually, so long as dividends are paid continuously by large firms even when earnings are just barely adequate to cover the "normal" dividend, the k-factor may well decline as N advances. Offsets, however, appear in the form of management bonuses, which may be considered as a form of dividend shared by a select few.

According to available data for the United States, in the years 1922 to 1943, from 30 to 56 per cent of net income was retained by manufacturing firms (except for 1936 to 1937 when an undistributed-profits tax was in effect). In larger firms, from 1940 to 1943 about 30 per cent of net income was retained, while in smaller firms the range was 50 to 64 per cent. See S. P. Dobrovolsky, *Corporate Income Retention, 1915-43* (National Bureau of Economic Research, 1951), p. 15. According to the same study, a 1 per cent change in net income was associated with an 0.8 per cent change in the rate of retained income (p. 25).

According to a survey of 295 large corporations, the percentage of net income retained was 44, 42, and 47 per cent, respectively, over the years 1953 to 1955 (see *Federal Reserve Bulletin*, June 1956, p. 586). With a corporate-profits tax

N is high and R is large, with ΔR relatively quite small compared with R as ΔN advances by one unit: with ΔR being small there is no reason to anticipate any large change in k so that, unless business-dividend policy is highly erratic, Δk will approach zero. Even if this were *not* the case, it could still follow that $\Delta Z > \Delta D_c$. Let us consider this.

So long as $\Delta Z > \Delta Y_d$, and as $\Delta Y_d > \Delta D_c$ whenever there are savings out of income, it follows that $\Delta Z > \Delta D_c$, so that the stability relation is necessarily satisfied; it is possible for $\Delta D_c > \Delta Y_d$ only through the avenue of dissaving, through enlarged expenditure out of wage income by wage earners to maintain their real consumption, and through enlarged rentier outlay. Yet dissaving is likely to be important only at low income levels; the surmise is that λA decreases in an employment advance. Further, $\Delta D_c{}^J / \Delta N \approx 0$ when income and employment are already high. If for wage earners we take $c_w = 1$, so that personal savings are zero, then it must follow that $\Delta Z > \Delta D_c$. The results are assured if we allow for a decrease in c_w, and thus some personal savings, for wage-earning groups. The appropriate curves appear in Fig. 14 (b); until D_c lies below Y_d, personal savings are negative.[21] Although D_c occasionally may rise at the same pace or even faster than Y_d, so long as there are personal savings the full D_c-function will lie below Y_d. Apart from some curious dissaving phenomena, D_c ought not, over an extended range, to climb faster than Z.

Somewhat more troublesome is the relation of $\Delta D_i / \Delta Z$. If real investment is taken as rising with N, then a nonequilibrium and explosive pattern is conceivable: there is implicit a built-in accelerator whereby enlarged investment is linked to the (virtual) employment increases. High accelerator values will, it is well known, defeat

---

of approximately 50 per cent, and considering that for our analysis R—"profits"—contains depreciation allowances and indirect taxes, then a size of k of something just over $\frac{1}{7}$ seems not too far-fetched.

[21] From eq. 18 and 19, then $\Delta Y_d - \Delta D_c = [\Delta Y_d (1 - c)] - [(Y_d \Delta c + \Delta C_s)]$, where $C_s = \lambda A$. The first bracket is positive; the term ΔC_s is likely to be negative, connoting smaller dissaving when N advances, so that on clearing this term becomes positive. On both scores, then, $\Delta Y_d > \Delta D_c$. As for Δc, ultimately for rentiers this becomes zero; for wage earners it can rise slightly (assuming *some* savings margin to begin with), while for profit recipients Δc is likely to fall as their personal savings mount (absolutely and relatively). On balance, therefore, the increment ΔY_d will outweigh ΔD_c.

equilibrating tendencies. For many purposes the explosive model may be little more than a geometrical design, for in the economy which it portrays as bordering on hyperinflation (despite constant-money wages), monetary policy doubtlessly will intervene to choke off investment and the inflationary binge. Further, if full employment is (roughly) an unequivocal quantity, so that there are limits on N, then Z will turn stiff and vertical, so that any flatness in D_i will assure the income-equilibrium outcome. In terms of the D-O-curves of Figs. 9 and 13 (b), for the nonexplosive case the D-O-curves will be steeper or rise at a faster pace than the industry-supply curves; in the nonequilibrating case the D-O-curves will be flatter than the supply curves.

FORCED SAVINGS

As an interesting sidelight of the foregoing discussion, we can reconsider the concept of "forced savings" which has tended to vanish from the literature since Keynes denounced it as a "very rare . . . phenomenon." The idea itself involved the belief that real consumption had to be curtailed as prices rose; Keynes argued that, until full employment was achieved, *aggregate* real consumption could expand with rising output and employment, so that "a forced *deficiency* of saving" was "the usual state of affairs." After full employment, he was willing to acknowledge, forced savings might develop if investment continued to expand.[22]

On an aggregate view, Keynes's main arguments are indisputable. Yet, in assessing the inevitable shifts in the distribution of income accompanying ΔN and rising prices, more remains to be said on the subject. For example, focusing merely on fixed income, it is clear that, beyond certain N-points and the associated price level, rentier real consumption must fall. Likewise, pensioners dissaving at low employment levels may also be denied their previous consumption intake as N advances. For both these groups, "forced savings" may be a very real, and common, experience at high N-levels compared to a recent historical past when N was lower. If we allowed for the possibilities of rising money wages, even without output and employment increases, these relations would become even more patent. Similarly, for salary recipients—though bonuses generally constitute

22 *General Theory*, p. 80.

a handsome counterweight as output, employment and profits rise. Wage earners employed at N_1 also suffer in a real income sense when employment expands to N_2 amid a price rise, so that "forced savings" may thus appear even among the wage-earning groups.[23] Insofar as those comprising the labor group N_1 perform some personal saving, the main consequence of an employment rise to $N_2 > N_1$, with price level $P_2 > P_1$, is that the (virtual) savings positions are eroded. When $c_w = 1$, so that the N_1-group is expending its full income, a subsequent N rise to $N_3 > N_2 > N_1$, with an ensuing price rise, may involve an actual cut in *per capita* consumption for the N_1 set. The real income relinquished by the latter—the "forced savings"—thus are released for consumption by the newly hired wage earners, $N_3 - N_2$, and by profit recipients. As described earlier for rentiers (see Fig. 10 [b]), it is the compulsory curtailment of their consumption which, in part, insures that the D-O-curves will be steeper than the industry-supply curves, rendering an ultimate equilibrium possible. Actually, in a money economy where many incomes are fixed while N and Z grow, and income fixity is typical of the "already employed" wage earners, it is partly through the existence of "forced savings" that Keynes's view of the "law of the marginal propensity to consume," whereby the increment in aggregate real consumption fails to keep pace with the increment in output, is validated. For though some new real consumption is made by those obtaining the money-income increment, there is likely to be a partially offsetting consumption cutback by other income recipients whose money income is constant.

CONCLUSION

In sum, on certain non-overly-restrictive assumptions it has been shown that it is possible to construct an aggregate supply schedule from the particular supply schedules of individual industries, which themselves rest on factor-price and productivity data in the component firms. Embedded in each point on the aggregate supply

---

[23] Keynes suggested that, through diminishing returns (and the implicit price rise), there could be "some sacrifice of real income to those who were already employed" (p. 81). But he went on to say that the idea of "forced saving" had not been extended to this case of "conditions where employment is increasing."

schedule are the supply prices (= expected market prices) for the output quantities in the particular industries among which the employed labor force is distributed.

From the self-same sums of expected proceeds and concomitant labor hire, income is disbursed according to the Y_d-formula. With income in the hands of factors, the question can be raised: how much of Y_d will be diverted to consumption outlay, given the product-supply prices as (virtually) ruling and given the volume of employment? The answer to this query reveals the appropriate D_c-point to attach to the particular N-position. Implicit in D_c, therefore, are exactly the same (supply) prices as are embedded in Z.

Investment demand, D_i, is constructed in a similar fashion. Investment outlay, of course, is not subject to an income restriction, as is D_c—which is contingent primarily on Y_d, itself a function of Z. Instead, the funds for D_i come from the usual sources: from bank lenders, from internal financing, and from private non-bank hands. At each Z,N-point the D_i-magnitude can, in principle, be elicited. Adding it on to the accompanying D_c-magnitude, the aggregate demand point (omitting the intended government outlay) can be derived. In this way, the full D-course can be constructed, embodying on its path exactly the same prices as are built into the Z-function at the corresponding employment-output positions. The equilibrium of aggregate demand and supply prevails at the intersection of the two curves, which entails an employment volume at which the expected sum of sales proceeds is exactly equal to the outlays forthcoming from consuming and investing groups.[24]

[24] The entire exposition has been conducted without bringing into play, either as an identity or as an equilibrium condition, the relation of savings to investment. Instead, what has been insisted on as a condition of equilibrium, in which goods are prepared for market in advance of purchase commitments, has been the equality between expected receipts (by sellers) and intended outlays (by buyers). Although this condition is sufficient to insure the global equilibrium, in order to guarantee that the structure is also in balance, and on only a slightly less aggregative view, it is necessary that: (1) the expected receipts from consumption output equal the intended consumption outlays, (2) the expected receipts from capital-goods production equal the intended investment-goods purchases, and (3) similarly for outputs designed specifically for government purchase. Thus, just as D is split into a tripartite division, Z likewise can be carved up. Condition (2) does entail the famous equality of saving and investment. But just as it is usual to insist that income must go to such a level that the two are brought into balance, we could, with about

MATHEMATICAL NOTE

In deriving formula 14, the necessary increment in aggregate proceeds required to accommodate an increment in employment in industry i would be given by

$$\frac{\partial Z_i}{\partial Q_i}\frac{\partial Q_i}{\partial N_i} = \frac{\partial(P_iQ_i)}{\partial Q_i}\frac{\partial Q_i}{\partial N_i} = P_i\frac{\partial Q_i}{\partial N_i} + Q_i\frac{\partial P_i}{\partial Q_i}\frac{\partial Q_i}{\partial N_i} \qquad (1$$

This follows inasmuch as, at the industry level, $Z_i = P_iQ_i$. Taking industry i as participating in a general employment expansion, a term such as $\partial N_i/\partial N$, representing a weighting factor, must also appear in eq. (1). Over the entire economy we can write:

$$\frac{dZ}{dN} = \sum_{i=1}^{n} \left(P_i\frac{\partial Q_i}{\partial N_i} + Q_i\frac{\partial P_i}{\partial Q_i}\frac{\partial Q_i}{\partial N_i} \right) \frac{dN_i}{dN} \qquad (2)$$

The formula bears an obvious family resemblance to the marginal-revenue concept, or better, to the marginal cost as seen by the buyer under monopsony, inasmuch as the second term is positive. By slight transformations, multiplying the first term on the right by Q_i/Q_i and N_i/N_i, and the second term by P_i/P_i, and remembering that $P_i(dQ_i/dN_i) = w$, the relation can be written in terms of the elasticity of supply $[E_{si} = (P_i/Q_i)(dQ_i/dP_i)]$ and the elasticity of productivity $[E_{qi} = (N_i/Q_i)(dQ_i/dN_i)]$.

---

the same neglect of other aspects of the general system, insist that income must stabilize at such a level as to accommodate an equilibrium between decisions to purchase consumption output and the expected sales value of consumption output. The focus on the balance in capital-goods markets is not always more revealing than the emphasis on the balance in consumer-goods markets; unintended investment and disinvestment can occur in either sector, through too slow or too rapid a pace of purchases. The absorption with the saving-investment tangle, as the literature of 20 years shows, has not always proved a felicitous means for portraying the forces of aggregate demand and supply in income and employment determination.

Chapter 3

Productivity and
Relative Shares

This chapter and the following one are devoted to the theory of relative shares, sketching its outlines by aid of the theory of activity just developed. The suppositions of a fixed stock of equipment, a constant price for variable factors, given productivity functions, a homogeneous labor force, fully integrated firms, and the absence of monopoly, will be retained for the time being, though several of the hypotheses will be dropped in the next chapter. The immediate emphasis will be on the effect of productivity phenomena in determining the relative wage share under conditions of pure competition. We begin, first, with a macroscopic view of the theory.

A MACROSCOPIC VIEW OF RELATIVE SHARES

Formally, the change in income shares and relative earnings as activity varies can be detected on an over-all view by observing the respective shapes and proximity of the Z-, FF'-, and W-curves. So long as the Z-function advances more steeply than W, the income shift is away from wage incomes and toward profits; relative shares would be maintained only if there were an equivalent rise in both curves. With a constant money wage, this can occur only if the Z-curve is linear, denoting a constant marginal product of labor under pure competition and $E_z = 1$.

THE FIXED SHARE. Fixed-income recipients inevitably are affected adversely by an income advance; not only will the relative position of rentier groups suffer by an income upswing, but also they are the only group whose absolute-income parcel fails to be enlarged. Benefit from the real-income employment growth is denied them unless the advance occurs to the tune of falling prices, though, with wage rates constant and the marginal productivity of labor declining, this prospect can be ruled out: rising prices must then accompany growing total production. Normally, the vacuum created by the falling rentier share will be filled by enlarged entrepreneurial earnings.

The rentier status tends to be maintained better when the Z-function rises slowly under conditions where the fixed portion is already small—a less than startling result considering that rentiers would have nothing to sacrifice when their income slice is already micro-

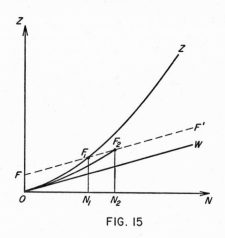

FIG. 15

scopic. Conversely, the rentier group is best able to sustain the relative real loss when its absolute cut is very large. With rising price phenomena accompanying the Z-upswing, with the fall in the real purchasing power of fixed incomes, an absolute *real* penalty is inflicted on rentiers. Small wonder, therefore, at the expression of chronic concern with inflation by rentier groups.

That rentiers are injured by an output and employment advance, in the usual case, is scarcely a novel conclusion. The proposition nevertheless must be qualified in that experience discloses that, at the low levels of depression activity, fixed payments are defaulted and contractual claims are abrogated. Hence, despite the binding legal covenants, the actual income experience of rentiers evidences a partly variable nature. This fact, insofar as it is valid, ought to be incorporated into the analysis. In Fig. 15 the Z-, W-, and FF'-curves are drawn as before. Where fixed charges are always honored regardless of the output and employment level, then the FF'-curve remains pertinent. Suppose, however, that ON_2 is a critical employment point in the sense that bankruptcies become rife if employment declines below this amount. (As a rough surmise, say that it is in the neighborhood of 15 per cent unemployment.) Then, when employment falls below the ON_2-figure, through mounting bankruptcies the rigid claims are scaled down in recognition of the facts of economic life. Thus the effective "fixed" cost curve between employment, ON_2, and zero is shown by the segment OF_2 rather than FF_2. Although other assumptions can be made, the fixed costs (as drawn) are portrayed as sliding gradually and continuously rather than in waves of business failures at several discrete employment levels.[1]

Allowing for the variability in FF' thus complicates the argument: in an employment downturn most of the Z-W-discrepancy will redound to the benefit of fixed claimants; by scaling-down claims the profit share will stay closer to zero rather than turning negative, as premised in a full meeting of legal claims. Of course, much of the argument hinges on the duration of the unemployment period. Once a cutback in claims occurs through a business reorganization, the rentier share is likely to be compressed permanently even in a subsequent upswing. Some "irreversibility" thus appears in the size of the rentier share, depending on the direction, the extent, and the duration of the employment move. "Fixed" incomes are correctly conceived as rigid only for temporary and minor output aberrations; otherwise they are more variable than a tight interpretation of the concept would suggest.

Output and employment levels large enough to permit the fulfillment of all fixed claims are thus advantageous to creditor groups.[2] Activity beyond this level portends some disaster for rentiers, menacing their real as well as their relative income position. Here, then, is a major income group with an inherent economic bias against full employment, especially when compared with unemployed labor and entrepreneurial agents whose status improves under an output advance. To be sure, insofar as rentiers are also dependent on profits and salaries for their total personal income,

---

[1] A curve drawn according to the latter image would display several discontinuities without modifying the main principles.

[2] Conceivably a slightly lower level might be even more desirable if the scale-down of claims were proportionately less than the fall in the price level. But this is a fine point that can be neglected in this over-all view.

their stake in depressed-employment levels becomes partially fragmentized: as rentiers their self-interest invites unemployment, as stockholders or managerial employees their position improves with high activity.

CHANGES IN RELATIVE SHARES. Some of the elements involved in altering relative shares may be put compactly and in sharper relief through some simple derivations.

For example, making use of the elasticity of aggregate supply, E_z (p. 29, for a small employment advance the change in the aggregate wage share is given[3] by

$$\frac{\Delta}{\Delta N}\left(\frac{wN}{Z}\right) = \frac{w}{Z}\left(1 - \frac{1}{E_z}\right) \qquad (w = \text{the constant money wage}) \quad (22)$$

Thus, if E_z is unity, the wage share will remain unchanged. With $E_z < 1$, indicating that the relative rise in aggregate employment is less than the relative movement in proceeds (as will be the case under diminishing returns), then the wage share will fall. The wage share will grow with rising marginal products and $E_z > 1$.

Formula 22 holds some very interesting implications. For one thing, it points up the prospect of an almost inexorable rigidity of the wage share once the proceeds level is already high—at least over short periods of time in which the Z-function is given, with the degree of monopoly and the stock of equipment approximately constant.[4] To illustrate, even if the value of E_z is absurdly low, such as $1/10,000$, which signifies only a 1 per cent increase in employment with a 10,000 per cent change in proceeds, and with an annual wage rate of $5,000, once income is in the neighborhood of $350 billion the fall in the wage share will be in the minuscule amount of $5/35,000$. Considering that values of E_z as high as $\frac{3}{4}$ or $\frac{3}{5}$ are not

---

[3] Differentiating, $\dfrac{d}{dN}\left(\dfrac{wN}{Z}\right) = \dfrac{w}{Z} - \dfrac{wN}{Z^2}\dfrac{dZ}{dN}$. Clearing the latter expression yields eq. 22.

[4] Compare M. Kalecki, "The Distribution of the National Income," in *Essays in the Theory of Fluctuations* (New York, Rinehart, 1939). Kalecki relies on a fortuitous rise in the degree of monopoly power over time to explain the stability of the wage share; this does involve shifts in Z over time, or a "long-run" Z- and W-conception. For additional data tending to confirm the stability, and with more empirically minded analysis, see E. H. Phelps Brown and P. E. Hart, "The Share of Wages in National Income," *Economic Journal* (June 1952).

to be precluded, the likely constancy in the wage share when the proceeds level is already high is driven home by compelling force by means of the formula. For small changes in the employment total, or even for changes of the order of 1,000,000 men in a work force of 65,000,000, and with wages, say, at $5,000 *and all of the added proceeds going to labor*, it constitutes a clue to the constancy of the wage portion: for a finite change of this order we would have to use the following formula[5]:

$$\frac{\Delta}{\Delta N}\left(\frac{W}{Z}\right) = \frac{w\Delta N}{Z_2}\left(1 - \frac{N_1}{Z_1}\frac{\Delta Z}{\Delta N}\right) = \frac{w\Delta N}{Z_2}\left(1 - \frac{1}{E_z}\right) \qquad (23)$$

where ΔN was the change in employment and Z_1 and Z_2 were the old and the new levels of proceeds, respectively.

The *change* in the share of fixed-income recipients is given by

$$\frac{\Delta}{\Delta N}\left(\frac{F}{Z}\right) = -\frac{F}{NZ}\left(\frac{1}{E_z}\right) \qquad (24)$$

The negative sign indicates that the rentier group always loses *relatively* after an N,Z-advance, with the decline most pronounced when F is large and N and Z are low, with E_z approaching zero.[6]

The change in the profit share is given by the sum of eq. 23 and eq. 24 with the signs reversed. Manifestly, the change in the profit share is always positive for an income advance—except in the event of some spectacular increasing-returns phenomena. Profit growth, we shall observe, is always facilitated by falling marginal products as employment swells, while a check on profits is provided by an already high employment and proceeds total which operates inevitably to narrow the gain possible at the expense of fixed-income categories.

Comparing the change in fixed incomes to wages directly, the appropriate formula reads

$$\frac{\Delta}{\Delta N}\left(\frac{F}{wN}\right) = -\frac{F}{wN^2} \qquad (25)$$

---

[5] Compare eq. 33, which incorporates productivity phenomena within individual firms.

[6] Actually, E_z is likely to be relatively high at low N,Z-levels, thus providing a counterweight to the decline.

Thus the fixed share always declines relative to the wage share as N,Z rise with wage rates constant; the relative diversion is strongest when the rentier sum is large absolutely, and the wage and employment level is small.

PRODUCTIVITY AND RELATIVE SHARES

The role of productivity in settling the position of Z relative to W has been alluded to at several places. Let us consider this in some detail; as before, both product and factor markets are regarded as purely competitive with individual firms animated solely by the profit motive.

At the level of the individual firm, with labor the only variable factor and the wage rate, w, inscribed as a datum, the firm will equate the marginal-value product of labor to wage rate. Thus:

$$P \frac{\Delta Q}{\Delta N} = w \qquad (P = \text{product price}) \qquad (26)$$

$$\left(\frac{\Delta Q}{\Delta N} \equiv \frac{dQ}{dN} = \text{marginal product of labor} \right)$$

Then,

$$\frac{dQ}{dN} = \frac{w}{P} \qquad \left(M = \frac{dQ}{dN} \right)\left(A = \frac{Q}{N} \right) \qquad (27)$$

$$E_q = \frac{N}{Q} \frac{dQ}{dN} = \frac{wN}{PQ} = \frac{M}{A} \qquad (Q = \text{physical output}) \qquad (28)$$

$$(PQ = \text{sales proceeds} = Z, \text{ in each integrated firm})$$

E_q is the familiar concept of the elasticity of productivity, signifying the relative change in output to the relative change in factor use, applied in this case to a one-variable factor situation.[7] Under the given hypotheses, E_q is thus equal to the ratio of the wage bill to total proceeds, and also to the ratio of the marginal to the average product of labor. Equation 28 conveys the important theorem that *the income share of labor*, wN/PQ, *depends on the ratio of the marginal to the average product of labor*. A significant inference can be drawn from it—namely, that a rise in the marginal product

[7] See, for example, my *Price Theory*, pp. 83–84, 86.

of labor will *not* increase labor's share in the income total unless the average product fails to rise proportionately. This is a result which is of major importance, and is a correct statement of a proposition which has often been distorted.[8]

Equation 26 is the root from which the others sprout; eq. 28 provides the coloration for the argument. According to the latter, if E_q is small then the wage portion will constitute an insignificant part of the income partition no matter how large the absolute size

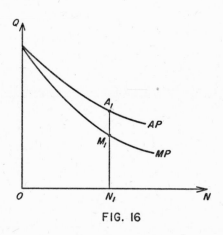

FIG. 16

of the marginal product of labor. Conversely, as the measure approaches unity, then labor tends to absorb all of income *even if its marginal physical product is small*. Exceeding unity, labor would amass all of income plus a transfer of wealth!—the latter result shows the fantastic implications of a hypothesis of rising marginal products when joined to the assumption of competitive-product markets.

Diagrammatically, in Fig. 16, the curve, *AP*, represents the average product, and the curve, *MP*, the marginal product of labor, with physical amounts of output measured vertically and amounts of labor represented on the horizontal scale. At employment ON_1, the wage share is given by $ON_1 \cdot M_1N_1$, while total output is

[8] One of the few writings to state the relation of the marginal product of labor to its income share correctly (though somewhat abstrusely) is the short article by A. L. Marty, "Diminishing Returns and the Relative Share of Labor," *Quarterly Journal of Economics* (November 1953).

$ON_1 \cdot A_1 N_1$. The ratio of the wage bill to total output is given by $M_1 N_1 / A_1 N_1$.

EXTENSION TO N-FIRMS. Despite their importance, the results so far seem only dimly related to macroanalysis, belonging in origin and spirit to the theory of the firm and marginal-productivity doctrine. However, the argument can be extended to encompass the economy by recalling the content of the Z-function. At the firm's level, proceeds $Z = PQ$ are simply the multiple of prices and quantities produced and sold. So long as each firm equates marginal-value products to factor prices, the macroanalysis properly ensues. Using subscripts to denote the individual firms, with many of them producing the same product in view of the competitive hypothesis, then[9]

$$\bar{E}_q = \frac{wN}{Z} = \sum_{i=1}^{n} \frac{Z_1 E_{qi}}{Z} = \sum_{i=1}^{n} \frac{Z_i}{Z}\left(\frac{M_i}{A_i}\right) \tag{29}$$

$\bar{E}_q$ can be interpreted as the "average" elasticity of productivity; it obviously is dependent on the elasticities within the individual firms where the latter are weighted by the importance of the firm in the division of the total proceeds. An E_q which is biased toward a large wage share in small firms (where size is measured in terms of the aggregate proceeds) will have less influence on the final income partition than a small E_q in large firms. The "average firm" would be one whose E_q moved identically with $\bar{E}_q$.

Equation 29 also discloses the importance of the "weighted" productivity phenomena: whenever diminishing returns preponderate within individual firms, with $A > M$, then the global $\bar{E}_q$ will reflect these facts and will also stand below unity.

MONEY WAGES AND THE INCOME SHARE. Interestingly, the absolute money wage fails to appear in these analyses of the relative wage share, leading to the conclusion that productivity phenomena alone

[9] Given

$$\frac{wN}{Z} = \frac{w(N_1 + N_2 + \cdots + N_n)}{Z_1 + Z_2 + \cdots + Z_n} = \frac{wN_1}{Z} + \frac{wN_2}{Z} + \cdots + \frac{wN_n}{Z} \tag{30}$$

$$= \frac{wN_1}{Z_1}\frac{Z_1}{Z} + \frac{wN_2}{Z_2}\frac{Z_2}{Z} + \cdots + \frac{wN_n}{Z_n}\frac{Z_n}{Z} \tag{31}$$

As $E_{qi} = \dfrac{wN_i}{P_i Q_i} = \dfrac{wN_i}{Z_i}$, then relation 29 follows.

govern the final result. This is an inference with overtones of immense practical importance, limited so far by: (1) the stringent competitive hypothesis; (2) the assumption of a homogeneous labor force, and (3) the postulate of labor alone comprising the variable factor category. All of these restraints would have to be lifted before the proposition could be evaluated properly for application to real affairs.[10]

One escape clause through which it could be contended that a money-wage rise would alter the relative wage share would be to demonstrate that a money-wage move altered the output level in such a way as to raise the M/A-ratios in individual firms. But this is likely to require an output and employment decrease generally, rather than the increase in employment typically averred by adherents of underconsumption theories of employment who counsel a rising money wage and "an income shift to labor" in order to combat unemployment.

The N-Factor Case. It is not too difficult to generalize the one-variable factor analysis and demonstrate that productivity phenomena also dominate the income division with n-variable factors, say of various grades of labor. The relevant formula is not vastly more intricate than for the one-variable factor instance. Thus the income share of factor i, when there are n-variable factors, is given by[11]

$$\frac{w_i N_i}{Z} = \frac{M_i}{n A_i} \tag{32}$$

Thus the ratio of marginal to average product still governs the result, though the income share is reduced in ratio $1/n$, with the denominator signifying the number of factors. Where $n = 1$, the result is as before.

[10] Some empirical evidence tending to support the argument on the ineffectiveness of money-wage changes in influencing the relative wage share appears in the study by Harold M. Levinson, *Unionism, Wage Trends, and Income Distribution, 1914–1947* (Ann Arbor, Univ. of Michigan Press, 1951), pp. 110, 114–115. Similarly, the view that the impact of labor unions on the relative wage share "has been minimal" appears in Clark Kerr, "Trade Unionism and Distributive Shares," *American Economic Review* (May 1954), p. 291. Martin Bronfenbrenner also concludes that the effect of collective bargaining in "changing the aggregate income distribution has been unimportant." (See his article, "The Incidence of Collective Bargaining," *ibid.*, p. 299.)

[11] See the Mathematical Note at the end of this chapter.

For any given factor, therefore, given the ratio of its marginal to average product, its relative income share will be increased if there are fewer complementary factor types associated with it in production. Thus, if other factors tend to become equally skilled and homogeneous, and *if the marginal and average products of the given factor remained unchanged* despite its greater use—a doubtful proviso—then the share of the factor in the income total will rise. In a sense, this amounts to an assumption of the given factor becoming more important compared to the other agents.

One qualification ought to be brought to the fore. It remains true that, if the product price and all variable-factor prices rose proportionately, and the amounts of factors used thus remained unchanged, then the relative distributive shares would hold firm. However, it is open to any grade of labor to alter its money wage relative to other labor groups, and, by so doing, it can conceivably revise the amount of its hire, with the substitution of relatively lower- for higher-priced labor tending to alter the productivity ratios and, thereby, the income shares. Through a higher factor price and a smaller output volume, any one labor group may even succeed in obtaining a higher absolute real income, though its relative advantage would be secured at least partially at the expense of other labor groups. All this remains to be explored further.[12]

CHANGES IN EMPLOYMENT AND THE WAGE SHARE. The preceding analysis revealed the productivity forces governing the wage share at any given output and employment position. Considering a variation in output and employment, our interest also extends to the changes in productivity phenomena which alter the wage share. At the level of the individual firm, the relevant elements are[13]

$$\frac{\Delta}{\Delta N} \left(\frac{wN_i}{Z_i} \right) = \frac{1}{A_i} \left(\Delta M_i - \frac{M_i}{A_i} \Delta A_i \right) \tag{33}$$

Normally, we are to the right of the maximum average product in the competitive case, so that, with continuous functions, both ΔM and ΔA will be negative. Further, inasmuch as M reaches a zero value while A is still positive, it follows that the decrease

---

[12] See Chapter 8.

[13] For $\dfrac{d}{dN} \left(\dfrac{wN_i}{Z_i} \right) = \dfrac{d}{dN} \left(\dfrac{M_i}{A_i} \right)$. Compare eq. 23, which skirts the productivity phenomena within individual firms.

$\Delta M > \Delta A$. Thus the wage share will fall, with the second term in the parentheses tending to temper the descent: the wage share thus tends to hold up better when the ratio M/A approaches unity and ΔA approaches ΔM. When $\Delta M = \Delta A = 0$, or constant marginal products prevail, manifestly the wage share will remain constant.

Extending the results to the economy, the formulae become rather complex not only because of the usual weighting problem but also because of the proceeds changes in the firm accompanying those in the economy. Thus,[14]

$$\frac{d}{dN}\left(\frac{wN}{Z}\right) = \sum_{i=1}^{n} \frac{1}{A_i} \left\{ \frac{Z_i}{Z}\left(\Delta M_i - \frac{M_i}{A_i}\Delta A_i\right) \right.$$
$$\left. + \frac{M_i}{Z}\left(\Delta Z_i - \frac{Z_i}{Z}\Delta Z\right) \right\} \frac{\Delta N_i}{\Delta N} \quad (34)$$

Considering that the whole second bracket is modified by M_i/Z, it is likely to be extremely small for each firm, so that the first bracket is likely to contain the decisive terms over the economy as well as in the firm. *Changes* in marginal product compared with average product will thus largely decide the nature of the change in the wage share. In this result, too, the absolute wage level is missing, seemingly divested of influence over the end result.

THE CONTINUITY POSTULATE. The derivations so far have been predicated largely on the belief that the expansion is housed within going firms. Misgivings may be aroused concerning the validity of the several propositions when the population of firms alters. The issue, of course, dissolves when the employment expansion is in fact uniform among all firms. Too, even in a disproportionate advance there are no real perplexities so long as the number of firms re-

---

[14] From eq. 31,

$$\frac{d}{dN}\left(\frac{wN}{Z}\right) = \sum_{i=1}^{n}\left\{\frac{\partial}{\partial N_i}\left(\frac{wN_i}{Z_i}\frac{Z_i}{Z}\right)\right\}\frac{dN_i}{dN} = \sum_{i=1}^{n}\frac{\partial}{\partial N_i}\left(\frac{M_i}{A_i}\frac{Z_i}{Z}\right)\frac{dN_i}{dN} \quad (35)$$

Performing the differentiation, we have:

$$= \sum_{i=1}^{n}\left\{\frac{1}{A_i}\left(\frac{\partial M_i}{\partial N_i} - \frac{M_i}{A_i}\frac{\partial A_i}{\partial N_i}\right)\frac{Z_i}{Z} + \frac{M_i}{A_i Z}\left(\frac{\partial Z_i}{\partial N_i} - \frac{Z_i}{Z}\frac{\partial Z}{\partial N_i}\right)\right\}\frac{dN_i}{dN} \quad (36)$$

Substituting ΔM's and ΔA's for changes in marginal and average product, respectively, then eq. 34 follows.

mains constant; the weighting process leads to the correct final results. When new firms appear on the scene, while old ones disappear, the difference in income shares, for example, made by entry and departure can also be calculated. Reflecting on the latter phenomena, however, suggests that the income transition accompanying an N,Z-advance is likely to be finite and discrete, containing jumps and leaps not amenable to the differential calculus and its economic progeny; namely, the marginal product.

Systematic analysis of change, if some average movement is to be detected, must largely presume general constancy in the universe of firms and some reasonable uniformity in the variations experienced by the greater part of the producing units comprising the economy: methodical inquiry would be checked in a world of free will where anything can happen. Macroeconomic analysis must accept such structural premises as an article of faith, for, otherwise, logical techniques would be stultified, either foredoomed as futile irrelevances or becoming so tenuous and contingent as to lose all didactic value: the admonition that anything can happen would be the culmination of all study.

Fortunately, there is no reason to assume that the facts are so perverse. There are strong currents of fixity underlying the diverse waves of change within the economy.[15] The population of firms particularly fails to exhibit the volatility of an unmitigated flux. Once granting the postulate of output and employment continuity within the present array of firms as the typical case, separate provision can be made for those cases in which new firms buck the economic tide, as ripples in a generally smooth surf.[16]

[15] Lest it be thought that the previous remarks constitute an invitation for the scrapping of analytic methods in favor of empirical and statistical-type techniques, it is only necessary to point out that the usefulness of statistical averages or trends is likewise contingent on a presumption of stability in the universe from which the data have been extracted. Otherwise, the calculations are of interest only in a historical sense rather than for any predictive merit in illuminating and foreshadowing the likely course of events.

[16] Clinging more sedulously to the continuity hypothesis than is warranted or necessary, if all firms increase output incrementally in an output advance, then with constant wage rates and diminishing marginal products the price level must always rise, with the magnitude contingent on the exact change in marginal products. Though the analysis would not apply to a *nonuniform*

ABSOLUTE SHARES AND ZERO INCOMES

Besides the changes in relative income as employment alters, there are at least three other questions that invite examination: (1) the movement in (per capita) real wages as employment alters, (2) the change in the *absolute* aggregate real-wage share as employment advances, and (3) the exact dimension of the income loss for those who remain unemployed as output settles at a given level of activity. The main ideas can be set forth briefly.

THE REAL WAGE. Singling out the set of individuals who remain employed whether total employment is N_1 or N_2, where $N_2 > N_1$, so long as production is accomplished under conditions of decreasing returns in competitive markets the real income of all wage earners populating N_1 must be affected adversely by the employment rise. Besides rentiers, a substantial set of wage earners may thus be injured economically in the advance toward full employment.[17] Thus, those employed at under-employment positions have a vested interest in maintaining the status quo and their ranks gain new adherents as employment picks up.[18] The conclusions, however, are

output expansion, the same elements of productivity and wage rate are inevitably involved. Thus:

$$\frac{\Delta P}{\Delta N} = - \frac{w}{M} \left(\frac{\Delta M}{M} \right) \tag{37}$$

As ΔM is always negative with falling productivity, the price level always rises. The wage rate is now shown to figure prominently, along with marginal-productivity phenomena, in governing the price level. On all this, see Keynes, *op. cit.*, Chapter 21, and my *Income and Employment Analysis* (New York, Pitman, 1951), Chapter 12, and "The Theory of the Consumer Price Level," *Canadian Journal of Economics* (1952). To tie the argument to the ordinary concept of the price level represented in index-number terms requires that the particular price changes be weighted by the quantities of goods included in the base-period market basket.

[17] This is a result with political overtones; it was undoubtedly overlooked by those who predicted a Democratic victory in 1952 because of the prosperous times. Although other issues may have been paramount, the rising prices fostered by the boom seem to have made new converts to the Republican party, exemplified in the many references to the "housewives' vote." Something of the same sort seems to have happened in Britain in 1955 and early 1956.

[18] Thus Kerr concludes that unions, by "the furtherance of a policy of continuing full employment," can reduce labor's relative share. (*Op. cit.*, p. 291.) This conclusion would be fully consistent with the hypothesis of diminishing

tempered by the psychic advantage of job security in booming labor markets and, if labor heterogeneity were recognized, the facts of "up-grading" as labor scarcities develop. A further qualification would have to be allowed if fuller employment compelled the introduction of equipment which raised the productivity of labor and the absolute level of real wages. The last reservation is likely to be unimportant whenever an up-climb and a down-swing occur precipitously in an unstable economy.

NULL INCOME. The discussion of relative shares has centered on the partition among those who actually derive income in the economic process. Yet a decline in employment plunges the earnings of the newly unemployed down to zero; they thus comprise part of the *null*-income set too often overlooked in distributive investigations.

Subtleties and imponderables of a definition of full employment can be waived at this place. On what may be plausible grounds, based on past experience and adjusted for estimated changes in the labor force, some level of employment might be selected and described as full employment, N_f.[19] When actual employment is N', the difference, $N_f - N'$, measures the unemployment so that the money-income loss of the unemployed null-income set is $w(N_f - N')$. Corrected for price-level phenomena, the actual income share relinquished through unemployment by the null-income set is thus

$$\frac{P'}{P_f}\left(\frac{w(N_f - N')}{Z'}\right) \qquad \begin{array}{l} (P' = \text{prices at } N') \\ (P_f = \text{prices at } N_f) \end{array} \qquad (38)$$

Under full employment, the income share that the null-income group would receive would be

$$\frac{w(N_f - N')}{Z_f} \qquad (39)$$

Thus, for the individuals affected within the null-income set, a rise in employment is an unmitigated boon and an employment drop a personal disaster.[20] It follows that it is inaccurate to describe labor

---

marginal productivity (relative to average product), though, so far as I can see, his conclusions rest more on data than on deductions from this principle.

[19] See Chapter 6.

[20] A correction, in personal-income calculations, would have to be entered for any transfer incomes received by the unemployed. This may generally be in the neighborhood of 25 to 40 per cent of their income while employed.

income, in a generic sense, as being ravaged by unemployment, implying proportionate suffering. Depressions touch mainly the unemployed, while the employed, individually, may experience an improvement in their personal well-being.

Profits will also be at a maximum under full employment so long as diminishing returns prevail. Thus unemployment carries with it a cut in profits; the profit sacrificed could be described in a way analogous to eq. 38 and eq. 39. An important difference lies in the fact that profit-recipients ordinarily are insulated from the complete income annihilation experienced by the unemployed.[21]

In sum, only entrepreneurs and the actual unemployed have an unequivocal stake in maximum employment, while rentiers and the employed find their interests best served at lower levels of activity. In a way, these results help explain the widespread fear and condemnation of inflation even when the economy is operating at restricted-output levels, and they suggest that, as measures to restore full employment become increasingly successful, resistance to further maneuvers toward the same end is likely to become more pervasive and articulate.

RENTIER REAL-INCOME LOSSES. That only the unemployed and the profit recipients relish a rapid employment advance is a disquieting result, for it entails that aversion to unemployment and deflation is far from universal. Rentier groups suffer a relative income loss as employment advances (see eq. 25) in amount $[(F/Z') - (F/Z_f)]$. In real terms, their relative *real-income* loss is equal to [22]

$$\frac{F\left(1 - \dfrac{P'}{P_f}\right)}{Z'} \tag{40}$$

Thus the real-income loss depends on the price-level movement. Insofar as the price level is constant, the real-income loss will be

[21] This assumes that (practically) all firms are profitable or unprofitable simultaneously. Otherwise, a depressed level of activity will create a class of null-income recipients among entrepreneurs in the same way as is true of wage earners. To a degree, this does happen as an income-employment drop leads to a chain of bankruptcies affecting only some firms.

[22] Measured in terms of the full-employment output, this becomes

$$\frac{F\left(1 - \dfrac{P'}{P_f}\right)}{Z_\cdot} \tag{41}$$

nil, while, in the unlikely event of a price-level drop, the rentier real position will actually be enhanced. There is a rather complete analogy between rentiers and those already employed whenever there is a rapid activity advance which signalizes a price-level upswing; the interlocked fortunes of this bloc obviously can create a hostile environment and raise obstacles to measures designed to promote greater employment.

THE AGGREGATE REAL-WAGE BILL. Though on strict short-period hypotheses the real wage (under pure competition) seems destined to fall with an advance in employment, it is also of some significance to inquire whether the *aggregate* real-wage bill will increase. Unless it does increase, it will be to the interest of labor as a bloc, employed and unemployed, to join together to check an advance toward fuller employment. Of course, if there were assurance that, when the real-income total rose everyone would participate in the welfare aggrandizement, the question would never arise; the facts, however, need not be so felicitous to labor as a group.[23]

The condition for a rise in the aggregate wage bill, in real terms and referred to the individual firm, is that

$$\frac{d(NM)}{dN} = M - \frac{NdM}{dN} > 0 \tag{42}$$

As before, M denotes the marginal product of labor. Examining eq. 42, the formula is closely reminiscent of the expression for marginal revenue; it reveals that the marginal physical product of an additional employee must outweigh the fall in marginal product of the group previously employed, multiplied by the latter number. To generalize the result for the economy, it would be necessary to put a money dimension on eq. 42, which can be done by multiplying the ruling price, P_1', and weighting the results for each firm by its advance in employment relative to the aggregate employment movement. Thus,[24]

$$P' \frac{d(NM)}{dN} = \sum_{i=1}^{n} P_1' \left(M_i - N_i \frac{dM_i}{dN_i} \right) \frac{dN_i}{dN} > 0 \tag{43}$$

---

[23] Compare I. M. Little, *A Critique of Welfare Economics* (Oxford, Clarendon, 1950), pp. 102–109, where he considers questions related to the distributive aspects of a growth in productivity.

[24] In both eq. 42 and eq. 43 the term dM/dN is regarded as typically negative; the negative sign has been incorporated in the formulae so that only the absolute values of the terms need be inserted.

Unfortunately, from the standpoint of unequivocal results, in some firms the inequality (eq. 43) may be positive and in other firms negative, so that the customary index-number dilemmas in measuring the change in real output and general well being would assert themselves. Nevertheless, if prices and money income have risen, it is only if eq. 43 is positive that the aggregate real-wage share can be maintained and any decline in the relative wage position be arrested.

Equation 42 is significant, for it places some restrictions on the production function within individual firms if we are to be sure that the aggregate real-wage bill is to increase. In each individual firm it would entail

$$\left(\frac{dQ}{dN} > 0\right), \quad \left(\frac{d^2Q}{dQ^2} < 0\right), \quad \left(\frac{d^3Q}{dQ^3} > 0\right), \quad \text{when } N = a, c > a > b \tag{44}$$

The first bracket in eq. 44 is merely a statement of the existence of positive marginal products while the second bracket expresses the conventional law of diminishing marginal productivity. The new complication is in the third bracket, which stipulates that the decline in marginal products must be at a falling rate; in diagrammatic terms, the *marginal-product curve must be convex to the origin*, at least to the right of the maximum average product position.[25] A concave marginal-product sector over the region where $A_i > M_i$ would signify a declining absolute real-wage take in the individual firm despite the greater employment.

These relations are of much interest in that generally they have been overlooked in the common surmise that the *aggregate* real-wage bill will grow with employment. It may—but this is an empirical matter depending on the ruling conditions and the exact nature of the production functions within the individual producing firms.

[25] Older drawings of the marginal-product curve seem to have taken this into account, whether by accident or design. In the modern textbook literature, with its family of total, average, and marginal-product curves for the individual firm, the drawings are as a rule faulty in the relevant range over which marginal products lie below the average: concavity seems to be drawn very much more commonly than convexity, with an apparent obliviousness of the implications.

NOTES: NON-WAGE VARIABLE-INCOME ALLOCATIONS

If the Z-category is broadened to include other components sharing in the allocation of sales proceeds, the necessary modifications can be made without undue difficulty. For example, the change in the total of user cost, regarded as depreciation sums resulting from the wear and tear on equipment, and recaptured by entrepreneurs through sales proceeds, for a small ΔN advance is given by

$$\frac{\Delta}{\Delta N}\left(\frac{U}{Z}\right) = \frac{1}{Z}\left(\frac{\Delta U}{\Delta N} - \frac{U}{Z}\frac{\Delta Z}{\Delta N}\right) \tag{1}$$

Although this can be converted into elasticity elements, the derivation above is easier to comprehend. Invariably, $(\Delta Z/\Delta N) > (\Delta U/\Delta N)$ while the ratio U/Z is likely to be quite small, of the order of $\frac{1}{20}$ or less. On the other hand, with diminishing returns the differential, $\Delta Z/\Delta N$, will grow so that the negative portion of the formula is enlarged. On balance, at high Z,N-levels the tendency will be toward a greater entrepreneurial recapture of capital through user-cost phenomena. At low employment levels the formula ought to approach zero values, for it is only when demand strengthens and promises additional buoyancy in the future that marginal user-cost phenomena will bulk large in entrepreneurial thoughts.

Interest payments, too, approximate a variable cost in that, with rising proceeds, more money is required by firms in order to finance the enlarged volume of transactions. While it is wrong to suppose that interest rates remain constant as Z,N-levels mount, for common experience is to the contrary, yet on this fiction, and letting r denote the interest rate (regarded as a short-term rate) and writing M for the supply of money, the *change* in the income share going as interest will be

$$\frac{\Delta}{\Delta N}\left(\frac{rM}{Z}\right) = \frac{r}{Z}\left(\frac{\Delta M}{\Delta N} - \frac{M}{Z}\frac{\Delta Z}{\Delta N}\right) \tag{2}$$

The ratio $\Delta M/\Delta N$ probably will become smaller as N grows on the ground, say, that a 5 per cent rise in the value of transactions does not require a similar rise in the stock of money.[26] This might be upset through strong diminishing-returns phenomena, whereby a 5 per cent employment expansion involves a substantially greater proceeds rise. In any event, as the velocity of circulation is greater than unity, it is highly certain that $\Delta M/\Delta N$ is less than $\Delta Z/\Delta N$. With $Z(\Delta M/\Delta N)$ in excess of $M(\Delta Z/\Delta N)$, the parentheses

[26] See William J. Baumol, "The Transactions Demand for Cash: An Inventory Theoretic Approach," *Quarterly Journal of Economics* (November 1952), p. 550.

will be negative, denoting a fall in the variable-interest share as the employment advance continues.

When excise taxes, T_i, are levied per unit of *output*, the relative intake of the tax collector will decline, as shown by

$$\frac{\Delta}{\Delta N}\left(\frac{T_i}{Z}\right) = \frac{1}{z}\left(\frac{\Delta T_i}{\Delta N} - \frac{T_i}{Z}\frac{\Delta Z}{\Delta N}\right) \tag{3}$$

With decreasing productivity, the ratio $\Delta T_i/\Delta N \approx 0$, implying that the entire parentheses become negative and the tax take declines relatively: although the tax collections bear a constant proportion to physical production, employment will increase relatively more rapidly than output.[27] A tax levied percentage-wise on sales proceeds would hold the tax share constant as proceeds grow; in this case, the relative tax take would change only with a change in the rate of taxation.

MATHEMATICAL NOTE

To derive eq. 32, assuming solely various grades of labor, total variable cost is given by

$$\text{Total variable cost} = w_1 N_1 + w_2 N_2 + \cdots + w_n N_n \tag{4}$$

With factor prices constant,

$$\text{Marginal cost} = w_1\frac{\partial N_1}{\partial Q} + w_2\frac{\partial N_2}{\partial Q} + \cdots + w_n\frac{\partial N_n}{\partial Q} \tag{5}$$

$$= \frac{w_1}{M_1} + \frac{w_2}{M_2} + \cdots + \frac{w_n}{M_n} \tag{6}$$

But for cost minimization all of the ratios in eq. (6) are equal (and the sum of the denominators equal unity), so that

$$\text{Marginal cost} = n\frac{w_1}{M_1} \tag{7}$$

Under pure competition, price equals marginal cost:

$$M_1 = n\frac{w_1}{P} \tag{8}$$

$$\frac{M_1 N_1}{Q} = n\frac{w_1 N_1}{Z} \quad \text{or} \quad \frac{M_1}{nA} = \frac{w_1 N_1}{Z} \tag{9}$$

[27] In this analysis, the recent argument that excise taxes lower incomes and fail to affect prices is rejected, for constant-factor prices have been assumed. Thus excise taxes *must* raise money costs and prices. See, however, Earl R. Rolph, *The Theory of Fiscal Economics* (Berkeley, Univ. of California Press, 1954), Chapters 6 and 7.

Chapter 4

Monopoly, Capital Accumulation, and Relative Shares

Continuing the theme of the preceding chapter with the methods and the analytic patterns already established, the following pages trace out the special influence of monopoly, of full-cost pricing, of the degree of integration, and of variations in factor prices, factor productivity, and the stock of capital equipment, on the income division.

MONOPOLY AND RELATIVE SHARES

Monopoly will be assigned a rather simple and unsophisticated meaning: it is meant to cover all those cases in which the firm equates marginal revenue to marginal cost, and perceives price to be higher than either.[1] The rule of profit maximization is thereby perpetuated, with entrepreneurs envisaged as motivated wholly by thoughts of pecuniary gain. Departures from the strict monopoly-pricing rules, as in the case of full-cost pricing, oligopoly, and price rigidity, will be appraised only briefly. The main objective of the study is to explore the impact of monopoly on the Z-W-spread rather than to cover these complicated matters in detail. Further, to evade certain problems of interdependence, it will be assumed that the relevant demand curve is subjective in nature, as perceived in the eyes of the seller, so that our derivations of demand elasticity likewise represent a subjective estimate. To assure determinate-

---

[1] The classificatory snarls surrounding the definitions of monopoly and competition are well known. For a recent attempt at restatement, as well as a survey of the literature, see Robert Bishop, "Elasticities, Cross-Elasticities and Market Relationships," *American Economic Review* (December 1952), with replies by E. H. Chamberlin and William Fellner in the December 1953 issue. For a further appraisal see my article, "Revised Doctrines of Competition," *American Economic Review* (May 1955).

ness and compatibility with objective market facts, it will be supposed that the price-output combination elected by the firm is consistent with the objective market quantities.[2]

Under monopoly, and on the pure profit-maximization hypothesis, product price, P, exceeds marginal revenue, MR, which is equated to marginal cost, MC. Taking labor as hired in a competitive market to be the sole variable factor, with a minimum of manipulation we can derive the ratio of the wage bill to proceeds in the individual firm merely by recalling the formula for marginal revenue involving the (normally negative) elasticity of demand, E_d: [3]

$$MR \equiv P\left(1 + \frac{1}{E_d}\right) = \frac{w}{M} \equiv MC \tag{45}$$

$$\frac{W}{Z} \equiv \frac{wN}{PQ} = \frac{MN}{Q}\left(1 + \frac{1}{E_d}\right) \equiv \frac{M}{A}\left(1 + \frac{1}{E_d}\right) \tag{46}$$

As E_d is normally negative, only its absolute value need be included in the formula inasmuch as the minus sign in the parentheses has already been altered to a positive figure. Generalizing these results to the economy,

$$\frac{W}{Z} = \sum_{i=1}^{n} \frac{M_i}{A_i}\left(1 + \frac{1}{E_d}\right)\frac{Z_i}{Z} \tag{48}$$

Under purely competitive conditions, the elasticity of demand is, of course, infinite, so that eq. 45 and 46 reduce to the earlier formula, eq. 28. In the normal monopoly case, E_d will take a finite value in

---

[2] See my "Demand Anticipations and Monopoly Equilibrium," *Journal of Political Economy* (1942) and *Price Theory*, pp. 354–364.

[3] For example, Joan Robinson, *Economics of Imperfect Competition* (London, Macmillan, 1933), p. 36. Remembering that $E_d = \dfrac{P}{P - MR} = \dfrac{P}{P - MC}$, and substituting $\dfrac{w}{M}$ for MC, then

$$\frac{W}{Z} = \frac{M}{A}\left(\frac{M(P - 1) - w}{P \cdot M - w}\right) \tag{47}$$

According to eq. 47, as $P \cdot M$ in the denominator is the marginal-value product, and as this exceeds the money wage, then the value of the bracket is less than unity. This formulation places a little more emphasis on the relation of productivity and price phenomena in influencing the wage share under monopoly.

excess of unity,[4] with the effect of cutting the relative wage share; with a generalized E_d of 2, say, the wage take under monopoly will be one half that under competition. Elasticities which approach unity in important firms will tend to compress the wage share most strongly, while, conversely, as the E_d-values become larger the income division will approach the competitive apportionment. Not only productivity phenomena, therefore, but also the reciprocal of the elasticity of demand—the degree of monopoly power [5]— influences the income division under monopoly.

There is one qualification, however, that must be brought to the fore and developed: the conclusion that monopoly must carry Z onto higher ground relative to W and reduce the relative labor share would be unassailable only if output in each firm under monopoly were exactly the same as under pure competition (or a structure in which price was equated to marginal cost). Manifestly, this is not so; monopoly also affects the composition of output for one thing and, for another, the opportunity for monopoly-pricing tactics makes possible output equilibria in particular firms at points where $M > A$.[6] Thus it is not possible to conclude abruptly that monopoly reduces the relative wage share. Nevertheless, envisioning an output and employment expansion—a movement along Z— in a mixed competitive-monopoly economy, and if it could be posited that (1) $A > M$, (2) $MR = MC$, and (3) E_d remained constant, then the conclusions would follow those of competitive theory: productivity phenomena would dominate the result. But if E_d falls because consumers become careless in their shopping habits as prosperity is extended, as some contend,[7] there will be an income shift from labor to profits. On the contrary view, where it

[4] If E_d were below unity, the marginal revenue would be negative.

[5] A. P. Lerner, "The Concept of Monopoly and the Measurement of Monopoly Power," *The Review of Economic Studies* (1933–1934).

[6] The prospect of increasing marginal products appears better founded when applied to an output expansion within a firm than over the entire economy. Evidence attests to higher rather than lower prices with a general strengthening of demand; although this is due in part to the rise in factor prices, it is also attributable to movements in raw-material prices where the latter reflect the declining productivity occasioned by the more intensive operations.

[7] For example R. F. Harrod, *The Trade Cycle* (Oxford, Clarendon, 1936), pp. 21–22, 85–87. See also the remarks of Helen Makower, "Elasticity of Demand and Stabilisation," *Review of Economic Studies* (October 1938).

is argued that cartels and restriction schemes become rife in depression, then with higher employment there will be a rising E_d[8] and the income shift will favor wages. In the absence of strong empirical evidence favoring one hypothesis over the other, the tentative assumption of constancy in the degree of monopoly power has been advanced.[9] This assumption relieves monopoly of any explanatory value as a determinant of *changes* in the income division as employment alters; monopoly would merely be charged with complicity for cutting the same *relative* slice from a varying income pie. Moreover, that monopoly can support output in certain productivity and demand configurations while a purely competitive—or a $P = MC$ type—adaptation cannot, eliminates any easy means of comparing the income result under the one pricing mode with that under the other. Although the income division for the same *employment* volume can be compared, as the output composition will differ, then not too much meaning can be assigned to the comparative results in this typical index-number riddle.[10]

[8] Kalecki, *Readings*, p. 213, and *Economic Dynamics*, pp. 17–18. Also, Joan Robinson, review article, *Economic Journal* (December 1936). Professor A. C. Pigou, in his *Employment and Equilibrium* (London, Macmillan, 1949, 2nd ed.), quotes Allen and Bowley to suggest that growing affluence leads to wider variety in consumption, and, thus, to higher rates of substitution and higher demand elasticity (pp. 82–83). In his *Industrial Fluctuations* (London, Macmillan, 1929, 2nd ed.), he wrote: "In practice, however, monopolists often decide . . . to exercise their monopolistic power *more fully* in bad times than in good . . ." (pp. 189–190). [Italics in original.]

A like view, that "there is greater likelihood in depressions that prices will approximate the monopoly figure than in periods of prosperity," is expressed by Moses Abramovitz, "Monopolistic Selling in a Changing Economy," *Quarterly Journal of Economics* (February 1938).

[9] J. R. Hicks, *Value and Capital* (Oxford Univ. Press), p. 84.

[10] A natural query at this stage concerns the question of how monopoly prices are to be entered into the Z-function. While under pure competition the Z-function embodies the supply prices of the associated output volume, given the employment level and the expected configuration of demand (pp. 25–27), under monopoly the very notion of a supply price is nebulous. Still, this problem is less formidable than might be supposed: assuming an expected volume and distribution of proceeds, monopolists will form subjective estimates of the demand for their products and implement decisions to produce output and hire labor on the basis of expected MR- and MC-values. Implicit, then, are the selling prices which the monopolists will stipulate for the planned-output volume, and it is these prices which must be included in the Z-function for the associated employment total as counterparts to the competitive supply prices

FULL-COST PRICING

Abandoning the pure theory of profit maximization, let us follow the analysis of "full-cost" pricing. Under this hypothesis it is contended that the firm will forego the immediate maximum pecuniary gain in favor of amassing merely "normal profits," obtained by charging a price adequate to cover average variable costs—"direct costs," as they are sometimes termed—plus a margin for overhead allowances and profit.[11] The effective pricing principle for this case is

$$P = \frac{wN}{Q} + K = \frac{w}{A} + K \qquad (49)$$

where K is the unit mark-up designed to protect depreciation and other overheads, including a "fair" profit; the A-term again denotes the average product of labor. As the firm's total proceeds can be written $Z(\equiv PQ) = wN + KQ$, then the ratio of proceeds to the wage bill within the firm is given by[12]

$$\frac{Z}{W}\left(\equiv \frac{PQ}{wN}\right) = 1 + \frac{KQ}{wN} = \frac{w + KA}{w} \qquad (50)$$

Thus the income division, given the productivity and wage phenomena, hinges on the absolute size of K. Holding K constant in the face of an output advance, it would be the change in A which controls the relative income parcels; a fall in A, curiously enough, would enlarge the relative wage slice. A decline in K would spur

---

contained in Z. Equilibrium will entail ultimately that for the monopoly firms the *expected* demand quantities are actually forthcoming, with excess demand zero. See my *Price Theory*, pp. 358–360.

[11] Although the modern challenge to the pure theory of profit maximization was thrown initially by Hall and Hitch in the 1930's, in more recent years the roll call of those partially embracing the doctrines is distinguished by the names of Chamberlin, Harrod, and Joan Robinson. P. W. S. Andrews has been especially persistent in advancing this argument. See his "Industrial Analysis in Economics," in *Oxford Studies in the Price Mechanism* (Oxford Univ. Press, 1951). For a review of the literature, see my "Revised Doctrines of Competition," *op. cit.*

[12] Writing the ratio of wages to proceeds, the result is less revealing from the standpoint of productivity, being $(W/Z) = (1 - K/P)$.

a shift to wages, unless neutralized by a higher A, while a higher K would send the wage portion tumbling.

Generalizing these results, the relevant formula reads[13]

$$\sum_{i=1}^{n} \frac{Z_i}{wN_i} = \sum_{i=1}^{n} \left(1 + \frac{K_i A_i}{w}\right) \frac{N_i}{N} \tag{51}$$

Large K's along with large average products in important labor-using firms thus enlarge the non-wage shares, while smaller K's and A's would mitigate the shift from wages.

Appraising a change in employment, the income change within the firm when the K-markup and wages are constant would be[14]

$$\frac{\Delta}{\Delta N} \left(\frac{Z}{wN}\right) = \frac{K}{wN} (M - A) \tag{54}$$

If increasing marginal products rule, the income shift will thus be highly disastrous to wage earners, for the term $M - A$ becomes positive: this is in strange contrast to the effects of increasing returns under a $P = MC$ hypothesis. Perversely, under diminishing returns and $A > M$, the policy of a fixed K would deflect income to labor and ultimately lead to stultifying results: it depicts a plunge of the profit share toward zero as prices rise under the impetus of diminishing returns and higher unit costs, in conflict with almost all evidence of the actual facts.

Rather than a fixed arithmetical sum, K may bear a constant ratio to price, being, say, 10 per cent of price proceeds. In this event, the non-wage share would always be 10 per cent and the wage take would be 90 per cent, assuming these to be the only income

---

[13] Thus:

$$\frac{Z}{wN} = \frac{wN_1 + K_1 Q_1 + wN_2 + K_2 Q_2 + \cdots + wN_n + K_n Q_n}{wN_1 + wN_2 + \cdots\cdots\cdots\cdots\cdots\cdots\cdots\cdots\cdots\cdots wN_n} \tag{52}$$

$$= \sum_{i=1}^{n} \left(1 + \frac{K_i A_i}{w}\right) \frac{wN_i}{wN} = \sum_{i=1}^{n} \left(1 + \frac{K_i A_i}{w}\right) \frac{N_i}{N} \tag{53}$$

[14] This comes from differentiating eq. 50 while holding K and w constant. If K varied, with w still constant, the following term would have to be added to eq.52:

$$+ \frac{A}{w} \frac{dK}{dQ} \frac{dQ}{dN}$$

claimants.[15] If the K-term is regarded as a variable (rising, say, as employment and output grow), all of the equations would have to be revised to incorporate this uplift. Ordinarily, the outcome would be unfavorable to wages and would foster accelerated price rises as N advanced and rapid price declines on an N-downturn.

After this examination, it is easy to discern the implications of price rigidity for distributive theory. Causes of rigidity are legion, and need not be explored at this point: an oligopoly market might be cited explicitly.[16] Whatever their origin, the income shift is aptly revealed by considering eq. 54 where, as average product falls, K diminishes—even to negative levels! In terms of the Z/W-ratio, the increment in proceeds would amount to the constant price times the marginal product of labor, while W would rise by the amount of the money wage. Eventually, the W-rise would outstrip the Z-move: persistent rigidity would ultimately carry the W-curve above Z. The rigid price hypothesis can, at best, masquerade as a description of price making only over a limited output and employment range.

NONINTEGRATION AND INCOME DIVISION

It is time now to relax the hypothesis of integrated firms and examine the distributive (and price) implications of the facts of nonintegration.

Recognizing interfirm purchases of materials, with a concomitant exercise of monopoly power, it is no longer permissible to assume that wage costs are the sole component in variable costs. When there are many stages before the final output is readied, the variable cost in the last stage will reflect the manifestations of monopoly power and productivity through the entire nonintegrated chain. It appears that, the greater the number of monopoly stages, the more baneful the ultimate results to the final purchaser, compared with integrated monopoly output.[17] The Z/W-gap will thus

[15] Equation 49 would now read
$$P = \frac{10}{9}\frac{wN}{Q} = \frac{10}{9}\frac{w}{A}$$
[16] See, for example, my *Price Theory*, pp. 426–433.
[17] See Lerner, *op. cit.*; also, *Price Theory*, pp. 305–308. Some welfare implications of monopoly and nonintegration appear in Lionel W. McKenzie, "Ideal Output and the Interdependence of Firms," *Economic Journal* (December 1951).

widen as N advances under the stress of monopoly and nonintegration, where only final factor payments are included in W; any systematic bias toward more interfirm transactions as employment spreads is capable of raising the average degree of monopoly within the economy.[18]

Visualizing all firms pricing according to competitive criteria, when output is nonintegrated a general production expansion marked by decreasing productivity (with the money wage constant) will tend to raise marginal costs for firms later in the economic chain: productivity consequences are transmitted from one to the other in a synchronized wave, just as in a fully integrated organization.

Formula-wise, viewing firm n as buying from i-suppliers, with each i-firm being integrated and hiring only variable labor and selling its output in competitive markets, the marginal cost for firm n for a small-output variation appears as[19]

$$MC_n = w \left(\frac{1}{M_n} + \sum_{i=1}^{n-1} \frac{1}{M_i} \left\{ 1 - \frac{Q_i}{M_i} \Delta M_i \right\} \frac{\Delta Q_i}{\Delta Q_n} \right) \qquad (55)$$

Symbols are as before, with the M's denoting marginal products of labor in the respective firms and the Q's signifying output levels.

[18] Until now, the exposition has been conducted on the assumption that all individuals are hired by firms and receive their income from them, though, obviously, this is not true. Insofar as services are provided directly to consumers, as by a doctor, the latter must be regarded in principle as a firm comparable to the giant corporations. The difference, less important for our purposes than may be presumed, is that there is always an instantaneous adjustment of expected sales proceeds and actual receipts compared with the case of output prepared in anticipation of sales.

[19] The total cost in firm n is

$$C_n = (wN + F)_n + P_1 Q_1 + P_2 Q_2 + \cdots + P_{n-1} Q_{n-1} \qquad (56)$$

With wage outlays comprising the only variable outlays in firms $1, 2, \cdots n - 1$, and with their prices equal to their marginal costs, then

$$C_n = (wN + F)_n + w \sum_{i=1}^{n} \frac{Q_i}{M_i} \qquad (57)$$

Equation 57 assumes homogeneous labor and a wage rate everywhere the same; this simplifies the analysis without real loss of detail. Under pure competition, the price of the output of firm n is equal to its marginal cost. Differentiating eq. 57, then eq. 55 emerges.

As the bracketed phrase is multiplied by the reciprocal of the marginal product, a fall in M_i inevitably will operate to lift marginal cost in firm n. The ratio $\Delta Q_i / \Delta Q_n$ (obviously positive) is dependent on the importance of material, Q_i, in the turnout of a unit of Q_n. With diminishing returns, ΔM_i will be negative, making the whole bracketed expression positive. Only with increasing returns in the i-supplying firms, and in n itself, can an output expansion in firm n lead to lower marginal costs. As this last possibility is precluded by virtue of the competitive hypothesis, the conclusion remains, therefore, that a nonintegrated model operates precisely like a fully integrated universe.

If the marginal product of labor in each supplying firm is constant, so that $\Delta M_i = 0$, a further simplification is possible. Thus:

$$MC_n = w \left\{ \frac{1}{M_n} + \sum_{i=1}^{n-1} \frac{1}{M_i} \frac{\Delta Q_i}{\Delta Q_n} \right\} \tag{58}$$

Each of the $n-1$ suppliers may also be conceived to buy materials from $(n-1)$ firms, who purchase from $n-1$ other firms, etc. Assuming that there is an "average" M_i, written $\overline{M}_i$, and that $\Delta Q_i / \Delta Q_n$ is constant (written m), and that there is some average here, too, then

$$MC_n = w \left(\frac{1}{M_n} + \frac{n(n-1)m}{\overline{M}_i} \right) \tag{59}$$

Thus the marginal product of labor in the given firm and its suppliers dominate the final result, with the influence of productivity phenomena in suppliers weighted by the importance of their output as input of the final product.

MONOPOLY AND NONINTEGRATION. When monopoly power is exercised in the supplying i-firms, even on the simplification that the latter are fully integrated and using only labor as the variable factor, the marginal cost for firm n will reflect the monopoly phenomena of its suppliers. The formula is cumbersome, but it indicates that a groundswell of monopoly among suppliers has a deep impact on the cost experience of a nonintegrated firm.[20]

[20] The basic equation for total cost in firm n is

$$C_n = (wN + F)_n + w \sum_{i=1}^{n-1} \frac{Q_i}{M_i} \left(\frac{E_i + 1}{E_i} \right)$$

Differentiating with respect to Q_n, formula 60 is derived.

$$MC_n = \frac{w}{M_n} + \sum_{i=1}^{n-1} \frac{w}{M_i(E_i + 1)} \left[E_i + Q_i \Delta E_i - E_i \left(\frac{Q_i}{M_i} \Delta M_i \right) \right.$$

$$\left. - \frac{E_i Q_i}{(E_i + 1)} \Delta E_i \right] \frac{\Delta Q_i}{\Delta Q_n} \quad (60)$$

In the formula, the demand elasticity, E_i, is construed with its natural sign. The quantity $\Delta Q_i / \Delta Q_n$ refers to the importance of product i in producing a unit of product n; this would be constant if fixed production coefficients were the rule through the economy. Where monopoly power is exercised by important i-suppliers (measured by $\Delta Q_i / \Delta Q_n$), the results are even more inimical to curbing cost movements within n. To derive the monopoly price to be charged by firm n, the appropriate equation would be eq. 60 multiplied by $E_n / (E_n + 1)$ the effect is to elevate the final price charged by firm n according to the monopoly power exercised by it in its own sales market.

A substantial simplification can be secured in eq. 60 if we assume the elasticity of demand and the marginal product of labor in suppliers is constant ($\Delta E_i = \Delta M_i = 0$). Thus:

$$MC_n = w \left\{ \frac{1}{M_n} + \frac{1}{M_i} \sum_{i=1}^{n-1} \frac{E_i}{E_i + 1} \frac{\Delta Q_i}{\Delta Q_n} \right\} \quad (61)$$

Also, if, in each of the $n-1$ suppliers, $E_i = \overline{K}$ and $\Delta Q_i / \Delta Q_n = m$, then

$$MC_n = w \left\{ \frac{1}{M_n} + \frac{\overline{K}m(n-1)}{M_i} \right\} \quad (62)$$

The price in firm n involves multiplying eq. 62 by $E_n / (E_n + 1)$. Assuming also $E_n = \overline{K}$,

$$P_n = w\overline{K} \left\{ \frac{1}{M_n} + \frac{\overline{K}m}{M_i} (n-1) \right\} \quad (63)$$

If each of the n-firms also has n-suppliers, with each in turn having n-suppliers, etc., the final result appears as [21]:

[21] If each of the $n-1$ suppliers has $n-1$ suppliers with $n-1$ suppliers, etc., we have an infinite series. In this case, firm n is presumed dependent for supplies directly or indirectly on all other firms. This is, of course, an exaggeration as a practical matter.

$$P_n = w\overline{K} \left\{ \frac{1}{M_n} + n(n-1) \frac{m\overline{K}}{M_i} \right\} \qquad (64)$$

The hypothesis of a universal $\overline{K}$ is equivalent to a supposition of an identical degree of monopoly power within firms; obviously it enables us to simplify and achieve determinate and comprehensible results. In the case of endless suppliers in a nonintegrated world, only a small m-value can compress the final price and limit the oppressive consequences of "universal monopoly."

The effect of a nonintegrated monopoly sequence on the income division need not be labored: clearly, it magnifies the rise in the final product price. Inevitably, because of its inflation through monopoly power, the Z-function will diverge farther from the W-function, with the implicit income shift being to the detriment of the wage share.[22]

PRODUCTIVITY CHANGES AND WAGE VARIATIONS

Factor productivity, until now, has been posited as given, so that the output of variable factors has followed a known pattern according to the defined production functions. This assumption can now be dropped, and, as part of the same general analysis, we can examine the consequences of a change in factor prices upon the position of the Z-function. A simple (and unreal) change in the produc-

---

[22] It remains to comment briefly on the implications of nonintegration for the theory of income and employment determination. On our methods (Chapter 2), as well as in all usual procedures, the intermediate purchases and sales of materials between firms are omitted. (Cf. Keynes, *op. cit.*, p. 24, n. 2.) The usual rationalization is that, as the sum of such purchases and sales are identical, deducting them from both aggregate demand and aggregate supply at each N-level will not influence the income-employment outcome.

In the analysis of income determination developed earlier, actual demand outlays were suspended against proceeds or expected outlays. If anticipated inter-firm transactions were always identical to realized transactions, their inclusion in both D and Z would fail to advance the analysis further. But it is possible that actual inter-firm dealings may depart from their *expected* magnitudes, though this discrepancy ought to be temporary so that we probably do not go too far astray in supposing their coincidence. This at least provides a partial extenuation for the customary procedure, although older theories of the business cycles tended to stress possible disruptions in these relations as being decisive. For example, see Pigou, *Industrial Fluctuations*, Part 1, Chapters VI and VII. The whole study might repay renewed investigation.

tivity of labor will be examined first under conditions where the stock of equipment is constant; workers, however, are assumed to evidence greater skill and diligence in applying themselves to the tasks at hand.[23]

Manifestly, every change in productivity and product prices at given N-points must shift Z relative to W, for so long as the money wage remains constant W will stay anchored firmly. The vital question thus concerns the volatility of Z.

It is just here that our methods fail to illuminate the income-sharing consequences of a rise in productivity. For the same proceeds as before, output undoubtedly will be greater and prices lower. But whether the Z-function will shift, and whether employment will be as large as before for the given proceeds level, remains rather fuzzy. In an economy which always maintained full employment, the upshot would surely be higher *aggregate* real income with product prices lower and real incomes generally enhanced. But exactly what will happen to the relative wage share is obscure, though the reason is not hard to find: it was shown earlier that the relative wage share depends not on the marginal product alone but also on the relation of marginal to average product. And although a rise in productivity signifies that aggregate output for the same labor force is greater than before, it tells us little about the new M/A-ratio compared with the old at each N-point. Without this added information, we are in the dark about relative shares. Assuming that production is carried on to stages of diminishing returns, and that the separate productivity curves are approximately linear, it can be proved that the wage portion will tend to rise.[24] Arguments on such lines, however, lapse into a review of special cases.

[23] This case often seems to be in the minds of efficiency experts, and curiously, socialist planners, who see limitless opportunities mainly by exhorting individuals to increase their intensity of application to the task at hand. It is of a piece with criticisms of whole nations or races as being indolent.

[24] Writing the marginal-product curve as linear and decreasing, as $a - bN$, the correspondent average-product curve is $a - bN/2$. Then

$$\frac{M}{A} = \frac{a - bN}{a - \dfrac{bN}{2}}$$

Thus a rise in productivity implies a larger a and a smaller b, leading to a higher M/A-ratio.

What can be asserted with confidence is that a higher marginal product for the same labor force will insure that labor's *aggregate* absolute real income will be improved and that real wages will be higher. The higher average product also entails greater total output and the general improvement of the real income of all groups. A sufficient uplift in the ratio of M/A can, of course, confine the benefits wholly to wage groups, though with product-price declines this outcome is unlikely considering the presence of the fixed-factor group.

A PARAMETRIC WAGE RISE. A more definite answer is warranted when we consider the effects of parametric money-wage changes. With a once-and-for-all wage rise which is independent of the employment level, we ought to be prepared by now for the conclusion that this is without bearing on the relative wage portion of the income total. Graphically, the effect of the wage move is to elevate both the Z- and the W-functions by the same proportions, keeping the ratio of Z/W constant. Hence, unless it can be shown that the degree of monopoly or the level of employment alters, the money-wage move will fail to improve labor's position in the income partition. With respect to monopoly power, there seems scant reason to expect that this must change when wage moves occur, so long as we adhere to the premise that firms are animated by the profit motive. The main reservations that must be interjected concern non-wage elements in marginal costs, which inhibit the price rise, and the existence of rentier positions: the income loss for the latter, in relative and in real terms, will eventuate as a profit gain so that the income reshuffle generated by a wage move resolves itself primarily into a struggle between entrepreneurial and rentier groups. Alternately, with fixed markups and rigid prices, a money-wage rise must erase some profit sums so that income will be diverted labor's way; from what has been said, rigid price policies are likely to vanish in the face of rising wage pressures. On the effects of the money-income change on aggregative demand, study is deferred until Chapter 6.

Consider, now, the case of money wages which rise continuously with employment so that w is associated with N, and $w + \Delta w$ with $N + \Delta N$. Diagrammatically, in Fig. 17, the W_1-locus pertains to a wage w_1; W_2 to w_2, etc. Imagining a continuous wage variation from w_1 to w_4 as employment advances from N_1 to N_4, the relevant wage-bill locus over this employment range would be given by W_n. A similar path could be described for the Z-function. It can be shown that the rise in Z will outstrip that in W by the amount of profit augmentation; this is, after all, the result we would expect from the earlier analysis.[25] Profits now mount for twin reasons: (1) the ordinary uplift due to diminishing returns and the inevitably

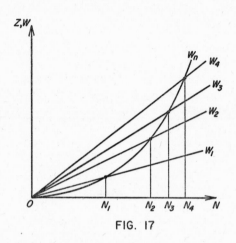

FIG. 17

higher prices and (2) the added price surge due to the higher wage cost. As an approximation, for a slight employment and wage rise in the individual firm, the profit increase can be represented by either[26]

$$\frac{\Delta R}{\Delta N} = \left(Z \left\{ \frac{\Delta w}{w} - \frac{\Delta M}{M} \right\} - N \Delta w \right) \frac{\Delta Q}{\Delta N} \qquad (65)$$

$$= \frac{1}{M} \left(N \Delta w [A - M] - Z \Delta M \right) \frac{\Delta Q}{\Delta N} \qquad (66)$$

[25] Analytically, the difference in the slope of Z and W is now given by

$$\frac{\Delta Z}{\Delta N} - \frac{\Delta W}{\Delta N} = \left(w + N \frac{\Delta w}{\Delta N} + \frac{\Delta R}{\Delta N} \right) - \left(w + N \frac{\Delta w}{\Delta N} \right)$$

[26] The basic equation is that, for profit maximization, $PQ - wN = R$. Remembering that dP/dQ is positive when output advances in response to rising prices, and that $w(dN)/dQ = P$, by making the appropriate substitutions formulae 65 and 66 follow.

Examining eq. 65, if $\Delta M = 0$, and the wage rate is doubled with $\Delta w = w$, then profits rise by the sum of original proceeds, Z, minus the augmented wage bill, $N\Delta w$. With diminishing returns, $\Delta M < 0$, so that the whole curved bracket is positive, with the relative wage change and the change in relative marginal productivity together influencing the profit rise. According to eq. 66, with $A > M$ and $\Delta M < 0$, profits rise by the sum of both terms, with the rise magnified when the excess of A over M is substantial and the slump in the marginal product of labor is heavy. While the formulae refer to an individual firm, generalization can come by weighting each equation by the importance of the employment change in the firm to that in the economy.[27]

A POPULAR CONFUSION. A popular fallacy, either deliberate and fostered, or a delusion pure and simple, ought to be exposed in passing. In mind is the plea often voiced by union spokesmen that a wage hike would "only add \$X to the total costs of the firm while total profits before taxes are \$gX, several times ample to absorb them." Not only is it well to disentangle this argument for its own sake, but also it illuminates some earlier remarks.

Obviously, if prices remained firm, the policy would shift income from profits to wage earners: this would simply be a manifestation of the rigid price hypothesis. In competitive sales markets, the crudity of the proposition is obvious: it ignores the relation of marginal costs and prices and argues as if firms would continue to produce the same output volume despite higher cost experience. In monopoly markets it pictures the firm as supinely acquiescing to a slash in its monopoly power, as reflected in its markup, and submitting to the dissipation of its profit share. A variant of this argument was promulgated by government control boards sharing responsibility for price and wage controls during World War II and its aftermath. Firms were often granted permission to raise

---

[27] The price rise necessary to induce each firm to augment its output would be approximately equivalent to

$$\frac{\Delta P}{\Delta N} = \left(\frac{1}{M} \frac{\Delta w}{\Delta Q} - \frac{w\Delta M}{M^2} \right) \frac{\Delta Q}{\Delta N} = P \left(\frac{\Delta w}{w} - \frac{\Delta M}{M} \right) \frac{\Delta Q}{\Delta N} \tag{67}$$

As $\Delta M < 0$ with diminishing returns, the ordinary price rise impelled by diminishing returns under conditions of greater output and employment will thus gain new momentum by a wage rise. Only increasing marginal products can serve to restrain the price surge after a wage lift. (See n. 16, pp. 57–58.)

prices "just enough" to enable them to recapture the proceeds of a wage boost at the prevailing output levels. Fundamentally, the premise involved was that the absolute price markup was fixed, and that, despite higher product prices, firms ought to be content with the same absolute profit sum as before; implicitly, firms were being asked to become willing spectators in observing their income share being whittled away. Similar thinking sometimes tended to ignore the roundabout echoes on costs through higher prices of materials in a nonintegrated structure. Manifestly, such rulings did deflect income to labor, mitigated only in comparison to rigid price provisos.

In competitive markets, the wage bill would rise proportionately with prices only under conditions of constant marginal products. As the marginal wage cost will stand above the average wage cost with decreasing marginal products, the necessary price proceeds required by the firm to implement a wage hike at a given output in competitive markets would exceed the rise in aggregate wage costs by the excess of marginal over average wage costs.[28] Only in conditions of constant returns does the crude practical precept dovetail with marginal insights; sheer analytic nonsense is perpetrated when productivity phenomena deviate from this simple norm.

VARIATIONS IN CAPITAL AND INVENTIONS

The stock of equipment has so far been assumed constant. For short periods of clock time—perhaps even extending for a year or two where the net investment is small compared to the total stock of equipment—this procedure is wholly legitimate; it becomes more

---

[28] In proof:

(1) The necessary change in proceeds after a wage and price hike is

$$Q\Delta P = \frac{Q\Delta w}{M}$$

(2) The change in the wage bill is $N\Delta w$

(3) $$\therefore \frac{\Delta Z}{\Delta W} = Q\frac{\Delta w}{M}\cdot\frac{1}{N\Delta w} = \frac{A}{M}$$

But as the average variable cost of labor, AC, is w/A, and the marginal cost is w/M, then

$$\frac{\Delta Z}{\Delta W} = \frac{MC}{AC}$$

dubious only over a longer temporal span. Assessing briefly some problems arising out of capital growth and new inventions, from one standpoint changes in the stock of equipment can be regarded as discontinuous and functionally independent of the volume of employment. Contrariwise, some functional interdependence can be entertained, marking a partial embrace of the acceleration principle; the tie, however, would be to employment levels rather than to output changes. Although a full analysis transcends the scope of this work, some of the formal implications can be sketched herein.

DISCONTINUOUS VARIATIONS. Where equipment does not vary in any systematic way with the N-level, every change in the capital stock will force the reconstitution of Z. However, with constant money wages the W-function will hold firm despite the changes in the stock of equipment. On the premise that the present quantum of equipment is an equilibrium amount for only a unique level of employment, on long-period analysis each employment level, given the interest rate, would invite an independent equilibrium capital adaptation. Some N-levels, therefore, would engender the partial rundown of the existing capital stock. Full adaptation on this interpretation must augment profits, pushing Z farther from W.

A more realistic short-period view would visualize new equipment erected on estimates of future earnings, and available thereafter despite earning disappointments. If the Z-curve somehow remained immutable despite the greater array of equipment, the total non-wage earnings would be pictured as unaffected, although some income shift from profits to fixed income might be admitted. This conclusion rests on the dubious proposition that, despite a greater quantum of equipment per head, the absolute interest and depreciation return would be unaltered. However, it is more plausible to suppose that the Z-curve moves leftward, shifting income from labor at each employment level. After all, this is what we would expect on an untutored approach: more equipment should enlarge the non-wage income by increasing the requisite total of proceeds at each N-position.[29]

This argument suffices, temporarily at least, for the "capital-

---

[29] This is implicit in the growth theory of Harrod which requires an income rise to justify the installation of new equipment at a given employment level. See his *Towards a Dynamic Economics* (London, Macmillan, 1948), Lecture 3.

deepening"[30] analysis, where new equipment largely supplants going varieties. In "capital-widening," new equipment duplicates and stands alongside existing varieties. To a degree, this should destroy some prevailing profit positions through the intensified competition if the new equipment signalizes the birth of new firms.[31] Further, whether the equipment is in the hands of new or old firms, for any N-level the degree of diminishing-returns phenomena will be checked: the marginal product of labor will increase and the "excess capacity" and check on price movements ought to redound to labor's favor. "Widening" thus suggests some relative income relations that seem the very opposite of "deepening."

Formally, the problems are the same when new equipment is created to produce new products rather than add to the output of going types. As there is likely to be some destruction of old monopoly positions, the results are akin to capital widening; in the creation of new monopoly havens the effects resemble those of capital deepening.

What makes the entire analysis of the swing in Z relative to W so elusive is that its resolution rests on the familiar imponderables; namely, the weighted M/A-ratios and the generalized E_d in the new position compared to the old. And though for any given amount of employment some remarks on absolute *real* income can be proffered, the diagnosis of the relative partition becomes rather hazy. Further, if the Z-function is dislodged, the equilibrium employment position is likely to alter through repercussions upon aggregate demand so that the new income allocation will have to be compared to the old—not at the same N-position, but at the new N-level. It is safe to surmise, however, that, if the wage share has tended to constancy over long periods of time, then either the M/A-ratios and the E_d-magnitudes must have remained constant or they must have operated systematically and fortuitously to neutralize each other's variation when the stock of equipment, the level of employment, and the nature of the product-mix underwent change.[32]

---

[30] See the use of these terms in R. G. Hawtrey, *Capital and Employment* (London, Longmans, Green, 1952, 2nd ed.), pp. 30–31.

[31] Wicksell appears to argue that, with more capital and unchanged population, the absolute as well as the relative profit share will diminish. See his *Value, Capital and Rent* (New York, Rinehart, 1954), S. H. Frowein, translator, p. 141.

[32] Kalecki initially insisted that there was a systematic long-run rise in

INVENTIONS AND INNOVATIONS. The discussion of new products leads naturally into a discussion of innovation[33] where new productive techniques, as a result of invention and cost turns in interest rates and wage levels, are introduced to produce going product varieties.

New techniques may, first, be "capital saving" involving simplifications in design, say, for a given output level. That is, to produce a given output, Q_1, where formerly $1000 of capital was used only $800 in constant prices is used now, while the amount of labor hired is assumed to be the same. The new processes must also be supposed to be cost-reducing so that the marginal-cost curve and thus output price must fall. The net effect is to pull the Z-function closer to W at each N-point so that the income shift is to labor and away from "profits." Real wages, on these assumptions of lower prices for given money wages and employment, will also rise.

"Labor-saving" (= "capital-using") inventions involve more capital used per unit of output with, say, $1000 now used whereas $800 was formerly applied. For the given volume of output, economies in labor cost must be assumed to outweigh the interest charges and depreciation allowances on the added $200 of equipment. Hence, if for the same amount of output more equipment and less labor is used, for a given amount of employment the stock of capital will be larger and presumably the marginal product of labor will be greater. Manifestly, these changes in productive techniques will not be undertaken unless the capital share can be widened. The effect of labor-saving inventions, therefore, is to lift Z relative to W, to the *relative* income detriment of labor at each employment position.[34] Real wages, however, with given employment levels ordinarily will rise with the greater amount of equipment per head.

---

monopoly power. (*Op. cit.*, pp. 210, 212.) In the revised account, his conclusion is qualified somewhat (*Theory of Economic Dynamics,* p. 34).

[33] To use Schumpeter's fruitful term. See his *Business Cycles* (New York, 1939), Volume I, Chapter II. For his earlier development of the idea in terms of "new combinations," see his *Theory of Economic Development* (Cambridge, Harvard, 1934), R. Opie, translator, Chapter II.

[34] I think Mrs. Robinson's definitions of capital saving and using inventions can often be interpreted in these terms. For example, in her volume, *The Accumulation of Capital,* she declares "capital-using innovations are favorable (income-wise) to the interests of entrepreneurs" (p. 172) while

Neutral innovations can be defined as those which leave Z stationary relative to W. Historically, in western economies the labor-saving invention is alleged to be most common[35]: automation is a continuation of this trend. On net balance a growth in the capital share would be expected,[36] mitigated by improvements in capital designs through entrepreneurial endeavors to cut their installation costs. After all, with more equipment per head we would expect a *relatively* lower wage share: in an agricultural economy using only the simplest and crudest equipment, just wages and rent, to the exclusion of "profits," would exhaust all of income.[37]

In both the capital-saving and the capital-using cases it has been argued that real wages at any given N-amount are likely to be higher; in the former this is likely to occur through prices falling relative to money wages, stimulated perhaps by new entry, while in the capital-using case it is likely to be the rise in the full marginal-product curve of labor or reduced real-output costs per unit of money wages that accomplishes the trick. In the neutrality case, merely the type of equipment is altered with neither costs being reduced—though a "superior" product is offered market-wise—nor labor productivity being enlarged. But the very statement of these matters bristles with index-number difficulties at every turn:

"capital-saving innovations, in a sense, reduce the need for capital relatively to labor, and have the same effect as an increase in the supply of capital brought about by rapid accumulation" (p. 166). Although there are many complications in all this, for the theory of relative-income division the linkages of the Z/W-curves are vital and they can be applied to a variety of these problems.

[35] See K. W. Rothschild, *The Theory of Wages* (New York, Macmillan, 1954), p. 117. For more discussion of inventions, see A. C. Pigou, *The Economics of Welfare* (London, 1932, 4th ed.), Part IV, Chapter IV; J. R. Hicks, *The Theory of Wages,* Chapter VI; Joan Robinson, "The Classification of Inventions," *Review of Economic Studies* (February 1938); O. Lange, *Price Flexibility and Employment* (Bloomington, Ind., Principia, 1944), Chapter XII; R. F. Harrod, *Dynamic Economics,* pp. 24–28.

[36] William Fellner, *Trends and Cycles in Economic Activity* (New York, Holt, 1956), p. 142n.

[37] Mention of rent suggests some reshuffling of income among "profits" and "rent." More will be said on this later, though it is apparent that, insofar as new equipment tends to check the diminishing marginal productivity of labor and render land relatively more plentiful, the rent share of the total will be compressed.

"new" and "superior" products, even though the *relative* wage share does not improve, do connote some betterment in labor's position.

CONTINUOUS VARIATIONS. Where the stock of equipment is assumed to vary continuously with employment, there are obvious parallels to the concept of continuous wage changes; the case involves leaping from one Z-curve to another as the N-level varies. As before, deepening and widening phenomena remain to be disentangled, with the one new inference being that, at each successive N-position, the total of fixed claims is likely to be inflated, immediately affecting the division between rentier and entrepreneurial groups.

Tieing equipment functionally to the employment level, so that its effects on expected proceeds are "built into" the Z-function, is likely to make Z "irreversible"; the growing stock of equipment accompanying the upswing will remain in operational readiness despite an N-contraction so that the proceeds level requisite to any given N is likely to depend on the direction from which N is approached. Income division inevitably will be subject to the same phenomena. When the introduction of equipment is contingent on wage changes, a connection of capital stock with employment could be maintained only if the money wage was itself functionally dependent on N. Irreversibility would appear in this case, too, with a reduction in wages.

Product variation motivated by a desire to circumvent non-price competition lends itself readily to analysis in terms of the techniques outlined. In general, a deterioration in the quality of the product sold at a constant price can be interpreted as a rise in the degree of monopoly power, raising Z relative to W inasmuch as the same amount of labor generally will be engaged in the pursuit of more proceeds after the product changeover.

Chapter 5

Distribution and Employment

Effects on the ultimate equilibrium of the shifts in income distribution as the Z,N-level varies can now be studied as a major illustration of aggregate supply-demand interdependence. Specifically, we will be concerned primarily with whether the distributive revision along a given Z-function is capable of influencing aggregate demand, and, thereby, the final Z,N-position and the income partition itself. Related to this is the question of how shifts in Z and W affect the Z,N-equilibrium; involved is the important issue of whether changes in money wages have an employment, aside from a price-level, effect. As a by-product, the analysis indicates how the outlay decisions of the respective income groups help to shape the final outcome and provides some useful insights into some basically different causes of price inflation. All of these matters are of vast importance analytically and practically, with wide ramifications for economic policy.

DISTRIBUTION AND AGGREGATE DEMAND

It was remarked earlier that, in the final equilibrium, the consumption outlay, D_c, had to equal the expected consumption receipts, C, while investment outlay, D_i, had to balance the value of investment output, I. Thus, $D_c + D_i \equiv D = Z \equiv C + I$, with $D_c = C$ and $D_i = I$ in equilibrium.[1] Our task now is to examine whether the relative income revision stimulates or retards the employment growth, and thus whether distribution itself appears as a determinant of aggregate demand and the ultimate income division itself.

Initially, we can suppose that D_i is fixed in money terms regardless of the Z,N-totals; entrepreneurs plan to make a given money investment outlay so that D_i maps as a horizontal line. If we sup-

[1] See p. 44.

posed that the D_i-projections were fixed in real terms, then D_i would tend to rise to the right parallel to the Z-uplift caused by price movements. If D_i rose at a faster pace, due to some built-in accelerator dependence on N, the explosive possibilities alluded to earlier would be a possible outcome.[2]

Whereas D_i is either unrelated to Z, or only partially and occasionally dependent on it, the functional connection of D_c and Z is inextricable inasmuch as $D_c = D_1(Y_d)$, where $Y_d = Y(Z)$, so that $D_c = D_2(Z)$: hence D_c becomes an implicit function of Z.

This opens the way for exploring some key relations of savings and investment, establishing the conditions under which $D_c = C$. Recalling that $D_c = cY_d + \lambda A$,[3] where c refers to the average consumption outlay out of personal-money income, Y_d, and λA denotes dissaving phenomena, then:

$$(D_c/D) \equiv [(cY_d + \lambda A)/D] = [(Y_d - S_g + \lambda A)/D]$$
$$= [(Y_d - S_p)/D] \qquad (68)$$

Here, S_g denotes gross personal savings out of personal income, while S_p is a net figure, after dissavings are deducted, so that $S_p = S_g - \lambda A$. Further, writing S_c for corporate saving, and neglecting government purchases so that $Z \equiv C + I$, we have

$$Y_d = Z - (1 - k)R = C + I - S_c \qquad (69)$$

After writing $S = S_c + S_p$, then it follows that

$$(D_c/D) = [C + (I - S)]/D \gtreqless C/Z \qquad (70)$$

Hence, whenever $I = S$, or decisions to save out of gross income, Z, are equal to the value of investment, then consumption expenditure, as part of total outlay, will be equal to the value of consumption output as part of total output. If savings run below the investment volume at some Z-level, then $D_c > C$, and vice versa if $S > I$. In general, $D_c > C$ will imply some expansive forces tending to raise output, money income, and employment; when the inequality is reversed, the outlay forces will press back on the economy, acting as a check on the Z,N-aggregate.

SHIFTS IN THE WAGE SHARE AND EMPLOYMENT. We now want to examine the implications for the $I - S$ discrepancy and the ultimate

[2] See p. 42.　　　　[3] See pp. 33–37.

Z,N-level of changes in the relative wage share as N varies under conditions of diminishing labor productivity.[4]

Understanding here has been advanced by some ingenious macroeconomic simplifications even though they are now superfluous for further analytic development. For example, it has been assumed as a tentative hypothesis that wage earners save nothing and that "capitalists"—non-wage income recipients—spend nothing, saving their full income.[5] In this kind of model it is not too difficult to prove that, as investment (= saving) increases, then capitalist income (= saving = investment) also increases. Further, when some allowance is made for capitalist's consumption, the non-wage income is shown to be equal to the investment aggregate plus capitalist consumption. Hence, it is concluded that, by enlarging either their investment programs or their consumption outlays, businessmen are in effect underwriting their own profits.[6]

Wage earners in the American economy do contribute in some measure to the savings stream.[7] Let us consider, then, the relation

[4] Alternately the analysis can be envisaged as involving a rise in the degree of monopoly power. So far as profits go, a rise in monopoly power is equivalent, in essentials, to a fall in the marginal (relative to average) product of labor.

[5] Originally, by M. Kalecki. See, for example, his *Theory of Economic Dynamics*, p. 45. A good part of the basic initial analysis is conducted on this basis by Mrs. Robinson in her *Accumulation of Capital*, pp. 43–45, 76, 255. Also, as an illustrative step in his theory, by Nicholas Kaldor, *op. cit.*; see the discussion at the close of this chapter.

[6] Profits, as a variable income, thus can be increased though profits as a *rate* of return may not be enlarged over time as the volume of investment and the stock of capital increase. Further, this way of putting it—of stressing investment as potentially expansible without limit—assumes either unemployed resources or chronic inflation. With inflation, as rentiers suffer there are contradictions in the income experience of capitalists so that analysis and understanding are better served by a breakdown of the capitalist-income category into at least the two separable pieces, of rentiers and entrepreneurs.

Too, the formulation in terms of "capitalist's consumption and investment" suggests that the relevant decisions are made by the same individuals. Before a decision to consume is reached, decisions to pay dividends must be made; thus consumption, saving, and investment decisions are not rendered by a single individual.

[7] Of personal savings in the national-income concept, wage earners in recent years have been responsible for about 20 per cent of the total. For a most important empirical study see I. Friend and I. Kravis, "Entrepreneurial Income, Saving and Investment," *American Economic Review* (June 1957).

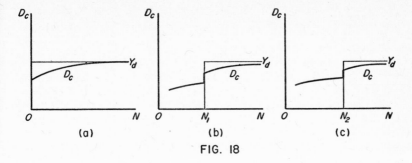

FIG. 18

of their savings to the wage bill; the study also involves an interesting exercise and new insight into the microeconomic composition of the consumption function.

In Fig. 18 (a) we have the income and consumption function of an individual who is never unemployed—he is the person who finds work even when employment is "very small," say the "first" one enumerated along the horizontal axis. His income curve is given by Y_d and his consumption outlay, related to aggregate employment, is shown by D_c: the outlay curve rises to the right, for, as prices rise, we suppose the individual to spend more and save less in order to maintain his real consumption.[8] Figure 18 (b) shows the same relations for an individual hired when employment is already at level $(N_1 - 1)$. In view of the consumption pattern of individual N_1, involving dissaving prior to his employment, the D_c-function exists to the left of N_1 and rises discontinuously at N_1, thereafter turning up continuously because of rising price phenomena. Figure 18 (c) shows the same relations for an individual hired only after employment is rather high, at $(N_2 - 1)$. If we are to take seriously the view that wage earners save nothing, then the D_c-curves must lie everywhere with Y_d. Allowing for the personal-income tax, the D_c-curves would be pulled proportionately below Y_d.

Aggregating the individual wage income and outlay relations of the sort described, we derive the curve field of Fig. 19 (a). Wage income $Y_d{}^w = W$, the wage bill. Consumption outlay is shown by

[8] The individual saves more when N is very low not only because his real income is high but also because with unemployment rife there is the understandable fear that the firing axe may hit him next. This worry diminishes as N grows. Also, when N is higher, there is less pressure on him to aid, by loan or gift, his friends or relatives who may be unemployed.

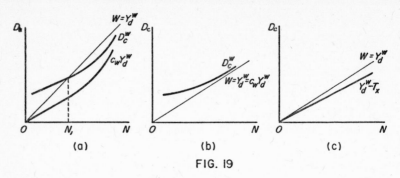

FIG. 19

$D_c{}^w$; at employment levels below N_1, as dissavings outweigh personal savings out of wage incomes, $D_c{}^w > Y_d{}^w$. To the right of N_1 there are some net wage savings after deducting dissavings; actual saving out of earned-wage income is given by the difference $Y_d{}^w - c_w Y_d{}^w$. As employment advances, $c_w Y_d{}^w$ turns asymptotically toward $D_c{}^w$, with dissavings approaching zero. Again, on the view that wage earners save nothing ($c_w = 1$), then $D_c{}^w > W \equiv Y_d{}^w = c_w Y_d{}^w$, for some dissavings are embodied in $D_c{}^w$, as shown in Fig. 19 (b). Including the inroads of personal-income taxes, the wage income before and after tax is as shown in Fig. 19 (c); appropriate adjustments would have to appear in $D_c{}^w$ and in $c_w Y_d{}^w$.

Concentrating on Fig. 19 (a) as a likely representation, until employment, N_1, all forces from the side of wage earners as a class are expansory; beyond N_1, as some net savings appear, there is some rein on the expansion. However, at N_2, say, as the N_1 set of wage earners strive to maintain their real consumption in the face of rising prices and decreasing real wages, then $c_w Y_d{}^w$ (and $D_c{}^w$) tend to curl up and approach W. At best, the slope of $c_w Y_d{}^w$ will equal that of Z as consumption outlays rise at the same pace as prices, at the expense of wage-earner personal savings. All of this suggests that, to arrest the decline in consumption intake, c_w moves more closely to unity.[9] As this tends to happen, and further expansory forces are released by $\Delta c_w > 0$, *the net result of the*

---

[9] Compare Chapter 2, where it was pointed out that the $D_c{}^w$-value, as N advanced, equaled $c_w W + N \Delta c_w + c_w w$; the second term reflects the impact of rising prices. To maintain consumption intake, $(c_w + \Delta c_w)/c_w$ would have to equal the relative price rise $(P + \Delta P)/P$.

strengthening of Z,N-equilibrium magnitudes must be a greater fall-off in real wages and a relative income shift from wages to profits, with a further price inflation.

This is a most interesting result, and a reversal of the usual statement which holds that *the income shift from labor and the fall in real wages is a damper on inflation,* a built-in restraint on inflation. But this cannot be entirely right; the rise in c_w seems almost certain —on all sides, in near full-employment positions, there is the complaint of the high cost of living and the inability to save out of wage incomes. The fall-off in the real consumption of wage earners is due to the fact that the rise in Z outstrips that in D_c^w. From the outlay side, however, wage-earner behavior is expansory and inflationary; that it is insufficient comes from the greater slope in Z—the shift to a higher profit share. The error in the conventional statement stems from its failure to distinguish between the aggregate-demand side, and the forces released there, and the more pronounced forces on the aggregate-supply side.

Just as the timidity of entrepreneurs in curtailing investment is alleged to be the cause of their low profits, in a similar vein it can be contended that efforts of wage earners to maintain their real standards only hasten the decline in their real positions and aggravate their fall, while serving to inflate and protect profits. As employment advances, therefore, the distributive shift tends to feed in part on itself by virtue of wage-earner behavior, tending to perpetuate the unbalance. If the *aggregate* real-wage bill of labor also falls,[10] then the income shift from labor is, of course, intensified by the efforts of wage earners to preserve their living standards by greater outlays. Their reduced savings margins also tend to inhibit their ascendancy to creditor or rentier status.

This has some implications for consumer credit and installment purchases. As households (of wage earners) go into debt to improve their current living standards, the results can only be unfavorable (relatively) to the wage-earning group as a whole compared to profit recipients.[11] The attempt to evade the income bounds when employment is quite full tends in part to cut their real wage— barring any important changes in productivity through added capital facilities.

[10] Compare Chapter 3, p. 61.
[11] See Boulding, *A Reconstruction of Economics,* pp. 255–258.

THE RENTIER-PROFIT SHIFT. Once employment and proceeds are ample to guarantee the payment of fixed charges, rentiers, as individuals or as a collective group, must observe their real and relative income status undermined as the Z,N-magnitudes move to higher ground. Endeavoring to pursue an unchanged real consumption, the $D_o{}'$ outlay curve will rise to the right, ultimately approaching the income level, FF', as in Fig. 10 (a). The reduction in rentier savings thus provides an additional outlay injection enhancing profits and simultaneously injuring rentier real-income.

Entrepreneurs, as individuals or as members of a class, are the only ones whose real position ordinarily is improved with higher Z,N-levels. As the number in the entrepreneurial group is (practically) constant, the enhancement tends to be on a per capita basis.[12] Profits, in an N,Z-advance, will increase in each firm by at least $Q(\Delta P/\Delta Q)$.[13] The excess of the profit increment over the change in the wage bill is given by[14]

$$\Delta(R - W) = [Q(\Delta P/\Delta Q)(\Delta Q/\Delta N)] - w \tag{71}$$

As the change in price $(\Delta P/\Delta Q)$ in each firm is equal to $-w(\Delta M/M)$, where $(\Delta M/M)$ is negative with diminishing returns, then eq. 71 can be written

$$\Delta(R - W) = w\left(\frac{Q\Delta M}{M} - 1\right) \tag{72}$$

Thus, where $\Delta M = 0$ the profit increment with an N-advance is nil. On the other hand, if ΔM is very large, as with a concave downward marginal-product curve for labor, the shift to profits will be extremely heavy, with the prospect that the aggregate real-wage bill will be lower.[15] Even where the total real-wage bill is higher, it still follows that real wages will fall so that wage-earner consumption

---

[12] This neglects financial phenomena such as stock-market trading which might show that the concentration of ownership tends to vary inversely with N as the number of stockholders increase through stock-splitting and greater public participation as profits rise. But this is hardly likely to affect the conclusions in any substantive way.

[13] More accurately, this ought to include a term for the employment change as in eq. 71.

[14] This assumes that labor is the only variable factor and that monopoly can be neglected. Differentiating $R = PQ - wN$ with respect to N yields eq. 71.

[15] See p. 62.

must in the limit be lower; a corresponding real-income reduction need never follow for profit recipients—given diminishing returns, that is.

Thus, while a constant c_r can maintain or even increase the real-consumption intake of entrepreneurial income recipients as N grows, a rising c_r almost certainly can strengthen their real-purchase intake.[16] Absolute savings out of profits are, in any event, likely to grow as employment advances except in rather unusual cases, and it is this savings swell which tends to equilibrate $D_c = C$ and $S = I$. Insofar as the average propensity to save grows with ΔN, then the ultimate income development will be checked and aggregate and relative profits will be restrained. From this relationship the entrepreneurial motto could well be "Consume more and grow rich!" The moral for each wage earner would be: *try* to consume more and become poorer! For the one, the injunction would be to spend, and for the other, to save in order to promote their individual self-interest. Entrepreneurs can thus, in a way, pull up their class by their own expenditure bootstraps; wage earners can at best assist their group to more employment even while individually their outlays inflict some personal real-wage harm. Ironically, the actual behavior patterns of the two groups are likely to be the very opposite of what seems to be the rational inference. Rising ratios of retained corporate income, for example, are likely to militate against growing profit levels within the income period in which they occur.[17]

A representative set of profit curves appears in Fig. 20. The curve R represents the course of profits which are zero or negative until N_1-men are engaged. The kR-function refers to dividend payouts; if k falls as N advances, then kR will be pulled lower in the field, and vice versa. The $(kR - T_x)$ function denotes the inroads of a progressive personal-income tax structure, while $D_c{}^r$ traces the consumption-outlay pattern.

[16] As stock-market prices are likely to be higher as N grows, the "paper profits" and realized capital gains are likely to stimulate consumption outlays by equity owners.

[17] In recent years, Kenneth Boulding has emphasized that consumption outlays are dependent on entrepreneurial profit disbursements so that the ultimate level of employment and profits hinges on the size of the k-factor. See his *A Reconstruction*, pp. 248–250. The point was made very clearly by Keynes in his earlier *A Treatise on Money* (New York, Harcourt, 1930), Volume I, p. 139. Compare p. 40.

There is one qualification to the proposition that greater corporate disbursements will swell corporate profits. Investment, it is clear, will also enlarge profits. Though the argument that retained corporate income serves to finance real-investment outlay *immediately* is patently false (in all but the unusual case), it is nevertheless possible for profit retention this year to facilitate plant expansion next year or the following year. Of course, in a frictionless economy in which funds were always available in the market, profit withholdings would always operate as a profit deterrent for investment would go on to the same extent over

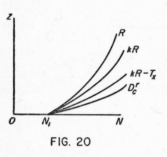

FIG. 20

time through market borrowing as by internal financing. But the facts are more stubborn and perverse: through money-market tightness, investment-banking reluctance, and its not uncommon desire to intervene and interfere in management policy, etc., then internal financing becomes vastly easier than market recourse; some investment, maybe a substantial part of it, is thus contingent on retained income. Hence, so far as profits go, the alternatives for firms *en masse* are either profits "today" via dividends and the return flow of consumption expenditure, or profits "tomorrow" via investment and its multiplier-income repercussions. The policy inference for high-level employment and income thus appears to be one leaning to profit disbursements in dull depression times (when new investment programs are unlikely to be imminent) and to favor profit retention in good times of high employment, when profits are already high *and when plans are on the drafting board and binding commitments are being made for near-future new plant and equipment*. Withholding is thus not always a menace to profits, though it may alter their time pattern. When equally satisfactory alternate financing sources are available, however, they do force a profit curb. Entrepreneurial adamancy and an overdose of tenacity in adhering to a "sound" dividend policy can undercut managerial self-interest and exact its toll by way of an implicit profit deflation.[18]

[18] Other than the desire to finance future expansion, the financial conservatism of corporations may have a more rational base; namely, to pro-

As a final remark at this stage, the effects of income redistribution as N expands have some obvious and important implications for the theory of the multiplier. As the rise in aggregate demand results in an income shift to profits, the implicit rise in the savings ratio tends to curtail the Z,N-exhilaration associated with multiplier theory, and the converse for an investment decrement. Distributive shifts thus operate as a stabilizing force—complicating the problem of policy measures during depression times even though the leverage effect of new investment will be at its greatest then while unemployment is rife.

MONEY WAGES AND EMPLOYMENT

The vastly important practical topic of the relationship of money-wage changes and employment concerns us now.[19] In view of the assumption of homogeneous labor, this amounts to a hypothesis of a proportionate wage change; the further intricacies occasioned by labor heterogeneity will be considered later.[20] Attention at this point will be directed primarily on the implications for Z,N of the redistribution compelled by money-wage changes, to the neglect of the repercussions on interest rates and investment, of the sort stamped into our thinking by Keynes.[21]

A simple problem can be used to launch this inquiry; namely, that of the effects of a shift in Z with W constant, that is, with money wages unchanged. In a wage analysis proper, both Z and W will be dislodged. The change in Z, W unchanged, may happen for several reasons: a cut in excise taxation might be cited as one example, although this creates the need to consider the total impact if there are new tax sources or new outlay magnitudes engendered by the altered tax policy. Alternately, a rise in labor productivity or a fall in monopoly power can edge Z closer to W.

With Z approaching W via a general drop in the Z-function, and

---

tect stockholders from the impact of the progressive income-tax structure. This is likely to be especially important in closely owned corporations.

[19] The analysis of wage changes and employment was described, not so long ago, as "in a fairly primitive state." See Paul A. Samuelson, "Economic Theory and Wages," in *The Impact of the Union,* p. 340.

[20] Compare Chapter 7.

[21] *Op. cit.,* Chapter 19.

with fixed payments assumed constant, one obvious effect is to decrease profits and shift income to rentiers: as prices are lower at each N-level, the latter are made better off. The round-about repercussions on the aggregate D_c-function will depend on the consumption-saving tendencies of the affected parties; if rentier consumption is unlikely to be advanced, the ultimate employment equilibrium might be lower in view of the cut in entrepreneurial intake. So far as wage earners go, the situation comes as an unmixed blessing, for prices are lower, their money wage is unchanged, and real wages inevitably are higher. From their side, the outcome is destined to be favorable to more consumption and thus higher employment, thereby providing some shield to protect the entrepreneurial share.

Rather innocently, this sketch abstracts from any repercussions on investment and to that extent is unrealistic: it is to argue that, despite their lower real income, entrepreneurs will continue to install the same volume of equipment. From the standpoint of consumption volume, they ought to do so; but construction of capital plant also rests on profit prospects even more than on purely physical output phenomena, so that, while short-run employment is facilitated, the long-run conclusion appears more dubious.

Technological change of the labor-saving, capital-using variety may elevate Z relative to W; the results are thus favorable to profits at each N-level with rentier income also higher if the new facilities require important contractual commitments. To maintain the employment level, the rise in D_c would have to match, at each N-point, the elevation in Z. Considering the shift against real wages and the higher "capitalist" saving propensities, the former N-level is unlikely to be sustained. "Technological unemployment" due to the failure of aggregate demand to keep pace with the necessary proceeds may well ensue as a consequence of the income shift impelled by the capital enlargement. Conversely, technological changes which push Z closer to W, either by increasing the degree of competition in the economy or by reducing the ratio of capital to labor, ought to enlarge N. These results seem reasonable enough: they stipulate merely that it becomes difficult to maintain employment when entrepreneurs have succeeded in installing labor-saving techniques, and vice versa. The failure, in the former case, is due not solely to the supply phenomena or Z-uplift, but also to the accompanying distributive revision which tends to thwart the appropriate rise in aggregate demand.

REDISTRIBUTION IN A PROPORTIONATE WAGE CHANGE. We turn now to the initial question; namely, of the relation of a money-wage change to employment. Suppose, as a purely illustrative exercise, that the national income is divided as follows:

HYPOTHETICAL INCOME DIVISION

	(1)	(2)
Wage incomes..........	$ 60	$ 66
Fixed incomes..........	15	15
Profits (and depreciation allowances)......	25	29
Totals............	$100	$110

That is, wage earnings constitute $60 or 60 per cent of the income total, while fixed incomes are 15 per cent and profits 25 per cent.[22] After a wage rise of 10 per cent, in a competitive framework where marginal costs consist wholly of wage costs, if the same output as before is to be produced then prices and proceeds must rise in the same ratio. The new income division is shown in column (2).[23] Examining this, wage incomes have risen by 10 per cent, fixed incomes remain firm, and profits mount by 16 per cent, so that the income turn is to profits.

Let us take it that real investment holds to its gait, rising in dollar value by 10 per cent to reflect the higher prices. Ruling out expectations of future price changes, there is every reason to hold that wage earners, whose pay envelopes have risen proportionately, will continue buying the same real market basket as before despite

[22] As we are working only with the three income categories, "profits" must be assumed to include any variable interest charges, excise taxes, and ordinary business taxes, including the corporate income tax.

[23] If $(wN/PQ) = M/A$ is to remain constant after the money wage and price rise, then w and P must rise in the same proportion. The fall-off in the relative rentier share is given by

$$\frac{\Delta}{\Delta Z}\left(\frac{F}{Z}\right) = -\frac{F\Delta Z}{Z_1 Z_2} \quad \text{(Compare, for the continuous case, eq. 24.)}$$

the price rise. Likewise, profit recipients can, at a minimum, at least maintain their real consumption *if the added profit income is distributed,* for the price rise is outstripped by the profit increase.

What fixed-income recipients do, compared to profit claimants, is thus the crux of the matter: this is an interesting and important result, which carries over with qualifications to cases of disproportionate wage movements.[24] If fixed-income groups cut their savings in order to maintain their real consumption, and if profit recipients seek to increase their real-purchase intake, the effect will be to increase money demand for consumption goods by more than 10 per cent, and thus increase employment through enlarged aggregate real demand. Conversely, if profit recipients merely sustained their previous real-consumption pattern while rentiers were compelled to restrain their original real-purchase volume, the effects would be detrimental to employment.

Schematically, as we are taking an uplift of Z at a given N-level, we are interested in the move in D_c. The initial and new ratios of the two are given by:

$$\frac{D_c{}^w + D_c{}^r + D_c{}^f}{Z} \gtreqless \frac{D_c{}^w + \Delta D_c{}^w + D_c{}^r + \Delta D_c{}^r + D_c{}^f + \Delta D_c{}^f}{Z + \Delta Z} \tag{73}$$

Stipulating that $(D_c{}^w/Z) = (D_c{}^w + \Delta D_c{}^w)/(Z + \Delta Z)$, so that the real consumption of wage earners is unchanged, then eq. 73 can be simplified to read

$$\frac{(D_c{}^r + \Delta D_c{}^r) + (D_c{}^f + \Delta D_c{}^f)}{D_c{}^r + D_c{}^f} \gtreqless \frac{Z + \Delta Z}{Z} \tag{74}$$

That is, if the relative money increment in consumption outlay of the combined groups rises in a lesser ratio than the rise in Z, employment will fall off. Clearly, a failure of rentier outlay to increase at the higher prices throws the whole burden of preventing an employment and output deflation squarely on profit recipients. Considering the importance of undistributed profits, the prospects for an unchanged real outcome appear substantially dimmed. It is as if firms were to pay out on balance an income sum of $10, which is then reduced by personal-income taxes to $8, and then expect a

[24] See Chapter 7.

return flow of expenditure of $12. In a "company town," as the
economy may be conceived, the realization of such an expectation is
hardly likely after a money-wage rise. Distributional effects which
point to constant real intake by wage earners, diminished intake by
rentiers, and merely sustained real intake by dividend recipients,
thus would confirm classical labor-demand ideas, of diminished
labor demand after a money-wage rise.[25] Thus, as a wage-price inflation persists, the income shift occasioned by it will curb the output development with only entrepreneurial
investment-enthusiasm capable of driving
the employment and price cart even higher.

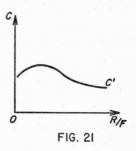

FIG. 21

To indicate that over a certain range the
income shift from rentiers to profit recipients is capable of enhancing aggregate
real-consumption demand, Fig. 21 is presented. Once curve C' reaches its peak, a
further relative income shift will reduce
the total real-purchase intake. The course
of C' depends not only on the degree of income shift between the
two groups, but also on the numbers contained in each class and on
the average strength of consumption and savings motives within
the separate categories.

The argument so far has compartmentalized rentier and profit
incomes as if they were self-contained islands in the income sea: in
practice, individuals almost invariably will draw income from both
sources. There will thus be some effect on consumption only insofar
as the income loss on one score is not counterbalanced by the gain
on the other; in general, a neat, net balance would not be expected.
On the presumption that the reaction to an income upswing is more
rapid than the adjustment to a decline, there ought to be some
temporary augmentation of consumption as profits go up. Once
more, the *number* of profit participants is worth stressing; if their
total outnumbers the size of the rentier group, the aggregate real-
consumption position tends to be better maintained after a wage
rise, and vice versa.

The significance of the respective real-consumption behavior
of rentier and profit groupings is also dependent on the magnitude
of the relative-income shift. For if the wage share, say, amounts to

[25] Compare Chapter 6, pp. 111–112.

90 per cent, then the effect of any likely rentier-profit income shift is dwarfed into insignificance; while, if the wage share is as low as 25 per cent, the rentier-profit tangle will be of primary importance. As matters stand, it appears that neither of these extremes is reached, with the wage share of gross proceeds approximating 55 to 60 per cent so that the changes are "unimportant and yet important." Hence, the disturbing conclusion that we face is that an important wage rise will threaten the employment level through inflicting a definite real loss on rentiers, and carry only a slight gain to dividend recipients, considering the impact of corporate and personal-income taxation and the tendency to profit retention.

WAGE-PRICE DISPROPORTIONALITY. The argument, so far, has assumed that prices rose proportionately with wage rates. This assumption must be tempered: in competitive price formation other costs enter into the marginal array, while, abandoning the competitive postulate, under administered prices or oligopoly situations, prices might hold rigid or move less than proportionately. Contrariwise, a wage rise may well serve as an excuse for a disproportionately greater price rise through a fuller exercise of latent monopoly power.

In the first case, of prices failing to rise proportionately, the outlook is distinctly more favorable for even an enlargement of the employment total, for now wage groups are in a position to increase their real consumption so that less reliance need be placed on the rentier-profit duel for output stability: the income shift is thus to wages *and*, in the probable cases, to profits, rather than to the latter alone. Conceivably, if prices fail to rise at all, say, even the profit share will be relatively reduced—as argued earlier, this is likely, however, at best within only narrow limits.[26] If, however, the reason that prices fail to rise very much is because wages are unimportant at the margin, then the stimulus from wage-earner consumption is also likely to be small since the average wage cost will be even lower than the marginal figure, in the usual case. The facts seem to indicate that wage costs (actually wages and salaries) amount on the average to about 55 per cent of the gross national product, with marginal wage costs undoubtedly being higher. Thus, the conclusion that prices ought to rise almost proportionately with wages, perhaps going up by about 80 per cent of the wage rise in purely

[26] See Chapter 4, pp. 70–71.

competitive circumstances. This proposition is threatened mainly by high marginal user-cost phenomena, which are likely to predominate when inflation—including wage increases—is foreshadowed, so that, when this applies, a wage rise can lead to even a disproportionately higher price rise; the employment total, and even the real wage, of labor groups may be menaced in this case. In a late stage of depression, where user-cost estimates may be high, a wage rise countered by a more marked price upswing can thus wreak new havoc by piling new unemployment on top of the existing idleness.

INCOME TRANSFERS AND AGGREGATE DEMAND. It will be convenient, in closing out this discussion of Z- and W-shifts, to consider the case of outright income transfers while the supply functions hold rigid.

Several possibilities come to mind, such as the reduction in fixed charges through (1) repayment of debenture debt, (2) a refunding of contractual interest obligations at lower rates, or (3) a switch to greater equity financing with a cutback in corporate contractual charges. Involved is an income shift between rentier and profit earnings with the net effect on the aggregate-consumption outlay function dependent on the numbers losing income, those acquiring income, their average income position, and their respective expenditure proclivities. At each employment level (for a small finite transfer) we have marginal-outlay relations of the following sort[27]:

$$\Delta D_c{}^r \gtreqless \Delta D_c{}^f \tag{75}$$

Depending on whether the marginal rentier outlay exceeds or falls short of that for profit recipients, the consumption influence will be either depressive or stimulating; this does assume, however, that sums formerly paid out to rentiers are actually disbursed as dividends.

Shifts can come about also through bonuses paid to wage earners —at Christmas time, say. Where these are not inviolate parts of the wage agreement, they will be made partly at the expense of profits.[28]

---

[27] Compare Harry G. Johnson, "The Macro-Economics of Income Redistribution," in *Income Redistribution and Social Policy* (London, Cape, 1954), Alan Peacock, editor, p. 25.

[28] It is interesting to quote Wicksell here. Writing in a related context he remarks: "According to Ricardo and Mill, if landowners remitted their rent, this would only result in tenants themselves now being able to live 'like

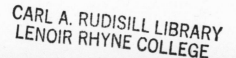

On balance, the effects on consumption ought to be stimulating. Practically all income transfers can be handled by means of eq. 75. Social-security tax collections from the employed and out-payments to the unemployed or to the aged are examples; insofar as the transfer contributions outweigh the transfer-income receipts, the discrepancy will be reflected in the respective ΔD_c-magnitudes. Loans between wage earners or family relatives would also lend themselves to treatment within the same framework; the net effect of "taxing Peter to pay Paul," a favorite maxim of critics of the tax system, can also be analyzed in the same way, provided that the particular tax can be identified as levied for Paul's benefit![29]

INFLATION AND REDISTRIBUTION

As the analysis has developed, at least three distinguishable causes of price movements which are likely to be denoted as inflation in popular discussions seem to appear. Yet their causes and consequences are likely to be in part different. Among the rising-price sequences we can enumerate (1) a price rise as N advances along a given Z-function with W also rigid, (2) a price rise due to a lift in Z while W stays in place, (3) a price rise due to a simultaneous upward lift in Z and W.

The first case might be termed one of "diminishing returns" or "employment" inflation, for, with wages constant and with the fall in labor productivity, the price rise is an inescapable accompaniment of the expanding activity. The only way that the upward pressure on prices can be averted would be through a money-wage cut, an increase in productivity, or a decrease in monopoly power, all of which are contrary to the hypotheses of the case. Diminishing returns with constant money wages render higher prices inevitable as output advances.

---

gentlemen.'" He goes on to point out that the price of bread would rise in view of the increased demand and greater output under diminishing returns. In our framework this constitutes a rise in D_c because of the income revision. See his *Value, Capital and Rent*, p. 39. (Ricardo, *op. cit.*, p. 75.)

[29] Government tax collections for transfer payments are never a full transfer because of the presence of administrative costs. Further, in the absence of government transfers, there probably would be greater charitable aids under private auspices, so that the ultimate issue is partly one of distributive incidence rather than pure transfer.

The second case might be called a "profit inflation": it could also be extended to include a nonequilibrium case, perhaps at "full employment," where there is a rise in D_c without a movement in Z. Alternately, demand upsweeps without changes in Z can be regarded as special causes of inflation, though, as ordinarily they will involve a new equilibrium along Z or a simultaneous change in the Z-function, they can be embraced as part of the cases listed. Returning to the elevation in Z, with W rigid, this can be a resultant of (1) a general enhancement of monopoly power at all employment levels, (2) a fall in labor's marginal productivity (relative to average) at each N-position, or (3) technological change and a shift toward the production of outputs requiring relatively less labor. A rise in user-cost estimates, too, can be at the bottom of this shift; e.g., heavier depreciation calculations because of forecasts of *future* inflation. In all these situations, with Z pushed parametrically higher, the price level will be propelled upward without any advance in the money-wage level.

The third situation is one of "wage-profit" inflation, or inflation pure and simple, embodying the spiral of popular conception. Once money wages go up, to maintain the same output and employment as before, prices also will have to rise.[30]

So far as distribution goes, in the first case it is the shift in income from rentiers and wage earners to profits that cramps the ultimate output-employment expansion; the shift to profits through diminishing M/A-ratios of labor productivity tends to check the output rise and thereby serves to protect the rentier and the wage position.

In case (2), the income shift at each N-position is immediately unfavorable to wages. Unless there is an unusual consumption binge by profit recipients, or gigantic investment plans are afoot, the result of this pattern of change in Z relative to W must be to reduce employment, while simultaneously, if the Z-dislodgment is large

---

[30] In the *Treatise*, Keynes distinguished "income inflation," akin to case (3) above, and "profit inflation," akin to case (2), although his concept properly referred to a given output level rather than a functional move in Z at all output or employment positions (Volume 1, pp. 155, 277). In the *General Theory*, the price rise as a result of diminishing returns (case 1) was introduced; situation (3) was elaborated as an instance of a change in the wage unit. These separate inflations ought to be kept distinct, for the appropriate economic policy to cope with them can be different. (Case 2 was not handled by Keynes in the *General Theory* except by implication.)

enough, establishing a higher price level. For rentiers the experience must be one of a real income cut without even the possibility of a rise in its class income, as would be the case for labor if employment somehow rose.

The real position of wage earners tends to be maintained with the price upsweep of case (3); in this situation it is only through the failure of entrepreneurial consumption to replace rentier retrenchment that invites unemployment. The cut in rentier consumption after each wage-price round thus imposes, apart from the monetary checks, one of the few natural obstructions to perpetual inflation via the wage-price spiral. The effectiveness of this restraint is, of course, contingent on the magnitude of rentier consumption in the total picture; where it is initially small, the roadblock that it is capable of erecting is likely to prove only a low hurdle and inconsequential barrier.

In all cases, a price rise is always detrimental to rentier interests and favorable for profits. Where labor's real wage falls (in case [1]) there are at least the higher employment and, usually, the higher aggregate-wage share as partial offsets. Finally, it ought to be reiterated that, in all the relative-income comparisons, the income concept that has been utilized—that of Z-proceeds—corresponds to the notion of gross national product. Relative-income experience may be somewhat different if other income concepts provide the basis for comparison.[31]

APPENDIX: MR. KALDOR'S "KEYNESIAN" THEORY

It is enlightening to consider the recent contribution of Mr. Kaldor to the theory of distribution, which he has labeled the "Keynesian theory" in the belief that it descends from key relations in the Keynesian system. Assuming full employment (initially), and dividing income, Y, into wages and profits, and writing s_w and s_r for the respective average propensities to save, with investment denoted by I, then[32]

---

[31] Compare G. L. Bach and Albert Ando, "The Redistributional Effects of Inflation," *The Review of Economics and Statistics* (February 1957). Their often unusual results can be traced to their use of national-income and personal-income concepts for comparative purposes. Of course, with undistributed profits, the personal-income concept will overstate the relative wage share and understate that of profits.

[32] See Nicholas Kaldor, "Alternative Theories of Distribution," *Review of Economic Studies* (1955–56), Volume XXIII, No. 2, p. 95.

$$I = s_r R + s_w W = s_r R + s_w(Y - R) = (s_r - s_w)R + s_w Y \qquad (1)$$

$$\frac{R}{Y} = \frac{1}{(s_r - s_w)} \frac{I}{Y} - \frac{s_w}{s_r - s_w} \qquad (2)$$

The conclusion is that, given s_w, s_r, the profit share "depends simply on the ratio of investment to output."[33] The interpretative value of eq. (2), according to Kaldor, is that the I/Y-ratio "can be treated as an independent variable, invariant with respect to changes in the two savings propensities" (p. 95). It is also pointed out that eq. (2) is meaningful only if $s_r > s_w$. Further, if $s_w = 0$, then[34]

$$R = I/s_r \qquad (3)$$

The "multiplier-type" relation—eq. (3)—reveals that profits exceed investment, depending on both I and capitalist consumption. These concepts are applied by Kaldor to problems of growth, of stagnation, and, in lesser measure, to cyclical oscillations, while certain limitations of the model are also explored. Concluding, Kaldor remarks that: "I am not sure where 'marginal productivity' comes in in all this."[35]

Equation (2) is the really intriguing formulation. As written, it makes profits dependent on investment and consumption outlays, with the latter being implicit through the savings propensities. Now if "full-employment" income prevails *by assumption,* as Kaldor initially declares, this is perhaps all that needs to be said: *supply phenomena and producing decisions do not matter.* Likewise, if growth is taken as a mechanistic phenomenon, moving somehow automatically at a given pace, supply phenomena are again irrelevant, impotent, or somehow subsumed within the hypothesis of automatic investment.

It is here that our development parts company with Mr. Kaldor's analysis—apart from rejecting his rigid (but ingenious) saving ratio simplification. If we envisage the economic system as sometimes running down to less than full employment, and conceive of it as a process in which entrepreneurs pay out proceeds in the expectation of recouping at least the same sums, and generally more, then supply phenomena *do* matter— *and marginal-productivity aspects do enter the picture.* In this conception, factor hire is undertaken in the light of expected proceeds, (expected) productivity, and factor prices. To overlook the productivity relations is to omit some important causal variables in the economic process; *aggre-*

[33] *Ibid.*   [34] *Ibid.,* p. 96.

[35] *Ibid.,* p. 100. Whatever importance is ascribed to marginal productivity is assigned to the dependence of the ratio of capital to output in the relation of R/Y. Thus it is not unfair to describe Kaldor as eliminating the influence of marginal-productivity ideas entirely.

gate demand does not exist independently of aggregate supply, at least for its consumption component. The wage outlays especially are contingent on entrepreneurial supply estimates, and, hence, on labor-productivity relations which govern labor hire. Just as Mr. Kaldor has shown that the profit share depends on the I/Y-relation, starting instead from the supply side it can similarly—and simultaneously—be shown that the wage share depends on the M/A-relation.[36] Inevitably, the profit share, in the two-factor case, would be equal to $(1 - M/A)$. In equilibrium, where aggregate demand, D, equals aggregate supply, $(Z \equiv Y)$, it follows that $(R/Y) = (1 - M/A)$, so that formula (2) above must be equal to $(1 - M/A)$.

Thus it is an incomplete view of the process to emphasize the investment volume and the consumption proclivities to the exclusion of productivity phenomena: equilibrium requires that both outlay *and* productivity conditions be satisfied. Emphasis on one set might be justified only if one were volatile and variable and the other rigid. But this has not been demonstrated—nor is it likely to follow when output is subject to diminishing returns along given productivity functions or when productivity is modified by virtue of technological advances.

In part, this chapter was undertaken to redress the balance and insert the variations in consumption-outlay behavior arising through the distributive revision in an output advance as a determinant of the ultimate income partition. Stress still centered on productivity, but recognition was extended to the fact that the income shift emanating on the supply side—in view of the causal role of entrepreneurial action—had its impact on demand. It is the hire decisions, the supply side, that make the wheels of production and employment go round; the actual demand outlays then play their part in the final equilibrium arbitrament of prices, output, employment, and the distributive shares. In a "forward-looking" economy, in which "today's" hire is directed toward physical output that will mature "tomorrow," it is the entrepreneurial anticipatory hire acts based on marginal productivity estimates that will prove decisive.

One final observation: Mr. Kaldor offers his interpretation on the ground that I, or the I/Y-ratio, is *the* independent variable, suggesting this as "the" Keynesian hypothesis. But this cannot be wholly right; it is to argue that the investment function is *the* income determinant, that the consumption function plays only an incidental part. Of course, it may be that the I-function is instable and thus, in a sense, strategic, while the consumption function is stable—and linear, as is entailed in the hypothesis of constant s_w- and s_r-ratios. But this is to minimize the effects of shifts in relative income and price-level phenomena on consumption as

[36] See pp. 51–53.

D_i and the Z,N-level alter. To hold s_w constant is to imply constant-money outlays out of wages ($\Delta c_w = 0$) for an individual employed at N_1 and N_2 where $N_2 > N_1$. This is, as argued earlier, most unlikely, as prices advance with ΔN. Further, the constant s_r-notion becomes even less plausible when applied to rentiers with a ΔN-move. On both these scores, then, Kaldor's technique understates the ultimate Z,N-level and the size of the shift to profits. For like reasons, plus the fact of retained earnings and corporate taxes, s_r as applied to profits is unlikely to hold firm. Finally, once we acknowledge the presence of retained earnings, it is probably illegitimate to argue that either s_r or I/Y will be invariant *or* wholly independent of one another. Once the hypothesis of rigid savings ratios is abandoned, then D_c does depend on Z where the latter, in turn, rests on productivity phenomena.

To argue that (most) savings come out of profits and that, therefore, investment determines profits is only slightly less tautologous than to argue that investment "determines" saving: one might almost say that by definition $I \equiv S \equiv R$. Yet investment, with consumption, determines income. To produce the income, however, requires employment which, in itself, entails some principle of factor hire. It is here that marginal-productivity ideas enter; paying labor its marginal-value product (under pure competition) the wage share "depends" on the ratio of marginal to average product, as well as on the level of investment.

Chapter 6

An Approach to the Theory of Wages

The way is now clear for an approach to the theory of wages.[1]
Prior to the appearance of Keynes's *General Theory,* economists
generally would have scouted the idea that their supply-demand
techniques were inadequate to cope with the theory of money
wages. Thereafter, the tide seemed to run the other way, with an
almost universal skepticism of the prospect of a determinate money-
wage theory; Keynes rejected the orthodox wage explanation on
the ground that its labor-demand function was based on the assumption that the level of income was given.[2] He argued that this
was a fatal defect in the theory since every change in money wages
was capable of altering the employment and the real-income position as well as money income and the price level. Since then, the
tendency has been to regard the level of money wages as an exogenously determined variable.

[1] The major portion of this chapter, omitting mainly a brief exposition of
the theory of income determination, is reproduced from my article, "A
Macroeconomic Approach to the Theory of Wages," *American Economic
Review* (December 1956), amended to incorporate the comment of Paul E.
Junk and my reply in the September 1957 issue. Permission to reprint has
been granted by the editors of the *American Economic Review.*

For a recent analysis devoted to much the same problem, see Martin
Bronfenbrenner, "A Contribution to the Aggregative Theory of Wages,"
Journal of Political Economy (December 1956). This article appeared prac-
tically simultaneously with my own and contains several interesting parallels.

[2] Keynes, *op. cit.,* pp. 258–259. In his Chapter 19, on "Changes in Money-
Wages," Keynes concerns himself with the effects of changes in the level of
money wages rather than with the problem of wage determination. Throughout the book he argues that the common wage controversies are disputes
mainly over the matter of relative wages of the different labor groups and
that the wage bargains are concerned with money wages; for, he declares,
there is no way by which labor, by itself, can determine its real wage.

Indeterminateness is always disquieting, particularly so in a problem which is of such vast practical importance and is so central in economic analysis; it is hard for an economist to have to admit that a typical case of price higgling, such as is found in a labor market, cannot be attacked successfully. It is to this problem of deriving determinate labor-demand and labor-supply functions free of the constant-income postulate that this chapter is directed. One major simplification will be made; namely, that the labor force is homogeneous rather than consisting of the heterogeneous groups that are found in fact. If a determinate theory can be obtained on this basis, it ought to be possible to extend it to the more realistic setting. The latter problem will occupy us in Chapter 7.

THE LABOR-DEMAND FUNCTION

From the analysis of income determination (Chapter 2), it is not too difficult to extract a demand curve for labor, D_L, that is compatible with the theory of income.

Given the stock of equipment and the labor-productivity equations, every change in the money wage will shift the marginal-cost curve of the individual firm, and thereby the supply curve of the industry; through shifts in the industry-supply curves, the full course of Z will be elevated or depressed. Analytically, at each employment position a rise in money wages will lift Z in amount:

$$dZ = \left(N + \frac{\partial R}{\partial P} \frac{\partial P}{\partial w} \right) dw \qquad (P \text{ denotes the price level}) \quad \textbf{(76)}$$

After the money-wage rise, the necessary increment in proceeds required to sustain the same employment and output level as before is thus equal to the money-wage increase multiplied by the employment total plus the increase in profits accompanying the price-level and money-wage changes. Further, it is readily shown that, when labor is the only variable factor (or other factors are assumed fixed), the shift to profits for a small wage increase within the individual firm is given by[3]

$$\Delta R = N[(A/M) - 1]\Delta w \qquad \textbf{(77)}$$

[3] See Note 2 in the Appendix to this chapter.

It is apparent from eq. 77 that, when the marginal product of labor is small relative to the average product, as it is likely to be in advanced positions of diminishing returns, the shift to profits after a wage rise is intensified. If $A = M$, which would entail the smallest ratio of A/M possible under pure competition, the increment in profits would be zero; all of the added money receipts would go to pay the higher wage bill. Of course, if the output that was most profitable before the wage rise is no longer the most profitable afterward, then eq. 77 understates ΔR.

As a wage rise lifts the money-income payments at each N-level, the D_c-component function of D must edge up. Since not all of the profit increment after a wage rise will be paid out, the added income disbursements appear as[4]

$$\Delta Y_d = (N + k\Delta R/\Delta w)\Delta w \tag{78}$$

Essentially, this is formula 76, reduced by the k-factor to take account of undistributed profits. Nevertheless, since the average propensity to consume, c, must be positive, the result of the increase in income payments to factors must be to propel D upward through the lift given to D_c by the augmented payments. Hence, in the chart field of Fig. 14, both the D- and the Z-function would have to be moved parametrically upward in order to reflect the rise in the money-wage level. Just as before, however, the amount of equilibrium employment can be ascertained at the intersection of the new Z- and D-curves generated by the money-wage rise.

The interesting point that comes out of the analysis in this: by varying money wages and observing the shift in Z and D from each point of intersection of the two curves, the equilibrium employment level can be elicited and thereupon linked functionally to the money wage, so that the relevant points for a labor-demand schedule can be derived. For example, in Fig. 14 the curves D' and Z' embody, say, a wage of w'. The equilibrium employment level of N_1 then becomes the labor-demand point for a money wage of w'. Implicit at the level of individual firms is the equating of the marginal-value product of labor to the money wage w', since firms are presumed to be hiring factors in accordance with the condition of profit maximization at the emergent-proceeds level Z_1. Without the equation

[4] Compare Chapter 2, pp. 39–41, and Chapter 5, pp. 93–94.

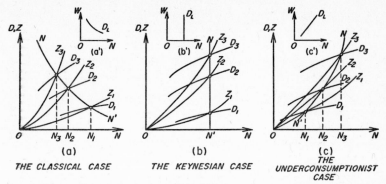

INSET DIAGRAMS (a', b', c') SHOW THE IMPLICIT LABOR-DEMAND CURVES

FIG. 22

of marginal-value product and factor price (under pure competition), the equilibrium would be incomplete.

Traditionally, the labor-demand curve, D_L, has been pictured as falling continuously to the right, signifying that more labor would be hired at lower money-wage rates, though to be sure in the tighter formulations of the "classical" position the vertical axis referred to real rather than to money wages. In practical precept, however, the well-nigh universal tenet was that a money-wage fall would, barring "frictions," eradicate involuntary unemployment.

Reinterpreting the underlying conceptual structure of the classical argument by aid of the D,Z-functions, in Fig. 22 (a) a rise in money wages from w_1 to w_2 is shown as lifting the proceeds function from Z_1 to Z_2, and the aggregate-demand function from D_1 to D_2. Equilibrium employment thus drops from N_1 to N_2. Likewise, a further wage rise to w_3 leads to an employment level of N_3, etc. In this way, a full dual family of D,Z-curves can be drawn, leading to a crosscut locus such as NN' which discloses the equilibrium path of N,Z-values traced by continuous wage movements and the resultant parametric shifts in the Z- and the D-curves. The small inset diagram (Fig. 22 [a']) indicates the corresponding form of the D_L-function, sloping continuously downward to the right: at each point on the latter, since it has been extracted from positions of equilibrium adaptations to proceeds flows, the conventional marginal-value-productivity relations are preserved despite the macroeconomic dress in which the analysis has been clothed.

It was the uncritical acceptance of the classical form of D_L that Keynes assailed; subsequent opinion has deferred to the view that the classical relationship can be sustained only under special provisos, particularly with reference to expectations.[5] Inasmuch as Keynes fostered the idea that little positive gain in employment could come from a wage change, we shall call a D_L-curve showing a zero demand elasticity and represented by a vertical line the Keynesian D_L (see Fig. 22 [b]).[6]

A more optimistic attitude on the effect of money-wage changes is often expressed by underconsumption theorists who argue that higher money wages induce greater consumer demand and higher employment. This suggests a D_L-curve that rises to the right, a phenomenon which is strikingly reminiscent of goods with snob appeal in product-price theory (see Fig. 22 [c]).

Formally, all of the D_L-functions of Fig. 22 seem plausible despite the fact that, from the standpoint of economic policy, their implications are vastly different.[7] Unless it is possible to do more to indicate at least the nature of the slope of D_L, wage theory will remain hemmed in despite the ability to define the relevant functions.

Something can be done to pierce the wall of darkness through taking into account the following considerations. In the upper reaches of D_L it seems reasonably certain that monetary policy will provide a decisive and restrictive influence; that is to say, higher money wages and a consequent higher price level are likely to engender tighter money, tending to put a brake on investment and, through some effect on the savings function, on consumption, thereby operating to decrease employment. Likewise, in an open

[5] See Keynes, pp. 262–265. Also, Don Patinkin, "Price Flexibility and Full Employment," *American Economic Review* (September 1948), pp. 556–560; reprinted with modifications in *Readings in Monetary Theory* (New York, Irwin, 1951), pp. 252–284.

[6] In fairness, however, his own position was not so uncompromising, for he declared that a flexible wage policy would not maintain continuous full employment "any more than . . . an open-market monetary policy is capable, unaided, of achieving this result" (p. 267). This suggests *some* responsiveness.

[7] A less plausible arrangement is sometimes suggested, with more emotion than reason, that a money-wage hike not only will lower employment but also will *depress* money income: thorough-going deflation rather than inflation is the outcome deduced from a wage hike. This would involve a rise in Z and a fall in D.

system, the export volume will also tend to decline under (reasonably) stable exchange rates and the ensuing price-level upheavals as money wages mount. All in all, the upper stretch of the D_L-curve is likely to be of classical form, even displaying a high elasticity.

Locating the "upper stretch" depends partly on historical, partly on institutional data. If the prevailing wage and price level represents the culmination of an inflationary climb, and if the monetary authorities are adamant about maintaining the (roughly) existing price level, then any rise in money wages which requires a directional move in the price level is likely to encounter tight money and a decrease in labor demand. In this case, the "upper reaches" of D_L lie just beyond the going wage scale.[8] Conversely, if the current economic position has been preceded by a marked deflationary spiral, and a price-level upsurge is regarded as tolerable from the vantage point of economic policy, then the "upper" classical-type D_L-stretch may be well above prevailing wage rates.

In the lower regions of D_L, through the cumulating strength of the Pigou effect, involving a rise in the real value of individual assets in the form of "hard" money, the fiduciary note issue, and usually government bonds, as the price level falls, it may be surmised that the D_L-curve will also be of classical form.[9] The loca-

---

[8] The argument, it is clear, presumes a constant-investment function, and a constant-consumption function, as well as defined productivity conditions, for otherwise the D,Z-field is indeterminate. If investment demand increased, say, "tight" money might become effective even without a rise in the wage level. For our purposes, some temporal constancy of D_c and D_i can be assumed.

[9] For a discussion of the Pigou effect, see Patinkin, *Readings*, pp. 258–270. The original elaboration appears in A. C. Pigou, "The Classical Stationary State," *Economic Journal* (December 1943), pp. 343–351. Milton Friedman has argued that, with 100 per cent money, the Pigou effect "in principle, would alone be sufficient to assure full employment . . ." See his article, "A Monetary and Fiscal Framework for Economic Stability," *American Economic Review* (June 1948). Reprinted in *Readings*, pp. 369–393. The quotation is from p. 387. It might be thought that the same forces which explain the depression trough could be used to explain the lower region of bb' in Fig. 23; that is, the need for some capital replacement and the rise in the average propensity to consume at lower aggregate real-income levels. But these factors explain only the volume of labor demand, or the D_L-quantity, but not why the D_L-quantity should *increase* as money wages and the price level fall. The increase in autonomous investment and replacement *over time* belong to a study of the dynamics of the labor market and of shifts in D_L over time.

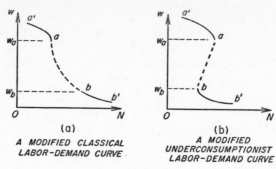

(a)

A MODIFIED CLASSICAL
LABOR-DEMAND CURVE

(b)

A MODIFIED
UNDERCONSUMPTIONIST
LABOR-DEMAND CURVE

FIG. 23

tion of this lower portion also depends in part on the course of the past price development.

Accordingly, the top of the D_L-curve ought to resemble the path aa' in Fig. 23 (a), and the lower sector should look like bb'. At a wage above w_a, monetary policy takes firm hold; at a wage below w_b, and its concomitant price level, the Pigou effect stimulates consumption demand, especially for services and luxury purchases, so that unemployment is absorbed. As an extreme illustration to make the point, though a cruel and prohibitive one from a policy standpoint, when prices fall to such levels that those owning "pennies" become "millionaires"—a calamitous prospect!—full employment may well be assured. Of course this is not to suggest that either monetary policy or the Pigou effect operates discontinuously, waiting for a particular price-level range; it is to aver solely that they dominate other factors only at certain wage positions. For example, to hazard a crude guess, in the current economy a wage move of, say, 20 to 25 per cent above present levels is likely to bring down the roof of monetary policy and thereby decrease employment; on the downside, to be effective, the real-asset influence on consumption might require a price fall extending beyond 50 per cent. Whatever the exact order of facts in these respects, the appropriate curve shape in upper and lower regions ought not to be in serious dispute.

For a fully determinate D_L, more must be known about the course of the curve in the arc between a and b. Over this range, monetary policy and the Pigou effect play a role, though ordinarily their importance will be neutralized by other factors. One such countervailing element consists of the expectations of future changes in wages as they vary in the range between w_a and w_b. Unfortunately, the little that can be said concerning the influence of expectations is scarcely calculated to impart determinateness to our curve; any movement from a wage intermediate between w_a and w_b may create a belief that the resulting wage level is only temporary and that further changes are foreshadowed, either in the same direction or in reverse. The influence on D_L is thus correspondingly vague: the range ab can contain either the classical or the underconsumptionist D_L-locus.

More of a definite nature can be said about the effects stemming from the change in interest rates and in the pattern of income distribution. That a money-wage rise, through its pressure on prices and money-income levels, tends to raise interest rates and in degree dampen investment has been well known since Keynes made it clear. Manifestly, this tends to buttress the classical D_L-arguments. Less, as a rule, has been said about the distributional effects. Yet every rise in money wages, and thus prices, will shift the relative income share in favor of entrepreneurs and against rentiers. Neglecting wage earners for the moment (by assuming that the price rise is proportionate to the wage rise so that their income is constant at the given output level), the rentier loss in real income is exactly counterbalanced by the entrepreneurial gain. Insofar as the real income sacrifice of the rentier class adversely affects its consumption, the counterbalance must be provided by increased consumption of the entrepreneurs in order that output remain unchanged. In view of the withholdings out of enlarged profit incomes, this counterbalance is unlikely, and hence, at least for important wage and price-level movements, the erosion of rentier real income offers a repressing influence via consumption, tending to fortify the classical view of D_L.[10]

Further light on the effect on employment, through consumption demand, likely to result from a wage increase can be obtained by re-examining eq. 76 and eq. 78. The former indicates the magnitude by which aggregate spending must increase in order for output to remain unchanged after a rise in money wages. Equation 78, on the other hand, indicates that a smaller sum will be distributed as

---

[10] Thus a price rise tends to obliterate the consuming power of Malthus' "unproductive consumer"—*Principles of Political Economy* (London, 1836), Book II, Chapter 1, Section 9.

income. Considering the corporate-income tax and the normal financial conservatism of corporations, k seldom seems to have been above $\frac{1}{3}$ and in recent years has approached $\frac{1}{4}$ of corporate profits *after* depreciation; including depreciation in R, a k-factor as small as $\frac{1}{7}$ cannot be precluded, though, for the profit increment being considered, the higher ratios are probably more valid. Further, through the inroads of a progressive personal-income tax structure, even if profit earnings are fully disbursed as dividends, the average propensity to spend, c, out of this income is likely to fall. On balance, therefore, in view of corporate withholdings and the personal-income shift toward profits, the demand increment is likely to be less than the necessary-proceeds increment.[11]

Now let us drop the assumption that the price rise is proportionate to the wage rise. Although in stable circumstances, and precluding a rise in the degree of monopoly power, the price rise is unlikely to outstrip the wage rise, it is distinctly possible that the price rise may fall short of the wage uplift, particularly if there are non-wage elements (such as user cost) present in marginal costs. This would portend an income shift favorable to labor, though it may be conjectured that the income shift will be small in view of the predominance of wage costs in marginal costs. Where the shift is not small, as in circumstances which trade-union spokesmen often unrealistically advocate—namely, that prices hold constant while wages rise without any changes in productivity—the upshot might be wholly favorable for consumption and would support the underconsumptionist conception of labor demand. But this assumes a placid entrepreneurial and rentier attitude in the face of a whittling away of their real income by labor; ultimately, it would require the suspension of the profit motive and the condition of profit maximization—which explains why these results do not usually follow upon money-wage increases.

The easing of the debt burden as prices rise might be deemed a factor tending to increase investment and compelling D_L to rise to the right through an exhilarating push on D_i. If excess capacity is present, however, the mitigated debt burden is likely to contribute mainly to swelling corporate reserves and savings, perhaps preparing the way for future investment by providing the internal

[11] Compare Chapter 2, p. 40, and Chapter 5, p. 98.

finance through profits for capital-expansion programs and by creating a better investment climate, rather than initiating an immediate burst of investment activity. Insofar as there is a more immediate and positive sensitivity of real-investment demand to higher profits and prices, there are also likely to be offsets because some investment programs will have been set up with the planned money expenditure fixed, and so will involve declining real investment as prices rise. Situations of the latter nature are not uncommon, as college and local school board building-fund administrators frequently testify in inflationary periods. Examples could be drawn also from the business world, where firms often organize their investment plans about a fixed-money budget. Real-investment inelasticity, and thus an inelastic labor demand, is implicit when purchase outlays are designed on a real-program basis, as in the case of government demand for military procurement.

In all, considering the catalogue of relations enumerated, unless there is a strong presumption that an expansion of real investment of fairly substantial magnitude waits on a price-level upsurge through the wage increases that are commonly made in practice, there seems to be good reason to assume that the shape of D_L within the "indeterminate" range of ab is of "moderately" classical form, as in Fig. 23 (a). However, there is no inexorable necessity here; the exceptions which justify the underconsumption D_L-pattern involve mainly the dynamics of expectations, which may hasten an immediate investment bulge in the belief that even higher prices are on their way—which is a valid argument—or an unlikely and fairly extreme income transfer to wage earners—which is a less reasonable belief. An appropriate diagram, however, appears in Fig. 23 (b).

THE LABOR-SUPPLY FUNCTION

It might be thought that, since a homogeneous labor force has been postulated, there could be no reason to analyze labor supply, for this would then be a very simple matter: if one person is willing to work regardless of real income, then all must be so inclined. However, it is more sensible to interpret homogeneity as meaning only *technical* homogeneity, so that, from the standpoint of productivity (as seen through entrepreneurial eyes), all individuals are alike;

this still permits differences in work attitudes or income-leisure preferences to manifest themselves. For our purposes, these attitudes are assumed to be given.

Unless it is presumed that wage earners are wholly imbued with a money illusion, the labor-supply function should be cast largely in real- rather than money-wage terms; even though wage earners may elect to ignore minor price perturbations at some stipulated money-wage level, there is little reason to suppose that they are utterly deluded.[12] Hence, if the S_L-function is formulated in terms of money wages, it will be imperative to specify the real wage attached to each money sum, for otherwise the construction is unlikely to prove serviceable.

The problem posed in thus a rather vexing one. If we are to use a diagram such as Fig. 23, where the vertical axis represents money wages, simultaneously we must take into account variations in real wages; for each money wage does not always represent the same real wage.

Fundamentally, the level of real wages attached to any money wage cannot be known until the (virtual) volume of employment, the output, and the price level for that output are also known. Hence the lead for deriving the S_L-function, despite the apparent paradox, must be through D_L. Consider how the latter is drawn: each money-wage labor-demand point on D_L assumes that entrepreneurs can hire as much labor as they require in the light of the income-determining forces operative at that wage rate. It follows that, after the labor-demand quantity is known, the price level and the real wage corresponding to the money wage likewise are disclosed. Thereupon, we can inquire whether the labor-supply quantity forthcoming is just equal to the quantity demanded, in the light of the underlying real phenomena, or whether it exceeds or falls short of the labor demand. The answer to this query furnishes the relevant supply point to set off against the demand point at the given money wage. Each S_L-co-ordinate thus depends on the implicit

---

[12] Cf. the original criticism of Keynes by W. W. Leontief, "The Fundamental Assumption of Mr. Keynes' Monetary Theory of Unemployment," *Quarterly Journal of Economics* (November 1936), pp. 195–196. Also, James Tobin, "Money Wage Rates and Employment," in *The New Economics* (New York, Knopf, 1947), Seymour Harris, editor, p. 580. For the incorporation of "money-wage illusion" during involuntary unemployment, in response to Junk's criticism, see p. 126.

phenomena in each D_L-point at a given money wage. In this way, a full S_L-path can be deduced.

The following definition of the S_L-function is offered so that the contrast between this supply function and a representation in which labor supply is contingent on either money wages or real wages alone will be clear:

$$S_L = \Psi(w, D_L, U) \tag{79}$$

where U denotes the leisure-income preference system while the other symbols are as before. As $D_L = \phi(w)$, then we may write

$$S_L = \Psi[w, \phi(w), U] \tag{80}$$

It is abundantly clear from eq. 80 that, although S_L is plotted against the money wage in the simple plane diagram, it is nevertheless *not* a function directly of the money wage but of the D_L and its implicit real-wage phenomena.[13] Real-wage attitudes, as represented by U, and real-wage potentialities through investment levels and productivity phenomena, as represented by $\phi(w)$, thus become parameters of S_L. Graphically, however, S_L is plotted against the money wage mainly because we are interested in using the S_L-function to aid us in disclosing the process of determining the money wage, and only thereafter in deriving the implicit real phenomena.

A curious sort of labor supply-demand interdependence thus emerges. The unusual concatenation of the two curves, generally conceived as independent, ought to prepare us for some rather odd functional forms in this analytic terrain, just as oligopoly has taught us to expect some queer and irregular curve types in product markets.

The three types of labor-supply functions that need to be reinterpreted in terms of the S_L-functional relation developed in eq. 80 are: (1) the case in which labor is positively responsive to real wages, with more labor forthcoming as real wages rise, which is the most common of the traditional supply conceptions, (2) the backward-bending S-curve in which labor offerings fall off in response to higher real wages over some "middle range" because of an urgent and unsatisfied income demand for leisure, and (3) the case of the perfectly inelastic labor supply, which is often taken as

[13] See Note 1 to the Appendix at the end of this chapter.

the typical case in statistical inquiries into the labor market.[14] The case of perfectly elastic labor supply, perhaps through trade-union action, is simple and will call for only brief mention; an amendment to it, involving involuntary unemployment, will be discussed at more length below.

All of these cases can, after a simple translation, be suspended against the D_L-function. For this purpose, the D_L-curve in Fig. 23 (a) may be regarded as typical. Clearly, the case of perfectly inelastic supply, which may be a valid account of the facts, promises analytic simplicity itself: this is represented by a vertical supply line and, if D_L falls continuously, there is a point of intersection which, in a competitive market, yields a determinate wage and employment position. Likewise, if the traditional rightward-rising labor-supply curve is regarded as valid, and if, according to the D_L-curve in Fig. 23 (a), real wages increase at higher money wages while employment falls off, then the traditional supply curve retains its customary form. However, if the stretch ab in Fig. 23 (a) is fairly steep, then the curve of labor supply is also likely to climb rapidly inasmuch as the real-wage rate is presumed, within this range, to increase very little despite the rise in the money wage; where the intersection of S_L with D_L occurs will depend substan-

[14] D. H. Robertson suggests, following Pigou, that the classical supply curve of labor must be taken as either perfectly vertical or horizontal. If so, there is no difficulty on the supply side. The perfectly inelastic case involves a submissiveness of labor to almost any real wage, which does not seem plausible especially below the Malthusian minimum or in upper reaches, considering the existence of personal debts which could lead more individuals to seek work temporarily to enhance their real asset position. The horizontal case appears more reasonable—within limits. See, however, his note on "Keynes and Supply Functions," *Economic Journal* (September 1955), p. 477. Also, A. C. Pigou, *Employment and Equilibrium* (1949, 2nd ed.), pp. 70, 86. Greater responsiveness of labor supply to real wages is noted by Pigou on p. 10.

Though qualified in part, substantially the same view of labor inelasticity is noted by Clarence D. Long from his statistical investigations in which he states that the labor force "appears insensitive to moderate variations in unemployment or in real or money incomes or hourly earnings." See his "Impact of Effective Demand on the Labor Supply," *American Economic Review* (May 1953), p. 466.

If the concept of labor inelasticity is interpreted literally, it would imply, too, that the labor force is insensitive to either income *or* indirect taxes so that arguments on taxes and work incentives become meaningless. I doubt that anyone would push the inelasticity argument to this extreme.

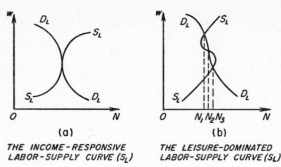

(a)   (b)

THE INCOME-RESPONSIVE   THE LEISURE-DOMINATED
LABOR-SUPPLY CURVE (S_L) LABOR-SUPPLY CURVE (S_L)

FIG. 24

tially on the position of the lower and highly elastic stretch of S_L, influenced largely by trade-union demands, minimum wage laws, and customary standards. In Fig. 24 (a), the intersection of the two curves is shown at a point where S_L is highly inelastic. Under this arrangement of the two curves, it is possible that, over a fairly substantial range, a money-wage change may occur without affecting employment, with the main impact being on the level of prices.

The S-shaped labor-supply curve gives rise to a configuration such as appears in Fig. 24 (b). This, too, discloses that whether the money-wage rate settles at one of the stable extreme points, or the unstable middle position, the change in employment is likely to be small in view of the assumed inelasticity of D_L in this range.

It follows that, if the demand for labor is highly inelastic, then the supply curve for labor is also likely to be highly inelastic, so that, despite even substantial changes in the going wage scale—say, of the order of 10 to 15 per cent—the accompanying variation in the level of employment will be minor despite the spin that will be given to the price level.

With the vertical Keynesian-type D_L, the possibility of thorough-going indeterminateness arises; either the accompanying S_L, which would also be vertical, merges with D_L, or it lies off to one side. Competitive market analysis would be unavailing in this case; the situation can be saved only if labor supply becomes perfectly elastic through trade-union wage stipulations, minimum wage laws, or common wage practice. Of course, trade-union price fixing always renders the money-wage level "determinate" though the labor hire is suspended in midair until the D_L-function is inserted. If we grant the wage adamancy of the unions and an obedience to its dictates by its membership, the procedure of regarding money wages as an exogenously determined variable is justified. But this resolution still evades the issue of why the union negotiations concentrate on a particular money wage. If a real-wage base is sought as the answer to this question, we are once again taken back to the D_L-function and its implicit real-wage outcomes.

Finally, if D_L contains a rightward-rising stretch (see Fig. 23 [b]), as argued in underconsumption theories, then real wages *fall* as money wages rise. Rather unexpectedly, the traditional labor-supply curve is likely to rise to the *left*, for this case, rather than to the right—at least over the backward-falling D_L-range. Although a determinate solution can be derived, the usual awesome possibilities of instability appear. Likewise, an S-shaped labor-supply function drawn in real terms, when translated into a correspondent of D_L in Fig. 23 (b), is likely to rise steadily to the right, at least in the portion where it ordinarily bends backward, showing a negative response to rising real income, and encounters the rightward-rising portion of D_L (which shows decreasing rather than increasing real wages). Thus, with the underconsumptionist D_L, the traditional labor-supply curve can occasion instability while the leisure-dominated S-curve is conducive to a stable wage-level pattern. Illuminating as these results are, they are unimportant unless there is strong reason to accept the underconsumptionist D_L-pattern as representative of labor market facts.

WAGE DETERMINATION AND CHANGES IN D_L

Under conditions of competition, it is to the intersection of the D_L- and the S_L-curves that we must look for the equilibrium wage and volume of labor hire. As a rule, stability requires that the D_L-function fall to the right and S_L rise to the right.[15] Because of the possibility of the combination of the underconsumptionist D_L and the traditional S_L, we ought to be prepared to find some instability in the labor market. But it may be surmised that this is not the most common case.

[15] See Melvin Reder, *Studies in the Theory of Welfare Economics* (New York, Columbia, 1947), pp. 112–115. For an analysis of the stability issue in terms of a likely D_L-function, see my *Price Theory*, p. 123, Fig. 4a.

Even more interesting than the stability question, which refers to given functions, is the matter of the interlocked nature of labor-demand and labor-supply shifts due to the interdependent relationship that has been revealed. For example, suppose that, as a result of a rise in the inducement to invest, the D_i-component of aggregate demand climbs higher, raising the D-function of Fig. 22 and the volume of labor demanded at each money-wage rate. With the labor-productivity functions unchanged, the D_L-curve will move rightward and each money-wage rate will now signify a *lower* real wage than before. Inevitably the D_L-shift will carry with it a displacement of the S_L-function, inasmuch as the latter is geared to the level of real income implicit in D_L. With the traditional

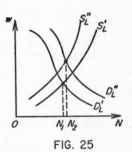

FIG. 25

labor-supply curve, for example, as D_L moves rightward from D_L' to D_L'' in Fig. 25, S_L moves leftward from S_L' to S_L''. Essentially, the effect is to curb the expansion in employment while accommodating an important wage movement and price-level upswing. It can be inferred from this that, if increases in investment demand occur, a rather small change in the employment figure is capable of accompanying a fairly sharp change in the money-wage level. Practically, this does not seem too far-fetched; often rather small changes in the employment total appear to be correlated with substantial pressure on the money-wage level. Functions which promise stability for small changes along their course thus need not exemplify "stability in the small" when even rather minor dislodgments in the full functions are investigated.[16]

However nominal in amount, greater employment, be it noted, can occur only if the marginal product of labor rises in consumer-good industries and the real wage of labor increases.[17] This does give us some clue to the conditions in which the new S_L-curve—S_L'' in Fig. 25—can intersect D_L'' to the right of ON_1: this can take place only if aggregate consumption *declines* after the investment bulge. But *this decline in real intake cannot hold for labor as a*

[16] For an analysis of stability as a first exercise in dynamics, see Paul A. Samuelson, *Foundations of Economic Analysis* (Cambridge, Harvard, 1947), Chapter 9.

[17] Compare Junk, *op. cit.*

group; we noted earlier in this chapter, however, that rentier consumption is likely to fall as money prices rise—in effect, as the wage rate moves up. The "forced (real) savings" of rentiers with fairly constant consumption intake of entrepreneurs can thus explain a possible rise in real wages after an investment upsweep and facilitate an employment advance in conditions where the S_L-curve is positively responsive to real wages. Rentier "forced-saving" can thus provide the elbow room for higher real wages.[18]

It is this analysis which is relevant to "full employment"—more precisely, the absence of *involuntary* unemployment. In these circumstances, only a decline in aggregate consumption, accommodating an increase in labor's real income and labor's aggregate consumption, can support an employment rise; investment is properly alternative to consumption in this case. Coincidence of declining aggregate (real) consumption with enlarged (real) investment seems so contrary to multiplier theory and depression and unemployment facts; we shall soon want, therefore, to give attention to situations of involuntary unemployment.

Similarly, the interlocked shift of the S-labor-supply function will be leftward for each rightward movement in D_L. As in the preceding case, this too implies some tempering in the employment expansion. By drawing the requisite figure, it can be shown that one sequel might be to reduce the number of intersections of multiple equilibria. In this case, it *is* possible for aggregate consumption to increase simultaneously with an investment upswing so long as the intersection of the new and the old D_L- and S_L-curves was located in the segment where S_L was "backward rising." Shifts in the underconsumptionist D_L, where credence is given to this possibility, can be handled in a like fashion.

The whole discussion of labor-supply phenomena has been based on the supposition that attitudes toward work are constant and are unaffected by shifts in D_L. Where this supposition is not justified by the facts, each demand change will require a reconstitution of the labor supply curve; with involuntary unemployment we shall argue shortly that something of this nature does happen because of

[18] Higher interest rates at the higher price level, by fostering entrepreneurial and rentier saving, can have the same effect. Likewise, any postponement of consumption by wage groups, on a belief that lower price levels are forthcoming, can also work to the same result.

labor-union demands for a higher wage floor, lifting the perfectly elastic stretch of S_L. Manifestly, there is no imperative reason why changes in individual work attitudes need accompany changes in labor demand. If there is interdependence here also, then traditional theory has been in error in treating the two functions as independent and alterable, as a rule, by separate sets of forces.[19]

Some final observations may be made at this stage, the first with implications for policy, the second, on techniques. If the D_L-curve is Keynesian, or classical and highly inelastic in the middle ranges, or slightly underconsumptionist, then even substantial wage changes will accomplish very little by way of more employment despite an (almost) proportionate effect on price levels.[20] Second, if the wage level is known to fluctuate with N, in the sense of $\Delta w/\Delta N > 0$, then the relevant Z-curve will be a cross-cut through a field such as that in Fig. 22 (a); the appropriate D-curve will be of the same nature, with their intersection yielding the equilibrium wage without recourse to separate diagrams for D_L and S_L. Finally, while the competitive market analysis for wage theory has been developed, both monopsony and monopoly structures, or even bilateral monopoly, seem far-fetched when applied to the concept of homogeneous labor.

INVOLUNTARY UNEMPLOYMENT

Let us now incorporate the presence of involuntary unemployment into the analysis and examine how wage-level pressures can build up in these circumstances. In a way, this analysis seems more general than full-employment equilibrium, for the common fact seems to be one of some flexibility and enforced inactivity in the labor market even amid peak boom phenomena.

The simplest, and reasonably realistic, procedure would be to draw the positive real-wage responsive labor-supply curve as having a perfectly elastic "going-wage" bottom, as at w_o for the supply curve, S_1, in Fig. 26. This might be regarded as given by minimum

---

[19] See, however, K. W. Rothschild, *The Theory of Wages*, pp. 26–31.

[20] Thus Pigou, while defending the substance of the classical labor analysis, declared: "The form of the book may suggest that I am in favor of attacking the problem of unemployment by manipulating wages rather than by manipulating demand. I wish, therefore, to say clearly that this is not so." *Lapses from Full Employment* (London, Macmillan, 1945), Preface.

wage laws, labor-union wage scales, or as a carryover customary wage standard from the historic past: in a sense it would also be legitimate to regard this wage level as an exogenous datum. In Fig. 26, with labor demand D_1 (constructed as heretofore), the equilibrium employment would be ON_1 while the full labor offering at the going money and implicit real wage would be ON_2, with the difference $(ON_2 - ON_1)$ constituting a measure of involuntary unemployment.[21] As drawn, and exaggerated purely for visual illustration, less than half of the labor force desiring jobs would secure employment.

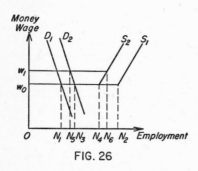

FIG. 26

Suppose, now, that through a strengthening of the investment function the labor-demand curve is shifted to D_2. In the absence of labor-supply and -demand interdependence, the immediate effect is to erase some involuntary unemployment, in amount N_1N_3.

However, with somewhat higher prices for consumer goods (when produced under conditions of diminishing returns) at the w_0 wage, there is now a leftward move in the positively responsive segment of S_1, to S_2, say.[22] Thus from the supply side, too, some involuntary unemployment is eliminated, with the total unemployment

[21] For similar measures, in D_L- and S_L-functions drawn entirely in real terms, see Oscar Lange, *Price Flexibility and Employment*, p. 6n, and Lawrence Klein, *The Keynesian Revolution* (New York, Macmillan, 1947), p. 87. Their functions, however, being cast in real terms, cannot illustrate the fact of market-wage determination without considerable implicit theorizing. If it could be used directly, the theory of employment could be compressed in just a few words.

[22] With some rectification for altered (= reduced, in this case) rentier consumption, we can derive a precise method for locating S_2. (See Junk, *op. cit.*) Each S_2-point would be located at the same ON-level as that point on S_1 related to D_1 and involving the same real income as the new D_2 point. For the case considered it would be necessary to complete the diagram by drawing in the implicit lower segment of S_1, below the perfectly elastic floor at w_0. As this extension is not necessary for the analysis here, the diagram has not been encumbered with it.

It might be noted that with constant-marginal products the labor-supply curve would become a backward L, and unresponsive to shifts in labor demand.

magnitude amounting in the end to $(ON_4 - ON_3)$ compared to the original $(ON_2 - ON_1)$ amount: involuntary idleness will be lower in the new investment situation so long as the real wage is reduced.

Considering the pressure on the labor market from both sides, from labor demand and supply, with the tightening of the market we can assume that events become propitious either for new wage demands by unions or higher wage offers by entrepreneurs faced individually by smaller pockets of unemployment; the latter sequence would be particularly relevant if we admitted more heterogeneity in the labor market. From either direction the sequel to the narrowed unemployment margin involves a raising of the wage floor, from w_o to w_1, with a consequent reduction in employment to ON_5 and an extension of involuntary unemployment to $(ON_6 - ON_5)$.[23] This case, then, could involve only a "small" employment change despite an investment and money-wage uplift.

On this interpretation it is the rise in labor demand and the decrease in labor offerings at the going wage level which absorb some of the involuntary unemployed, tighten the labor market, and lead causally to higher money-wage levels. Of course, trade-union demands for money-wage hikes may be quite independent of the size of the involuntary unemployment gap, but they are likely to be most successful and reflect market forces most closely when, through rising investment and the multiplier, the labor market has first been tightened compared to an easier (past) situation. And the higher money wage, when won, has in part the effect of increasing involuntary unemployment and easing the labor market— given the juxtaposition of the classical labor-demand curve and the flat-bottomed positively responsive labor-supply curve.

It is possible to interpret the perfectly elastic bottom of the labor-supply curve of Fig. 26 as reflecting either a "money illusion" or a surreptitious introduction of an exogenous wage under the guise

[23] This analysis is consistent with the view that real wages rise in a downturn due to the lesser flexibility of money wages compared to prices. This would involve a D_L-decrease from D_2 to D_1 (Fig. 26), a rightward shift in S_L from S_2 to S_1, while the money-wage floor remained at w_o. See Albert Rees, "Wage Determination and Involuntary Unemployment," *Journal of Political Economy* (April 1951), pp. 151–152, and Clarence Long, *op. cit.*, *American Economic Review* (May 1953), p. 459, n. 3.

of market determination, though other interpretations are equally plausible. For example, workers may be entirely cognizant of real-wage phenomena and yet, if the law compels them to accept a nominal minimum wage, or if union loyalty leads them to observe the announced money wage standard, then there is no "money illusion" with which to charge them as individuals, though there is illusion in the "system." Likewise, in the argument above it is the tightening of the labor market through demand-and-supply changes which is regarded as causal in lifting the money-wage floor, though the analysis is unable to account for the exact magnitude of the elevation.

APPENDIX

A mathematical restatement of the argument is not intended here; only the main ideas connected with the derivation of the D_L- and the S_L-functions are considered.

NOTE 1.   THE DERIVATION OF D_L AND S_L

In general, the aggregate supply or proceeds function may be written

$$N = N(Z) \tag{1}$$

Both N and Z have the meanings already assigned to them. Usually, beginning with Keynes, the inverse function has been used to denote aggregate supply; this also becomes more convenient for our purposes. Thus

$$Z = Z(N) \tag{2}$$

Holding constant the stock of equipment, the productivity functions of labor in the individual outputs, the degree of monopoly, and the prices of productive factors other than labor, and disregarding the problems of nonintegration, then the money-wage scale alone becomes a relevant parameter for our analysis. So eq. (2) becomes

$$Z = Z(N; w) \tag{3}$$

In the same way, aggregate demand, D, in money terms can be written also as a function of the level of employment and the money-wage level. Thus

$$D = D(N; w) \tag{4}$$

Implicitly, through its dependence on N where, according to eq. (1), N depends on Z, aggregate demand also rests on the latter value.

Equilibrium requires that $D = Z$, or

$$D(N; w) = Z(N; w) \tag{5}$$

In eq. (5) we have one equation and two unknowns. Taking w as a parametric constant, w', the level of employment, is therefore determinate at each wage rate. Thus

$$N = \phi(w) \equiv D(N; w') = Z(N; w') \tag{6}$$

But eq. (6) represents simply the demand for labor at each wage rate. Thus, inasmuch as the N-quantities extracted in eq. (6) represent D_L, we can write

$$N \equiv D_L = \phi(w) \tag{7}$$

This is the demand function for labor, where w represents the money wage with real-wage implications, as disclosed in eq. (5), and as argued earlier.

The labor-supply function has been made dependent, at each money wage, on the corresponding amount of labor demand (eq. 80). Thus, S_L can be written, as described earlier, as

$$S_L = \psi(w, D_L, U) = \psi[w, \phi(w), U] \tag{8}$$

The term U represents the leisure-income preference function and may be taken as given.

Writing $D_L = S_L$ and solving for w, the equilibrium money-wage rate for a competitive market can be elicited. In order that an equilibrium wage rate exist, it is of course essential that certain restrictions be placed on the shape and the position of the two functions; visualizing the curves, these would amount to an assurance that the curves intersect, requiring in principle that the simultaneous equations be compatible. Additional restrictions concerning the slope of the curves would be necessary in order to insure the stability of equilibrium. For the case of involuntary unemployment, S_L would be discontinuous, perfectly elastic at some money wage until, say N_o labor volume, and thereafter positively responsive to higher real wages.

NOTE 2. THE PROFIT INCREMENT AFTER A WAGE RISE

To derive the increment in profits on the assumption that employment and output are constant despite the rise in wages, and bearing in mind that at the level of the individual firm price = marginal costs, then

$$P = \frac{w}{f} \tag{9}$$

This is the formula for the marginal-value product of labor equaling the money-wage rate, or for price being equal to marginal cost on the assumption that labor is the only variable factor. (It need hardly be mentioned that $f \equiv dQ/dN$, which is the marginal physical product of labor.)

For the same output as before, the change in price after the rise in the wage scale is

$$dP = \frac{\partial P}{\partial w} dw = \frac{1}{f} dw \qquad (10)$$

The necessary change in proceeds in order to maintain the output constant would then be

$$QdP = \frac{Q}{f} dw \qquad (11)$$

The increase in profits, after deducting the increase in the wage bill, which amounts to Ndw, would be:

$$dR = \left(\frac{Q}{f} - N\right) dw = N\left(\frac{1}{f}\frac{Q}{N} - 1\right) dw$$

$$= N\left(\frac{A}{M} - 1\right) dw \qquad (12)$$

In eq. (12), A is written for average product and M for marginal product (see eq. [5], above). Inasmuch as the ratio A/M ordinarily will exceed unity under competitive conditions, there is a positive increment in profits ensuing from the wage rise and output constancy. In the limiting case $A = M$ so that the change in profits is nil.

Of course this formula underestimates the profit increase in that it assumes that the output at which profits are maximized will remain unchanged. If this assumption is not satisfied, and globally it would be satisfied only under a Keynesian D_L, the profit increment will be even larger than the total indicated in eq. (12).

Chapter 7

Relative Wage Changes and Employment

It is time now to discard the hypothesis of a homogeneous labor supply and to consider some aspects of labor heterogeneity. Effects of particular wage changes on employment levels can also be analyzed as part of this set of problems.

THE HOMOGENEOUS-LABOR POSTULATE

If wage earners were actually alike in ability and temperament, the foregoing analysis obviously would be relevant. Although the facts belie this hypothesis, let us examine some more realistic circumstances which would justify the retention of the general structure already erected.

Conceivably, individuals may differ in ability and yet be compensated on a uniform scale, as if their talents were roughly similar. Keynes appeared to subscribe to this view, and it is one partly borne out by virtue of collective wage bargains covering vast numbers of laborers, treating each member of some broad grouping as if alike in efficiency. Practices which confer institutional uniformity where nature has been more erratic with its endowments have some interesting consequences for the laws of returns.[1] If individuals A and B are each paid $50 per week, and A is twice as productive as B, then the hire of B after A is already at work will entail rising marginal and average costs even with fully divisible equipment and the absence of supervisory inefficiencies. On the premise that firms hire first those individuals whose productivity relative to wage cost is greatest, a tailor-made explanation of diminishing returns, rising prices, and the shift to profits as output advances is ready at hand.

[1] *General Theory*, p. 42.

131

Schematically, if the individuals compensated uniformly possess the same relative efficiency wherever they are hired in the economy, or if they are so specialized vocationally that they seek employment only in the one industry, then the Z-N-function holds firm, without emendation. If the physical productivity of laborer A exceeds that of B in industry X, while the reverse relation prevails in industry Y, or the disproportionality is more limited, more remains to be said: unless each Z-sum is always disbursed in a particular way on the expectation of a unique composition of aggregate demand, the possibility arises that if N individuals are employed the hire may consist in one case of the set A, C, E in industries X_1, X_2, X_3 and in the other B, D, F, in X_4, X_5, X_6. Proceeds may thus not be uniquely associated with output; the Z-N-function could be retained only on the assumption that the "hiring path" was unique. This signifies that if N_1 persons are hired, or for $N_2 > N_1$, the individuals comprising the N_1-set are always the same ones hired by the same firms for the same outputs.

Empirically, it does appear that there is considerable temporal stability in the economy, in the sense that if gross national product is at \$425 billions over years close in time, the composition of output and employment will show strong parallel features. (Even statistical projections based on index numbers or the use of output totals which refer to an underlying product mix make this assumption, explicitly or tacitly.) Sectors of variability seem more limited than the regions of constancy in the economic universe, though this presumption weakens as time passes. Further, even though talents and temperaments differ, the diversities are not necessarily critical from an entrepreneurial standpoint: the philosopher and the garage mechanic, when hired as operatives in a mass-production plant, are not vastly different when put to work on a conveyor system: army privates with wide disparities in talents appear as reasonably standardized specimens when summoned to perform most military tasks. Where job specifications are such as to evoke equivalence, the postulate of homogeneity assumes wider significance than might be surmised at first glance.

EFFICIENCY WAGES. A second hypothesis would be that wages are paid strictly according to efficiency, so that, if the productivity of A is always twice that of B, then A's earnings are precisely twice B's. Complications arise again when in some activities A is more adept than B, while in other occupations the disproportion is reduced or even reversed. Still, if it is posited that wages are attached to the occupation rather than to the person, then the expected allocation of proceeds would determine the wage bill and the employment structure and there is no indeterminateness. There would have to be the addendum, however, that greater proceeds always involve the hire of the same individuals as at lesser proceeds plus some new labor. Otherwise, more proceeds might conceivably mean the hire of fewer men if the greater expenditure were directed to higher-priced labor.

To preserve the Z-function intact under the hypothesis of efficiency earnings, wherein a unit of standard labor is accepted as the base and those who are, say, twice as efficient are denoted as two "individuals," or two wage units, *it becomes necessary to associate the Z-level to the wage bill, W, rather than to employment, N.* Even if the wage structure holds firm, however, a given Z-outlay sometimes means more, and at other times less, employment (measured in numbers), depending on the distribution of the Z-sum[2]; for example, if low-wage individuals are hired, a particular Z-sum will signal more employment in terms of numbers. The allocation of proceeds, the composition of output, and the structure of employment for each Z-sum would thus have to be subsumed among the data.[3]

A CONSTANT-WAGE STRUCTURE. This turn toward wage units leads to the query of whether the premise of a constant-wage structure does not provide the best resolution of the problem, rendering superfluous the hypothesis that wages are wholly proportionate to efficiency, or even to define the latter idea precisely. All that would have to be invoked would be the notion that labor is somehow graded and compensated according to some empirical standard based on ability and union-management agreement concerning sex, age, seniority, etc. This approach would be akin in spirit to the concept of noncompeting groups of traditional theory.[4] Let us

[2] Compare Keynes, *General Theory*, Chapter 20. Keynes's whole argument is written in these terms, though there has been a tendency to ignore it.

[3] See p. 26.

[4] The concept of a constant-wage structure is itself ambiguous. If it is assumed that all labor is specific, with occupational choice confined to one type of income-creating activity against the alternative of leisure, then the

consider this, for once it is shown that the analysis can be preserved for a given wage structure, the probe can be pushed on to discover the consequences of variations in the relative wage scale.

As always, the lead is contained in the dependency of N on expected proceeds, Z. The most obvious approach would be to isolate the largest labor group—denote it as category A—from the standpoint of numbers and homogeneous by virtue of equivalence of compensation. In Fig. 27 the Z-function is drawn on familiar lines, with Z associated this time to the hire of the N_a labor category, rather than to aggregate employment. The concomitant wage bill linked to A-labor is now W_a. For each Z-sum and the associated N_a-magnitude there is, however, an implicit volume of total hire and an aggregate wage bill covering all labor groups. Thus the full W-function can be sketched, comprising the total wage bill over all industry; the W-curve will be smooth so long as the advance of Z and N_a involves a continuous employment expansion for all sorts of labor. If wage payments to $B, C \cdots N$ labor classes outstrip the W_a earnings, then the W/W_a ratio will rise; if N_a expands more rapidly, the ratio will be cut.

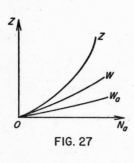

FIG. 27

In this way, the analytic apparatus can be preserved fairly intact and applied to proceeds and earning levels. Usual D-functions can be attached to the Z-curves, affixed at each point to appropriate N_a-levels but revolving functionally about Z- and W-magnitudes directly, with dependence on N_a being more tenuous and remote. Undoubtedly, the Z-N-diagrams would then become somewhat less revealing, for they would show employment only of A-labor rather than the aggregate work force, although the full wage bill is also disclosed. Nevertheless, differences with the earlier analysis are

---

meaning of a rigid-wage structure is directly comprehensible. When labor is versatile, two distinct interpretations are possible: either the wages for the individual are the same regardless of occupation, or are fixed per person occupationally, with individual A, say, capable of earning \$50 in activity X and \$75 in Y. It would seem that the supposition of occupational wage constancy has stronger empirical content. On this basis, rather than being handed a few broad labor groupings, as in the noncompeting classical categories, there are literally endless classes.

confined more to details than to principles, or theme: from the equilibrium intersection of $Z = D$, the Z-, N_a-, W_a-, and W-magnitudes can be uncovered. Employment of every labor type is implicitly involved, as N_b, $N_c \cdots N_n$ hire amounts are embodied in the W-point associated with each N_a-position.

Rectifying the analysis to take account of labor heterogeneity thus fails to upset the theory of determination of the Z,N-level, though it does complicate it. Again, the analysis rests on the proviso that the structure of output and outlay accompanying each Z-N_a-level is unique, or largely so[5]; it is most meaningful if there is a major labor category which can be regarded as essentially homogeneous.

RELATIVE WAGE DETERMINATION

Some aspects of relative wage determination can now be considered. Our main objective will be to indicate how a determinate demand curve for a particular grade of labor can be derived and a wage established in a competitive labor market.

For each wage rate, w_a, for A-labor, and given an accompanying wage scale for all other labor, as $w_b{}^1$ for B, $w_c{}^1$ for C, etc., the respective labor-demand quantities are perfectly determinate, with each entrepreneur, in the light of expected proceeds, selecting the work force he deems most profitable after assessing their price-productivity ratios. In terms of Fig. 27, measuring N_a horizontally, the Z-function and D fall into place for each w_a. Considering a rise in w_a, and supposing all other wage rates constant—which is tantamount to the partial equilibrium analysis of product markets—the Z-function may be presumed to move leftward. If the A-group is important enough so that its wage increment affects aggregate demand, the D-function will also shift leftward.[6] As a rule, as a

---

[5] This attention to structure is not new despite some recent work insisting that the problem was overlooked; it was recognized by Keynes as necessary for a systematic association of employment levels and expenditure flows. (*Op. cit.*, Chapter 20.) Some remarks on the structural aspects of aggregation appear in Hans Brems, "Employment, Prices, and Monopolistic Competition," *Review of Economics and Statistics* (November 1952), pp. 316, 317. Compare the criticisms of A. F. Burns, *The Frontiers of Economic Knowledge* (Princeton Univ. Press, 1954), pp. 3–25, especially.

[6] We consider this in the next section.

wage rise for fully homogeneous labor is expected to reduce total employment, we can surmise this result to be even more likely when the wage rise in question is confined to a particular type of labor for which substitute varieties are available: the $D_L{}^a$-curve ought thus to be of classical form. Together with the $S_L{}^a$-supply curve, the particular labor-market equilibrium ought to be determinate, with demand quantity equaling supply quantity or with involuntary unemployment (see Chapter 6). On a particular equilibrium approach, with wages of other labor as parametric constants, the proceeds-employment equilibrium and the equilibrium in labor market A seem fully assured.

In product-price theory, an impact on the demand quantities for products $B, C \cdots N$ are recognized as the price of A-rises.[7] Much the same story applies in labor markets; upward pressures will be exerted on wages for $B, C, D \cdots$ labor as w_a rises. Manifestly, the full change in the demand quantity for factor A cannot be written until after the general equilibrium wage-price adaptations are completed. If $w_a{}^2$ leads in the related labor markets to new employment levels $N_b{}^2 > N_b{}^1$, $N_c{}^2 > N_c{}^1$, etc., then pressures are released, ordinarily, to strengthen wages in these interdependent markets.[8] The rise in substitute wage rates would serve in part to restore the demand for labor A.

Once variations in $w_b, w_c \cdots w_n$ are recognized, immediately the question arises of whether there is a determinate equilibrium wage, hire, and proceeds structure or whether chronic inflation and wage-price spirals are in the offing. On usual reasoning it can be concluded that the results are equilibrating so long as $w_a{}^2$ remains firm, and so long as the uplift in aggregate demand, D_c, is inadequate to increase the $D_L{}^a$-quantity after the increase Δw_a ($= w_a{}^2 - w_a{}^1$) and the concomitant movements in $w_b, w_c \cdots$ etc. If, however, each wind of change from other markets alters $w_a{}^2$, which in turn affects them in the same direction, and back again *ad infinitum*, the outcome can only be chronic inflation. If involuntary unemployment prevailed initially in A, and if it grew as w_a rose, there would be an obvious

[7] In price theory, income is taken as a datum in drawing a particular equilibrium demand curve. The same restriction need not hold for factor markets.

[8] The accompanying wage moves can come also from an uplift in labor-supply curves in the latter markets, for labor-supply attitudes in $B, C \cdots N$ can alter consequent upon a change in w_a.

damper on sequential wage hikes and the spiral process would culminate without any substantial price-level upheaval. Unemployment is clearly an effective wage- and price-level stabilizer in the event of an initial wage move and a "rolling" wage upturn. Supporting the belief in a wage anchor at $w_a{}^2$, if the Δw_a rise is attributable originally to union wage demands and an uplift in a horizontal labor-supply curve in A, the new perfectly elastic labor-supply curve for A will throw a rein on the inflationary sequence. Similar perfectly elastic supply curves and involuntary unemployment in $B, C, D \cdots$ would also inhibit any tendencies of $D_L{}^a$ to rise to the right. Trade-union action, which in itself is capable of initiating an original perturbation, thus winds up as a pillar of price-level stability and responsibility.

While the foregoing sketch is a purely experimental (mental) derivation of $D_L{}^a$, in practice w_a may rise for any of the usual reasons: (1) there may be some variation in its supply curve—for which altered union action provides an obvious background, or (2) a change in the consumption function or investment and government demand may provide the spark, or (3) there may be a change in the productivity of factor A. While (1) involves a shift in $S_L{}^a$, both (2) and (3) entail shifts in $D_L{}^a$ as initially responsible for the pressure on $w^1{}_a$ and the roundabout impact in other markets and feed-back reverberations on A. In the case of an investment upsweep, in the heterogeneous labor case the prospect of a rise in the equilibrium hire of A, say, is even more certain than with homogeneous labor. For a rise in the real wage of A after the enlargement in its demand is now clearly possible, despite its greater hire, so long as the accompanying rise in the price of consumer goods leads to "forced savings" or a consumption-intake diminution by both rentiers *and other labor groups* whose money income is (largely) constant.[9]

While wage interdependence has been assumed, a comment might be in order on its causes. Labor A, for one thing, may be regarded as a roughly similar category hired in several major industries and subject to almost simultaneous bargain. Concretely, in recent years wage variations in the automobile, steel, coal, and electrical industries, for example, have tended to move in fair synchronization. Generally, the pattern established in one or more of these

[9] Compare Chapter 6.

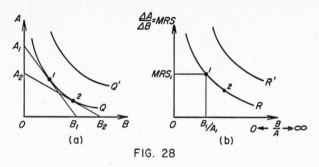

FIG. 28

groupings has been transmitted and transformed into a host of less spectacular agreements in, say, transport, textile, rubber industries, etc. Sometimes the list varies between originators and followers, with some not participating immediately while still others join the swell. In any event, these "key bargains," as the mammoth industry agreements have been termed, tend to set the money-wage level. As other agreements are reached by mimicry, the general concept of a proportional wage movement and a new "wage scale" becomes reasonably applicable: the interlocked supply phenomena lift all labor-supply curves upward, upsetting the past structure while establishing a new one. Insofar as there are laggards, as inevitably occurs, the scale move is disproportionate.

Alternately, wage moves for one type of skill, as a result of buoyant investment or consumption tendencies, will place pressures on substitutable grades of labor as the latter tend to be utilized more in order to trim costs. Substitution thus appears as a force insuring the direction-wise tether of the wage chain, given a rise in activity. A general increase in aggregate demand which pushes all labor-demand quantities rightward may be interpreted as evidence of labor-complementarity, tending to raise all wage rates and encouraging the widened use of all labor groups.

WAGE CHANGES AND THE ELASTICITY OF SUBSTITUTION. The concept of the elasticity of substitution may be invoked to furnish part of the answer as to how the respective labor groups will fare, in hire and relative income, after a change in relative wage rates. In Fig. 28 (a), isoquants Q and Q' are drawn, with each showing the various combinations of factors A and B yielding the respective output volumes. Along the course of each curve, and for each combination of A,B, the relative marginal products, M_b/M_a, or marginal rates of substitution, MRS, can be discovered. Plotting these relations, of relative factor quantities and concomitant MRS-values, the curves R and R' in Fig. 28 (b) can be constructed. The elasticity of R (or R') at each point is known as the elasticity of substitution, E_{ss}, and refers to the relative change in factor use compared to the relative change in the marginal rate of substitution. It is written as[10]

$$E_{ss} = \left[\frac{B}{A} \Delta \left(\frac{A}{B} \right) \right] \Big/ (\Delta MRS/MRS) \tag{81}$$

The value of E_{ss} can range between zero—the case of an utter lack of substitutability of factors—to infinite values when A and B are perfect substitutes. In the latter event, $\Delta MRS = 0$, and in the former, the variation is boundless.

Let us now apply the concept. If the relative wages are those embodied in the factor-cost line A_1B_1 in Fig. 28 (a), the minimum cost-factor combination for output Q is located at point 1. If w_a rises relative to w_b, shifting the factor-cost line to A_2B_2 the new equilibrium factor combination for output Q appears at point 2. In Fig. 28 (b) the rectangular area enclosed by the axes and point 1 is $(MRS_1)(B_1/A_1)$. In the light of the fact that the equilibrium MRS is also equal to the ratio of factor prices, it follows that

$$MRS_1 \cdot \frac{B_1}{A_1} = \frac{P_b \cdot B_1}{P_a \cdot A_1} \tag{82}$$

Thus the relative-factor income is disclosed by the area formed between the axes and the particular co-ordinate on the R-curve.[11] By properties analogous to those by which the rectangular areas under a demand curve disclose total revenue, and the manner in which this sum is linked to the elasticity of demand, the ratio of factor incomes represented in formula 81 depends on the elasticity of the R-curve in Fig. 28 (b), or, simply, on E_{ss}. Thus a relative rise in w_a, which induces the use of more of factor B and less of factor A at an output level Q, involving a shift in factor use from point 1 to 2, will raise the income of factor B relative to that of factor A if curve R is elastic as one moves down its course. Factor

[10] See Allen, *op. cit.*, pp. 341–343, and my *Price Theory*, pp. 67–71.

[11] See J. R. Hicks, "Distribution and Economic Progress," *Review of Economic Studies* (1936–1937).

A, on the other hand, can benefit only if E_{ss} assumes values between zero and unity over the stretch in question.

The E_{ss}-measure thus constitutes a convenient index of relative income variations *if output (and income) remain constant*. But this becomes part of the point in dispute: in terms of the Z-N-functions, the E_{ss} assumes that, with changes in w_a, the Z-function in the N_a-field of Fig. 27 moves leftward and intersects the new D-function at the same Z-level as before, even though N_a-hire falls off. So long as N_a is lower, the $D_L{}^a$-curve will of course be of classical form; its exact elasticity, however, is partly contingent on whether Z moves up or down as w_a rises. If output and proceeds vary, then E_{ss} fails to be wholly serviceable in revealing the changes in factor hire and relative factor income. It is on questions of this sort, particularly the income variation resulting from a relative wage turn, that we now embark. Ultimately, these matters involve the purchasing-power aspects of a relative wage change.

RELATIVE WAGE CHANGES AND EMPLOYMENT

Let us now examine some particular wage changes, drawing our categories a little differently than heretofore. First, we will examine the effects of a wage change confined entirely to labor employed in investment-goods industries—admittedly, a (partially) unreal simplification. Reversing this, we shall then consider cases in which the wage rise extends only to consumer-goods industries: this will recall certain of the arguments of Chapter 5. Thereafter, a wage rise limited to one grade of labor extensively utilized and a movement in a particular industry will be investigated. Pondering this breakdown, it appears that the demand curve for a particular type of labor is likely to reflect the classification which most nearly fits its use.

WAGE CHANGES IN INVESTMENT-GOODS INDUSTRIES. A wage change affecting one or a few industries is a special case of the analysis of disproportionate wage changes, sometimes with some special peculiarities. Consider first the case of a wage hike confined to investment-goods industries. Immediately, it would seem that this must lower the marginal efficiency of capital so that investment employment would suffer. Still, several supporting hypotheses are necessary before this conclusion can be established solidly.

First, if the demand for *real* investment is utterly insensitive to price changes, the effect of the wage rise must be to *increase* the money volume of investment and, through the multiplier, aggregate money income and aggregate employment will expand. If the multiplier were constant at 3, say, and if \$1 billion of investment were put in place, the total income generated would be \$3 billion, consisting of \$1 billion of investment and \$2 billion of consumption. If the same real investment comes to cost \$1.2 billion (because of a 20 per cent wage and price rise), money income will grow to \$3.6 billion. Employment in consumer industries, and thus total employment, will be increased because of the extra wage exactions in investment industries.

Schematically, to derive the total employment change, ΔN, we can write

$$\Delta N = e_c \frac{\Delta C}{w_c} + e_I \left(\frac{I + \Delta I}{w_I + \Delta w_I} - \frac{I}{w_I} \right) \tag{83}$$

Symbols e_c and e_I denote the ratio of consumption and investment outlay that goes as wage income (perhaps equal to about $\frac{2}{3}$), while the other letters have the same meanings as before; for simplicity, the relative wage share is assumed to be unchanged before and after the wage move. According to the assumption of constant *real* investment, with investment employment unchanged, the bracketed term becomes zero while ΔC is positive and implies an employment expansion.

Assuming a lesser real-investment inelasticity, total investment expenditure may still rise, to \$1.1 billion, say, rather than \$1.2 billion. The results still remain favorable to consumption-industry employment, though in part offset by the unemployment in investment goods through the failure of I-outlay to expand to \$1.2 billion. Assuming the relative income division in I- and C-industries to be about the same, it can be concluded that the employment gain in C, through the money income rise of \$200 million, will overshadow the loss in I through the real-investment decline of \$100 million (measured in the new prevailing prices): whereas the labor-demand quantity for investment-industry labor diminishes as its money wage rises, the labor-demand curve for consumption-industry employees moves rightward.

As a general relation, if money-investment demand is inelastic in the sense of aggregate money outlay increasing after a price rise due to a wage boost, then $\Delta C > O$; so long as the income enlargement in consumption industries exceeds the difference between actual money proceeds and those premised on perfect money-demand inelasticity in investment industries ($=$ constant real investment), the results are likely to be favorable to employment (so long as wage discrepancies in I- and C-industries are generally small). If the money-demand elasticity for I-goods is unity, then $\Delta C = O$ and the first term in the bracket of eq. 83 is zero, so that the total employment fall is shown by the second bracketed term.

A wage boost in I-industries when there is an elastic (money) investment demand is thus entirely adverse to aggregate employment, for not only does it lower direct employment and total earnings in investment industries but also it exerts unfavorable indirect ramifications in consumption-goods industries: both ΔC and ΔI become negative so that all elements in eq. 83 operate to depress N. Hence, at the peak of a boom, or whenever investment decisions are figured closely, a wage and price hike for capital goods may well touch off a downward employment and income spiral. Conversely, whenever money-investment demand is elastic, a wage cut is conducive to greater I- and C-employment. Hence, in a depression when investment is already practically zero, a wage cut can hardly diminish I-outlay and I-employment; instead, it may promote an upsweep. Historically, therefore, the arguments of those who suggested cuts in labor costs in construction industries during the 1930's, assuming that the reduction would be confined solely to those industries, were not necessarily in error. The impetus would be greatest if the immediate wage cut was believed to be temporary and subject to a reversal in the form of a wage rise before too much time elapsed.[12]

Undoubtedly, real-investment demand is often highly inelastic, especially when government military programs are included. Wage and price climbs for these items can be depicted as contributing to employment and real-income growth. In the field of consumer durables, such as automobiles and houses, it is also not unlikely that

---

[12] Analogously, a wage boost in I-industries believed to be the first in a future series might also accelerate current investment. In these cases, rather than being concerned with wage hikes of the "once-and-for-all" variety, the analysis is bound up with the dynamics of expectations. Compare pp. 116–117.

real demand is often strongly inelastic for moderate price changes —say, of the order of 5 to 10 per cent from prevailing levels. Wage maneuvers in these industries thus can be defended as fostering purchasing-power impacts favorable to employment whenever the higher prices are largely counterbalanced by easier installment or mortgage terms, so that even the immediate upshot need not be a reduction of direct employment, or by a concomitant decline in personal savings. In the longer future, as consumer payments become rigidly committed in greater amount out of the income flow, the employment outturn may be less favorable; but this analysis belongs to long-period temporal investigations, which is not part of our present inquiry, though it would repay careful study.[13] The point remains that there is likely to be some warrant for the arguments stressing the favorable purchasing-power effects of wage rises in key durable-goods industries; while direct employment in those industries may fall slightly or at best hold firm, the indirect effects may be expansory. Unsavory features lie not in the employment effects but rather in the discriminatory wage scale that comes to be erected, with anomalies in output, labor hire, and rational resource use.

CONSUMPTION INDUSTRIES. An appraisal of a general wage change in consumption industries seems logical enough after the analysis of wage moves in investment goods. Actually, the consumption-industry analysis has already largely been detailed, for it is embodied in the analysis of wage moves and rentier-profit consumption patterns already investigated in Chapter 5; there is no need to repeat the argument here. The one new point consists of the muting of the real effect of the multiplier, for the consumer price rise destroys part of the real consumption intake of wage earners in investment-goods industries. This, too, points to lower aggregate consumption and a reduced employment total.

The argument is not altered in fundamentals if the wage moves of the various labor groups in consumption industries are disproportionate, with some rising by 10 per cent, others by 3 per cent, others not at all. If all firms use the various grades of labor in the same ratio, then marginal costs and prices will rise proportionately

[13] The analysis of installment phenomena, despite some recent studies for the Federal Reserve system, still appears as a virgin field for investigation, as is true of almost all temporal clock-time sequences.

in all firms to reflect the uniform labor-cost rise. Where, as is inevitable, use of the diverse labor grades differs, then prices will rise disproportionately at a given output volume. As before, the analysis of the effect on real consumption is largely contingent on the profit-rentier income tangle and the reduced real consumption of investment-industry wage earners, with the one new feature being the relative price disruption. Insofar as this permits a switch to substitutes by fixed-income groups and investment-industry wage earners endeavoring to maintain their real-consumption position, there will be some expansion in output of the relatively lower-priced goods and contraction of those which have risen most, with the consumption-industry employment fall being partially checked. Nevertheless, if wage discrepancies do not bulk large among the various consumption-industry labor grades, then only minor dikes are erected by the availability of substitute products to stem the employment downturn.

AN INDUSTRY WAGE CHANGE. Let us turn to problems of a wage rise confined to a particular industry, as an offshoot of those problems in which ratios of labor use differ.

A rather academic case is that of a single firm selling in competitive markets and confronted with a wage rise; at best it might pertain to a firm which sells in a world market without having any domestic competitors. Clearly, the effect is to decrease output and employment within the firm, with the change in the wage bill within the firm depending largely on the shape of the marginal-cost curve, the relative importance of wage costs, the elasticity of substitution, and the extent of the wage move. Total proceeds of the firm must be smaller in view of the product-price constancy and curtailed output: the firm's contribution to the income stream thus will be contracted. Expenditures on other products by income recipients dependent on earnings within the competitive firm will fall off, leading ordinarily to a multiplier chain of diminished income and employment.

Consider now a whole consumer-good industry, A, subject to an upward wage tug. For simplicity, assume the numerical income division of situation (1) on p. 97, Chapter 5, as prevailing initially, and that situation (2) represents the required proceeds after the wage rise in order to maintain output and employment within the industry. Further, it can be assumed that entrepreneurs fully expect expenditure on their product to grow to 110 from the former 100, so that they pay out a wage total of $66 and raise dividend payments in the expectation that gross profits will be $29 rather than $25.

Immediately, from wage earners and profit recipients within industry A, expenditure on outputs of other industries $B, C, D \cdots$ will rise. Growing income and employment among the latter will lead to a new flurry of demand augmentation, etc. This is, after all, nothing but the multiplier at work, with the output of industry A, originally subject to a wage rise, temporarily (and hypothetically) denied participation in the augmented demand-expenditure stream. A's higher income payments thus constitute a form of additional money investment: it is as though the extra $6 of wages, plus the added dividends out of the anticipated $4 profit increase, were paid to a new income group—the "A-employed."[14]

As a chain of money income is created equal to the multiplier aggregate of the extra $10[15] of income disbursed in the initiating A-industry, output and employment increments appear along the line of $B, C \cdots$ industries. Ultimately, whether the A-industry will continue to produce the same output and offer the same employment as before will depend on the elasticity of demand for its own wares, where elasticity itself is a compound concept made up of the ordinary demand elasticity along a curve drawn on the premise of constant-money income, plus a term to include the shift in A-demand due to a rise in money and real income in $B, C, D \cdots$ etc. If the general income augmentation is able to lift the outlay on A from $100 to $110 at the former A-output, then its former output volume will persist. If the income rise boosts demand for the constant A-output sufficiently to lift proceeds above $110, then A's employment and production can even advance beyond its former levels. With an outlay on A of less than $110, its output—and employment—must necessarily suffer. Nonetheless, so long as outlay on A exceeds $100, an income multiple will be generated in $B, C \cdots N$.

In investment-multiplier sequences, it is well known, the income chain will be elongated sufficiently to provide a savings margin equal

14 Except that the actual marginal propensity to consume is likely to be lower than if the sums were really granted to previously unemployed individuals.

15 Less any income withholdings for taxes, undistributed profits, etc.

to the initial investment. However, the sums saved need not be loaned back entirely to the enterprise undertaking investment—other sources of permanent "finance" can be found, from the banking system or dishoarding.[16] In the illustration considered now, though the added money value of A's output is temporarily held aside, and treated as investment, it too must find a market. *The sum needed for equilibrating the wage hike and the market proceeds is exactly equal to the sums "saved" by those in the income chain.* Thus, if the wage boost raises the value of A's given output by $10 and the multiplier is 3, then the full "savings" out of the income increment of $30, and in amount $10, must be diverted to A and expended there. Otherwise A's production will slump and the subsequent income chain will be compressed. Considering that the wage hike and higher prices in A (and elsewhere) can induce fixed-income recipients to spend more in order to maintain their real consumption, any enhanced rentier outlay will permit a corresponding counterbalancing saving by those in receipt, directly or indirectly, of fresh income after the wage lift in A. Likewise, any diminution of personal savings by former B, $C \cdots N$ income recipients can maintain A-employment. If the added outlay by them on A consists of a transfer from outlays on B, $C \cdots N$ products, aggregate money income on balance is unaffected though a distributive shift is implicit; any saving in A will thereupon reduce employment.

This suggests, too, that if the expected profits increment consequent upon the wage hike in A does not immediately occasion larger dividend disbursements in A, then the multiplier sequence itself will be smaller. With steeply rising supply curves and shifts to profits in B, C, $D \cdots$ industries as expenditure is deflected to them, then the whole income enlargement is likely to be restrained: the income effect on A will inevitably be low, almost surely too small to sustain the previous output. Thus employment in A will slip back to lower levels, in part offset by higher output and employment in B, $C \cdots$ industries *so long as aggregate outlay on A exceeds its initial level.* Generally, it would seem that some direct unemployment in the A-industry would have to be set against some indirect employment.[17] Yet, with lower wage rates in the latter industries, it

---

[16] See p. 44.

[17] One interesting by-product of this analysis of a wage rise confined to industry A is that the labor in this industry which continues in employment en-

does seem that a surprisingly respectable purchasing power argument for wage increases in particular industry-sectors may often be made. An A-demand, inelastic at the expense of savings, appears involved.

The last remarks are particularly germane for monopoly markets where a wage rise may be followed by an increase in the degree of monopoly power; as the relative wage bill is likely to be smaller than in competitive cases, a wage rise will lift the proceeds necessary to maintain employment significantly, while providing a relatively small income-distribution subject to multiplier forces. Wage boosts in monopoly industries are hence unlikely instruments for enhancing the aggregate employment total.

WAGE CHANGES AND PRODUCTIVITY. Although the subject is too vast to be tackled here, there looms on the horizon the great debate over the proper relation of relative wage movements to productivity. Insofar as technological improvements occasion unemployment, interest in wage boosts to lift employment secures a strong hold on imagination for policy purposes. Nevertheless, as there are more routes to full employment than there are roads to Rome, wage manipulation is hardly a feasible device except in a centralized economy, for there is no way of implementing equitable and functional adjustments and placating the various wage groups. The scale cannot be lifted proportionately by fiat if wages are to play their part in resource adaptation; alternately, to rely on the market mechanism to assure the greatest wage pulls on the scarcest labor categories, so that labor is rationed among its manifold uses, can just as easily pull up the full scale through trade-union pressure without accomplishing the allocative purpose.[18] Always in the foreground, justifiably

---

joys a real income boon relative to all other labor. The only comparable improvement consists in the earnings of those newly employed in $B, C \cdots N$. Similarly, any unemployment in A creates a new null-income group ousted from the income circle and thus injured by the wage policy. Rentiers and wage earners whose money income remains constant are also hurt despite any general employment, output, and income enlargement.

[18] One thoughtful attempt at formulating a functional wage policy under productivity improvements is suggested by A. P. Lerner, *Economics of Employment* (New York, McGraw-Hill, 1951), Chapters 14–16. See also, Erik Lundberg, R. Meidner, G. Rehn, and K. Wickman, *Wages Policy Under Full Employment* (London, Hodge, 1952), Ralph Turvey, editor and translator, and H. W. Singer, "Wage Policy in Full Employment," *Economic Journal*

alarmed at suggestions of wage rises which threaten its income place, are rentier groups. Entrepreneurs are bound to be almost equally concerned, considering the disproportionate cost-profit impact of uneven wage advances. Criteria for a proper money-wage policy are thus inextricably mixed up with the quest for an optimal policy of resource use and a desirable price-level course over time.

APPENDIX: A SYMBOLIC STATEMENT

For an industry wage change in A, if total outlay in the economy is constant with those in the $i = B, C \cdots M$ industries shifting expenditure from their products to A then the employment change, ΔN, is given by

$$\Delta N = \left[e_a{}^1 \frac{Z_a}{W} - e_a{}^2 \frac{(Z_a + \Delta Z_a)}{W + \Delta W} \right] + \frac{Z_i}{W} (e_i{}^1 - e_i{}^2) - e_i{}^2 \frac{\Delta Z_a}{W} \quad (1)$$

The e's refer to the ratio of wages to proceeds before the wage change in A (noted by superscript 1) and after the wage change (superscript 2). If employment in A, N_a, is unchanged, the employment *decrease* is given approximately by the last term. If $\Delta N_a < 0$, then the first bracket is also negative.

If total outlay is higher, with outlay in the i-industries as large as before, then the last term becomes zero. If the enlarged outlay, as distinct from the expenditure shift, is spread between industry A and the i-sector, then new terms must be added to include these sums: wherever spent the added sums serve to maintain or increase the employment total. For a decrease in outlay the ΔZ terms must contain a new deduction. Thus, only if outlay on A is inelastic at the expense of savings, or if the consumption propensity of A-income recipients is high will a wage increase result in an employment rise.

(1947). Compare, too, the strongly reasoned article by M. W. Reder, "The Theoretical Problems of a National Wage-Price Policy," *Canadian Journal of Economics* (1948), and comment and reply by B. Higgins and Reder in the May 1949 issue. The subject has had far too little attention.

Chapter 8

A Modified Liquidity-Preference Theory of Interest

The theory of interest has not been neglected since Keynes wrote; more attention has been devoted to it than to all the other income categories combined. Largely this chapter will attempt to repair some shortcomings in the present state of the theory.

In a way, the interest study constitutes a detour, though it is one that must be taken in view of the confusion on the place of interest rates in distribution theory. Borrowing at interest leaves a trail of fixed payments in its wake, helping to shape the magnitude of this category. However, the payments do not comprise recompense for the imputed importance of a distinguishable productive agent over the period in which they are made: except in a stationary model, they will seldom reflect the value productivity of existing equipment—as older writings wrongly contended. In the economy of fact, fixed-interest payments constitute merely one mode of reimbursing those who have participated in financing the capital installation; as the payments may bear only a faint resemblance to original productivity conjectures, they must be viewed essentially as transfers.[1]

Current interest rates, rather than the inherited contractual arrangements, can affect activity through two channels. Extensions of employment require financing; interest charges contingent on the activity level are thus embodied in the total variable-cost function.[2]

---

[1] Compare the cogent attack on traditional income categories by E. R. Rolph, *The Theory of Fiscal Economics,* Chapter 4.

[2] Compare p. 63. Thus interest-rate increases can raise prices (in degree) and in this aspect can be viewed as inflationary. It is through choking off investment demand and cutting borrowing generally that the deflationary impact dominates. In the field of public-utility regulation, however, through petitions for rate increases, an interesting and unusual inflationary influence

Further, interest rates influence investment demand. It is in income determination, therefore, far more than as a variable-income share in distribution, that interest rates merit attention—even in the former area some regard it as an esoteric fascination with trivia.

Following a common practice, discussion will be couched for the most part in terms of "the" interest rate. Manifestly, this is a gross oversimplification, for there are myriads of loan prices, depending on the time length of the transaction and the attendant default risk. Still, before tackling the more difficult problem of the interest structure, some important insights can be obtained by an examination of a single loan market; namely, one in which perpetual debts are created and traded.[3]

We commence first with a brief restatement of the liquidity-preference theory, and thereafter indicate certain revisions whereby it might be strengthened pending the development of a more far-reaching theory of asset prices. There is no need to defend the liquidity-preference theory against its alternative, the loanable funds approach. Not only is the former more clearly articulated in the literature—despite confusions of its own making!—it also has the merit of treating money as a stock rather than embarking on a tortuous study of income flows and the splintering off of income streams of saving and investment which, in the final telling, may have little to do with the interest level.

LIQUIDITY-PREFERENCE THEORY

Let us sketch what seems to be the commonplace version of the liquidity-preference theory. Taking the quantity of money as a

---

of an interest rise can be detected. (I am indebted to Dr. Joseph Rose for this observation.)

[3] Working in terms of a definite maturity, say of twenty-year bonds, dealings in old issues would introduce a medley of interest rates by the back door. Analyzing a very short interest rate, conversely, suppresses many of the crucial issues, particularly those associated with the hazards and the uncertainties of the future.

A minor tantalizer on a perpetual loan concerns the manner of debt extinction. The borrower can be conceived to buy back the bond originally issued, which is fully analogous to what takes place on a dated instrument, or he can be conceived as turning lender himself, acquiring an offsetting asset to mark off against the liability created earlier.

datum and distributed among participants in the economic process, each pool of money held reflects a demand for money—the most liquid of all assets. The fundamental question of monetary theory, with implications for interest, price, and activity levels, is to explain why individuals choose to retain money, which is an idle, non-interest-bearing stock, in lieu of the available goods or interest-yielding securities, either of which ought to hold greater attractions. Following Keynes, it is customary to distinguish the motives for holding money[4]:

1. THE SPECULATIVE MOTIVE. Once money savings out of income are amassed, on an individual plane the immediate issue concerns the choice of money versus gilt-edge bonds as an asset, on the proviso that the sums involved are ample to render the choice meaningful.[5] Manifestly, the best reason for holding money rather than bonds is a belief that bond prices may tumble, with the capital loss exceeding the interest return by the date the downturn occurs. As the conviction that interest rates can only go up in the future is bound to gather strength as current interest rates go lower, more money will normally be held at lower interest rates. It was this pattern which Keynes characterized as the *speculative motive* for demanding money. It is also known as "liquidity-preference proper"[6] or the demand for "bear hoards."[7] Functionally, the demand for money, L_s, is tied to the ruling rate of interest, i, as $L_s = L(i)$, with the L_s-curve sloping down to the right, resembling any normal demand curve. Following Keynes, it is usual to argue that

[4] It is on the demand side that Keynes's discussion was at once deft, illuminating, and profound; while his treatment emphasized the motives for holding money, he acknowledged that, in practical affairs, tidy compartmentalization was impossible. The leading alternative to his design is to classify the demand for money by means of borrowing sources, such as households, governments, and business firms. As exemplified in loanable-funds theories, this procedure involves needless repetition in examining why each source requires funds.

[5] The choice between demand and time deposits is always available. For large sums time deposits are inconvenient and potentially costly if withdrawal is refused when a sudden expenditure decision requires funds for its implementation.

[6] G. Haberler, *Prosperity and Depression* (New York, United Nations, 1946, 3rd ed.), p. 210.

[7] Joan Robinson, *The Rate of Interest and Other Essays* (London, Macmillan, 1952), p. 14.

there is a floor beyond which interest rates cannot fall because of a pervasive feeling that the rate must soon go higher. At this lower limit, "liquidity-preference proper" turns absolute and the demand function appears perfectly elastic.

2. TRANSACTIONS DEMAND. In an older terminology, the speculative demand for money represents a demand for the money item as a store of value rather than as a medium of exchange; the demand for money as a medium was termed by Keynes as the *transactions* (and *income*) motive, L_t, for holding cash. This includes the necessary exchanges between firms in a nonintegrated structure and the money sums for income payments and outlays; the price-level and output composition are thus simultaneous determinants of the volume of cash required once the lags between receipts and outlays are recognized.

Much more can be done to decompose the transactions demand for money; it will be affected by such institutional matters as whether incomes are paid weekly or monthly, and whether the time patterns of D_c-outlays are smooth and continuous or hit peaks and touch troughs, as well as the degree of integration and the time structure of inter-firm payments. But these interesting questions of monetary theory can be put aside here and regarded as affecting mainly the magnitude of L_t.[8] Normally, the transactions demand is written as independent of the rate of interest. Until interest rates are so high as to inspire efforts to economize in transaction balances, it is probably not too inaccurate to describe L_t as interest inelastic and as responding less than proportionately to transactions.[9]

[8] For a discussion of factors determining the velocity of circulation, and thus L_t, see Irving Fisher, *Purchasing Power of Money* (New York, Macmillan, 1926, rev. ed.), Chapter V. Also, Arthur Marget, *The Theory of Prices* (New York, Prentice-Hall, 1938), Volume I, Chapters XI, XIII. For some calculations of velocity see J. W. Angell, *The Behavior of Money* (New York, McGraw-Hill, 1936), Chapters IV–V. See also an interesting recent study, with new velocity estimates, by Richard T. Selden, "Monetary Velocity in the United States," in *Studies in the Quantity Theory of Money* (Univ. of Chicago Press, 1956), edited by Milton Friedman.

[9] It has been argued in recent years that a doubling of transactions (proceeds) will not require a commensurate build-up in the money supply. (See W. Baumol, "The Transactions Demand for Cash," *op. cit.*) The argument is based on the interesting revelations of inventory theory developed by T. Whitin, *The Theory of Inventory Management* (Princeton Univ. Press, 1953).

3. PRECAUTIONARY DEMAND. Normally, all of us hold more cash than we expect to spend in the course of the day. There is good reason for this, for we do not know what contingencies will arise: the unexpected friend whom we wish to take to lunch, the opportunity to make an unintended purchase, the small loan or contribution we do not wish to refuse, etc. For business firms, analogous situations develop; any number of unexpected cash demands may appear. The demand for money to protect against unforeseen circumstances is called the *precautionary* motive, and it too is largely interest inelastic. Further, even with full certainty on the course of interest rates and outlays, some sums will be demanded because of the inconvenience of investing small amounts. By stretching the thought, this demand can also be subsumed under the precautionary motive.

4. THE FINANCE MOTIVE. Funds to finance projected real-investment operations prior to the actual activity, or to finance any planned increase in output, must finally be included. Once the activity is set in motion, this demand is transformed into one for transactions balances; but the effect on the demand for money is likely to be felt in advance of the actual rise in income. In an addendum, Keynes referred to this as the *finance* motive, L_f, described as midway between a transactions and speculative demand.[10] Prior to implementing a decision to put equipment in place and execute real investment, for example, businessmen require "finance" to assure them that their plans can be fulfilled. During the gestation and installation process, as the sums are spent, finance holdings are indistinguishable from transactions balances. Once the investment process is consummated, and the savings are amassed and available for loan, businessmen can issue bonds to absorb the money savings (identically equal to investment), and fund the initial, short-term "finance."

THE LIQUIDITY-PREFERENCE THEORY: DIAGRAMMATIC ANALYSIS. Given the factors of demand for money, and the money supply

[10] This was described lavishly by Keynes as the "coping stone" of his theory. See J. M. Keynes, "Alternative Theories of the Rate of Interest," *Economic Journal* (June 1937) and "The 'Ex-Ante' Theory of the Rate of Interest," *ibid.* (December 1937). Also, D. H. Robertson, "Mr. Keynes and Finance," *ibid.* (June 1938) and the comment by Keynes, and the further note by Robertson (September 1938). Also, Joan Robinson, *The Rate of Interest and Other Essays* (London, Macmillan, 1952), pp. 20–22, 80–87.

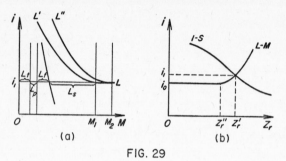

FIG. 29

(taken as a fixed quantity), the interest rate can be determined. Let us depict the liquidity-preference theory diagrammatically.

In Fig. 29 (a), the $L'L$-curve is the composite demand curve for money, embodying transactions demand, L_t; funds desired for precautionary purposes, L_p, equal to the lateral distance $L_p - L_t$; finance demand, L_f; and the speculative demand, L_s. As drawn, L_t and L_p are interest inelastic, while L_f is slightly and L_s is highly interest sensitive. It is the extreme responsiveness of the latter that creates the liquidity floor and the perfectly elastic (lower range) composite $L'L$-curve. Given the $L'L$-function and the money supply, OM_1, the interest rate is determinate at i_1. If $L'L$ rises or falls for any reason, the interest rate will go in the same direction; with $L''L$, say, resulting from a rightward shift in L_t, the interest rate will go above i_1 so long as the money stock remains at OM_1.

Ordinarily, the analysis is pursued to show the effect of an increase in the money supply. In Fig. 29 (a), the argument would be that, if the money supply increased through banking policy from OM_1 to OM_2, the interest rate would settle at the ordinate intersection of the new supply curve and the rigid $L'L$-function. So long, however, as a range of perfect elasticity of $L'L$ was encountered, the interest rate would hold firm whether the money supply was increased or decreased. Similarly, if $L'L$ moved rightward to $L''L$, with money supply now OM_2, the interest rate would remain anchored at i_1. What would take place, if income and transactions balances changed, would be a diminution in idle speculative holdings of money and an increase in (active) transactions balances. Once interest is at the perfectly elastic liquidity floor, it becomes possible for income to rise or fall without pressure on interest rates, or for money supply to alter without affecting interest.

One objection to the diagrammatic argument of Fig. 29 (a), even by proponents of a liquidity-preference approach, is that it is too partial a view of the economic process, for it subsumes income levels as constant in determining the interest level. As income is affected by the level of investment, and investment is in part dependent on interest rates, the hypothesis of constant income in interest determination is considered vulnerable. A more general equilibrium approach is ordinarily advocated, in which income and interest are determined simultaneously.[11]

In Fig. 29 (b), if we are given the consumption function, the investment function, and the definition of (real) income, we can link the income level to the interest level: that is, by varying the interest level and noting the equilibrium level of income accompanying it, we can trace out the investment-saving, I-S, curve.[12] Likewise, the L-M-curve rests on the functions connecting the demand, L, and supply of money, M.[13] Up to a level of real income equal to Z_r'' it is possible for real income to increase and transactions demand for money to rise, without putting any further pressure on interest rates, implying that, in terms of Fig. 29 (a), we are moving along the liquidity floor of perfect elasticity. Beyond real income Z_r'', an output and employment rise will lift the interest level. Interest and income, in equilibrium, are determined simultaneously at i_1 and Z_r', respectively. A rise in investment or consumption demand will move I-S rightward, with rising effects on both i and Z. An in-

[11] Compare J. R. Hicks, "Mr. Keynes and the 'Classics'; A Suggested Interpretation," *Econometrica* (1937) for the original diagrammatic extension. Reprinted in *Readings in the Theory of Income Distribution*. Also A. H. Hansen, *Monetary Theory and Fiscal Policy* (New York, McGraw-Hill, 1949), Chapter V. For Hansen's insistence on the need for a simultaneous determination of interest and income, see his comment, in reply to Mr. Edward Nevin on "Professor Hansen and Keynesian Interest Theory," *Quarterly Journal of Economics* (November 1955). Also, Hansen's "Classical, Loanable-Fund, and Keynesian Interest Theories," *ibid.* (August 1951).

[12] Given the consumption function (in real terms) $C = C(Z_r)$, the investment function $I = I(i)$, and $Z_r = C(Z_r) + I(i)$, by varying i, then Z_r can be ascertained and the course of I-S can be plotted. The curve is one of "investment-saving," for at each point along its length the savings and investment sums are at their equilibrium levels, with income at the appropriate levels to insure their balance.

[13] Thus $L = L(Y,i)$, through transactions and speculative demands primarily, and $M = \overline{M}$. With $M = L$, and taking Y as a parameter, L-M is traced out.

crease in money supply will depress L-M, though the liquidity floor at i_0 is likely to be maintained.

MONEY SUPPLY-AND-DEMAND INTERDEPENDENCE

We turn now to certain shortcomings in the liquidity-preference theory due primarily to its omissions. The following considerations are designed to strengthen the liquidity approach, and not to supplant it. We commence first with some analysis of the interdependence of money supply and demand, which has generally been overlooked, and with important implications for monetary policy. As a first step, it requires a detailed study and dissection of the speculative motive.

The following variables ought to be included explicitly in the L_s-function:

$$L_s = L(i, A, \theta, e) \tag{84}$$

The symbol A refers to the total assets owned by individuals.[14] θ is written to indicate the "state of expectations" about the future interest level: temporarily we take this as a datum to be analyzed at more length later. The letter e is designed to refer to the *number* of individuals among whom the asset total, A, is distributed, for unless this is specified a shift, say, of $50 billions from 10 million people to 20 million people can affect the function. Although this matter normally will be ignored, it is well to state it explicitly.[15]

Initially, it is the A-concept that we want to decompose. Ruling out the presence of any claims in the economy other than money and perpetual bonds, the A-total must contain both. Individuals who hold money are in a position to exercise a demand for it and help locate and shape L_s.[16] Likewise, if they hold bonds—the al-

[14] Compare A. H. Hansen, *Monetary Theory and Fiscal Policy*, p. 56.

[15] Considering the presence of institutional investors and corporate entities, the concept of the division of assets is even trickier than described. But it is largely irrelevant for the major argument.

[16] This is an illustration of "own-demand," long ago analyzed by P. H. Wicksteed, *The Commonsense of Political Economy* (London, Routledge, 1933 edition), L. Robbins, editor, Volume II, Book II, Chapter IV. It is surprising that there have been so few references to Wicksteed and his "communal demand" concept in the theory of liquidity preference. Among the few who have recognized the concept is G. F. Thirlby, "Demand and Supply of

ternative asset in our simple model—they can demand amounts of money in excess of their present cash holdings. Denoting A as the value of assets, M for money, and B for the *value* of bonds, all held by the non-bank public, then[17]

$$A = M + B \tag{85}$$

Neglecting e and θ, eq. 84 appears as

$$L_s = L(i, M, B) \tag{84'}$$

According to eq. 84', the demand for money for "bear hoards" depends, in part, on the quantity of money. Hence we have an interesting case of supply-demand interdependence in the making though there is no indeterminateness in deriving the demand function for money; given M and B, the full L_s-course can be traced.

As B denotes the *value* of bonds, it is equal (for perpetual obligations) to

$$B = \frac{\text{annual contractual interest payments}}{\text{market rate of interest}} = \frac{\lambda}{i} \tag{84''}$$

Thus, eq. 84'' can be written as

$$L = L\left(i, M, \frac{\lambda}{i}\right) \tag{84'''}$$

It may be surmised that, if the demand for cash and bonds is complementary as A rises, then as the value of B is enhanced upon an interest-rate fall, the bear demand for cash would increase.[18] Hence

Money," *Economic Journal* (September 1948), who uses it in the context of a loanable-funds theory.

[17] For an account of the interplay between the value of bonds and the demand for money, see A. P. Lerner, "Alternative Formulations of the Theory of Interest," *Economic Journal* (June 1938), reprinted in *The New Economics* (New York, Knopf, 1947).

It is undoubtedly harmless to speak of the "speculative-motive" or "liquidity preference proper" in terms of individuals or persons. Yet, if this motive has any strength in influencing interest rates, it must be through its effect on the decisions of investing institutions rather than persons. To represent the reality of this matter, the term "non-bank" public normally will be used.

[18] Lerner was particularly explicit on the enlargement of B as the interest rate fell. Despite the frequent references to this article, his diagrammatic discussion seems to have escaped the attention it deserved; otherwise the interdependence examined above would have come to be recognized long ago. See *The*

the value augmentation of B with a drop in i serves to increase the elasticity of L_s. This is predicated on the desire for more cash balances as wealth positions are enlarged; if this does not follow, and if only uncertainty of the future interest course colors L_s, then the "wealth effect" is zero. Further, if i is held constant and λ is treated as a parameter, then, in a model in which new bond issues are forthcoming, B will be enlarged at a given i and will operate to shift L_s to the right, tending to raise the interest rate unless new supplies of money are created.[19]

Let us apply these ideas. Returning to the simple Fig. 29 (a), in which income is taken as a datum, an increase in the money supply, unless the liquidity floor were tapped, would lower the interest rate and a decrease in money would raise the rate. Despite the shift in the inelastic supply curve of money, the usual contention is that the liquidity curve $L'L$, say, would stay rigid.

But this must be wrong. For $L'L$ rests (in respect of its L_s-component) on the existing M and B total. (See eq. 84′). If either total changes, then the full L_s-segment will alter, and the whole L-function will be dislodged. To illustrate, in the usual analysis of an increase in the money supply the L_s-component of money demand remains totally unaffected, as if $\partial L/\partial M = 0$. It thus presupposes that, somehow, the M-total can be increased without an alteration in B, as if the non-bank public somehow can own more money without surrendering bonds. Curiously, a change of this nature could occur only if the non-bank public awakened one morning to a money "windfall" which augmented their cash holdings without modifying their interest-bearing bondholdings. Actually, when commercial banks buy bonds and increase demand deposits, the individual bondholdings must

---

New Economics, pp. 647–649. See also Ralph Turvey, "Consistency and Consolidation in the Theory of Interest," *Economica* (November 1954), p. 301, for a brief discussion of the influence of the number of bonds.

[19] This accords with the commonsense view, though sometimes it has seemed to be denied. Conceivably, the demand for "bear hoards" may largely be independent of the size of λ so that money and bonds would be noncomplementary, with the wealth effect serving to enlarge individual bond holdings rather than cash holdings. It would be surprising, however, if B (or λ) did not have some influence on L_s, for, after all, larger cash holdings and bond holdings generally go together. If the B-effect were nil, it would imply that the "marginal utility" of bonds was constant as wealth increases—an assumption ordinarily reserved for money!

diminish so that *at the rate of interest at which the bonds are transferred* we must have $\partial B/\partial M = -1$.

This fact conceals some important implications. In Fig. 30 we assume that LL is the original L-function, based on the amount of money, M_1, and interest claims, λ_1. The interest rate is therefore determinate at i_1. Suppose, now, that the banking system has acquired bonds at an interest rate of i_2, with the new-money total at M_2 and the new sum of interest claims outside the banking system at λ_2. In view of the equivalent exchange of money for bonds, then

$$M_1 + \frac{\lambda_1}{i_2} = M_2 + \frac{\lambda_2}{i_2} \tag{86}$$

or,

$$M_2 - M_1 = \frac{\lambda_1 - \lambda_2}{i_2} \tag{87}$$

The interesting result is this: though $A(= M + B)$ is the same at i_2 whether the individuals hold more bonds and less money or vice versa, *this is not true at any other rate of interest.* Compare the asset position $A_2 = M_2 + \lambda_2$ and $A_1 = M_1 + \lambda_1$, with $A_2 = A_1$ and $\lambda_1 > \lambda_2$. If the interest rate rises to $i_1 > i_2$, then $A_2 > A_1$, inasmuch as A_2 contains fewer bonded assets to depreciate in value as i mounts: the non-bank public thus becomes partly insulated against an interest-rate rise. The contrary holds for an interest fall to $i_1 < i_2$. In this case,

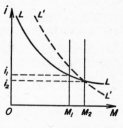

FIG. 30

$A_1 < A_2$ for the A_1 asset composition contains more bond instruments and has more "price-leverage" for an interest fall.[20]

In words, suppose that the money supply is initially \$50,000 and λ is \$1,000, so that at 2 per cent the total asset value of $M + B$ is \$100,000. Let the money supply increase to \$75,000 with a decrease

[20] The proof can be developed as follows. Write ΔM for the left-hand side of eq. 87 and $\Delta\lambda$ for the numerator on the right. Then

$$\Delta M = \frac{\Delta\lambda}{i_2} \tag{88a}$$

If $i_2 \lessgtr i_1$, then

$$\Delta M \lessgtr \frac{\Delta\lambda}{i_2} \tag{88b}$$

in λ to \$500, or $\lambda/0.02 = \$25,000 = B$. Thereafter, suppose that the interest rate rises to 4 per cent. Although the money holdings will still be \$75,000, the value of the bond assets will slump to \$12,500, making $A = \$87,500$. If λ had remained at \$1,000, the A-total at 4 per cent would be: money \$50,000, plus bonds \$25,000, totaling \$75,000. Hence, in a situation in which bonds have been exchanged by non-bank holders for cash, the asset totals are identical at the interest rate at which the exchange is consummated, but thereafter, if interest rates rise, the asset composite with fewer bonds will show the larger dollar value; conversely for the interest fall. Thus, if LL in Fig. 30 traces the L-function when the money supply is OM_1, then the dashed line, $L'L'$, denotes the new liquidity function after the money supply has been increased to M_2 and the non-bank bondholdings decreased. The asset shift must affect the liquidity function so long as the value of assets has some influence in shaping the course of L_s.

This is an interesting result, with implications for monetary policy. In technical terms, we have deduced that the L-function, besides being dependent on M, so that there is interdependence between money supply and demand, is also "irreversible": the trail "down" after an increase in the money supply need not coincide with the path "up" after a corresponding decrease in the money supply. This proposition deserves to be developed further.

IRREVERSIBILITY AND MONETARY POLICY. Figure 30 reveals that, after LL is transformed into $L'L'$, to lift the interest level from i_2 back to its former i_1-height requires a smaller decrease in the money supply than the former increase of $\Delta M = M_2 - M_1$. This "irreversibility" aspect suggests that the effect of a money change depends on both the composition of assets and the direction of money movement.

That this conclusion, which seems so queer at first sight, is justified can be seen from the following considerations. Once the community holds more money and fewer bonds, as at M_2 compared to M_1, if the banking system wants to absorb the ΔM created earlier, more bonds will have to be sold than were acquired previously in increasing the money supply. The reason is that originally the bonds were bought at the "high prices" accompanying the interest rate of i_2, while in their disposal by the banking system they must be unloaded at the "low prices" implicit in $i_1 (> i_2)$. In the return to i_1, the non-bank public would own more bonds than originally, so that, if they also owned the same amount of money as before, M_1, there would be some pressure on the demand for money, tending to lift the interest level above i_1. To restore the interest rate back to i_1, therefore, would require a lesser diminution in the money supply than the original increment needed for i_2.

For monetary policy the argument suggests that, in the case of open-market operations, the twist of the money screw required to re-establish a former higher interest level needs to be shorter than the earlier turn of money injection undertaken to induce a given degree of ease, as reflected in interest rates. It further suggests that, if the total of outstanding bond holdings (measured in original par values) increases *after* the OM_2 money amount has been created, then the subsequent security sales and money absorption by the banking system to tighten credit needs to be even smaller.[21]

THE LINKAGE OF MONETARY POLICY AND EXPECTATIONS. Omitted so far are the possibilities of interdependence between θ, the state of expectations, and changes in the money potential through central bank action.[22] Yet this nexus is vital and may be decisive in that, with modern publicity and awareness of central-bank actions, money-market participants are likely to anticipate the results sought by the authorities. Moves toward monetary easing are thus likely to be parent to the belief that future rates will be lower, serving to shift the L-function leftward. The converse holds for tightening maneuvers. Normally, the psychological chain reaction

[21] In terms of the L-M-curve of Fig. 29 (b), the drop in L-M for a money increase will, for the same money decrease, lift L-M above its original level. To restore the original interest rate, a smaller money contraction is necessary. The argument has skirted the loanable-funds theories of interest determination. It may be surmised, however, that lurking in the demand curve for loanable funds, as a determinant of the demand for money to hoard, is the matter of the existing total and composition of assets, with the magnitude of the latter being susceptible to a "built-in" variation at each rate of interest—as we move down the demand curve for hoards. The demand curve for loanable funds thus also comes to depend on the existing money supply. And once a market interest rate is established, with banks acquiring bonds, the matter of "irreversibility" arises. Further, on the supply side of loanable funds, with banks and "dishoarders" regarded as lenders, the very same elements appear.

[22] Compare the observations of Keynes, *General Theory*, pp. 197–198. These connections have been overlooked too often in the textbook exposition of Keynesian ideas.

between monetary policy and the market response ought to operate to implement the objectives pursued by the central bank. Perverse repercussions may arise through a belief that the monetary policy, by its timidity, is doomed to fail, or that soon it will have to be reversed through the realization of some foreseen train of events, of political or economic origin; in this case, a move to increase the money supply will, through its effect on θ, drive the L-curve rightward, rather than to the left, thereby tending to raise interest rates.

MONEY SUPPLY AND BANK-LIQUIDITY DEMAND

We turn now to two further shortcomings of liquidity-preference theory, the repair of which ought to make the analysis a more useful tool for understanding interest phenomena. The first matter is its incomplete definition of the money supply; the second, its omission of commercial banks "own-demand" for liquidity.

THE MONEY STOCK. Money ordinarily includes the total of demand deposits plus outstanding currency. The definitional haze is indeed thick when one contemplates the almost endless chain of money substitutes, ranging from time deposits to short-term Treasury bills, to long-term government bonds, extending finally to assets of almost any variety. Generally, and this is the element distinguishing demand deposits and currency from other assets, the latter must first be converted into the former forms before payment is effected.[23]

For the theory of interest-rate determination, the demand deposit-currency aggregate is not wholly satisfactory, for, with excess reserves possessed by commercial banks, the demand-deposit dimension is an amorphous one, capable of instant change. That it does not do so is due solely to the liquidity attitude and the expectational horizons of the commercial banks. If vault cash in the hands of commercial banks is to be included as money, then potential vault cash or demand deposits based on utilization of ex-

---

[23] Time deposits, often convertible into money without delay, pose the definitional test. Institutionally, as cash payment can be deferred, it is best to omit them from the money class in its purest form. This will be our practice, although it is not entirely a happy solution. It will still avoid error if the ratio of time deposits bears a fairly constant proportion to demand-deposit and currency totals.

cess reserves also must be included, for both cash payment and deposit expansion are alternative means of expanding the bank's earning assets. Denying vault cash a money status, then the susceptibility of the money supply to immediate change tends to impair an analysis based on the premise that the money supply is fixed.

Commercial-bank motives for liquidity, as exemplified in vault cash and excess reserves, ought not to be put on a plane different from the selfsame urges of non-bank institutions.[24] To include commercial-bank demands in the total demands for liquidity, the total money supply must be defined to mean the total money *potential*, that is, all currency outstanding (outside the Treasury and central bank), plus the *maximum* demand-deposit potential based on the existing volume of actual reserve balances multiplied by the coefficient of expansion.[25] Thus, if the currency supply is $30 billion, reserve balances $20 billion, and the required reserve ratio 20 per cent, then the deposit potential is $100 billion and the money potential is $130 billion.[26]

[24] The reason for this anomalous treatment, a defect of the liquidity-preference approach, has been due generally to a lack of clarity on the definitions necessary to bring them into the same framework. One of the few to recognize these shortcomings has been Henry Wallich, "The Current Significance of Liquidity Preference," *Quarterly Journal of Economics* (August 1946), pp. 500–501, 504–505.

To anticipate a possible query, the problem cannot be resolved by treating the money supply as a function rising to the right, rather than as a perfectly inelastic supply curve. For the rising supply function would involve treating the stimulus toward liquidity for bank lenders on a different plane than for other lenders, which entails a false dichotomy; further, there would still be the obligation to explain the limits to the money potential.

A treatment of some aspects of these problems, more suitable for a loanable-funds theory rather than for liquidity preference, is in J. J. Polak and William H. White, "The Effect of Income Expansion on the Quantity of Money," Staff Papers, *International Monetary Fund* (August 1955), especially pp. 422–428.

[25] In view of the "internal drain" of currency into circulation as the money supply is expanded, the deposit potential is actually somewhat smaller, requiring some reduction in the expansion coefficient. Further, in view of the lack of uniform reserve requirements, a weighted average coefficient ought to be used.

[26] After my own ideas on this subject were developed, a check of much of the literature on liquidity preference revealed that only Joseph F. McKenna

This is the appropriate concept of "money," M^p, if we wish to incorporate commercial-bank liquidity demands on the same psychological plane as that of the non-bank public into a comprehensive L-function. Unless the money supply is envisaged in this way, every new bank loan accomplishes a change in the money media. Further, where commercial banks hold some vault cash because of a prospective daily imbalance between currency deposits and withdrawals, these sums can be regarded as held for "transactions" purposes. Likewise, some excess reserves will be held as a precaution against an unfavorable clearing-house turn; the remainder, however, constitutes a sum available to sate liquidity motives.

Under the revised definitions, when commercial banks evidence a demand for bear hoards, L_s, this is exemplified in their holding of *excess* reserves (and possibly vault cash), rather than in amounts of demand deposits as in the case of the non-bank public. Thus, if banks desire some excess reserves, it is this excess-reserve volume multiplied by the deposit-expansion coefficient that must be included in the L-function, at every rate of interest, and added laterally to the demands of the non-bank public for liquidity.[27]

has suggested that the money supply be defined in an analogous way. He devotes only a few lines to the subject and does not extend the idea, so far as I can see, to any of the interesting and important policy implications. See, however, his often ingenious applications of *Aggregate Economic Analysis* (New York, Dryden, 1955), p. 109.

[27] Two queries arise: (1) Ought the expansion potential of the central bank to be included in the definition of the money potential? As central banks are animated by motives of economic stability or control rather than by profits, the answer is given in the negative. Their actions over the money supply must be viewed as an exogenous influence prompted by extra-economic considerations. (2) There is the matter of commercial-bank borrowings at the Federal Reserve bank through the rediscount counter. Considering the tradition against continuous indebtedness to the central bank, the positive influence of rediscounts on reserve balances might be regarded as temporary and the reserves so created ignored. Alternately, rediscounts might be visualized as entailing simultaneous dealings by the banks in two (or more) loan markets, as borrower in one and lender in the other; as this involves questions of the interest structure and the interdependence of loan markets, this study might be deferred. Some may prefer to subtract the total borrowings via rediscounts from the excess reserve balances to derive a net figure. For the immediate task of reconstructing the L_s-function, the question is probably of marginal importance.

To illustrate, in Fig. 31 the LL-curve is the one used until now, while $L'L'$ includes commercial-bank liquidity demands of excess reserves multiplied by the expansion coefficient plus vault cash. The money total, in the sense of the money potential, is given by M^p, while actual currency and demand deposits are denoted by M^a. As shown, including the extra money potential and commercial-bank own demands, the interest rate is the same, at i_0. That this must be so can be gathered from the fact that the interest rate must settle at such a level as to lead the non-bank public to hold willingly the existing stock of cash. However, it is not possible to understand the effects of central bank action in creating money without apprehending the behavior of commercial banks toward lending and liquidity. Further, the liquidity desires of the latter may often, in degree if not in direction, move differently from that of non-bank individuals. In short, monetary and interest changes will be perceived indistinctly unless money is defined in the broader context of M^p and commercial-bank liquidity demands are included in the composite liquidity function. It is worth pondering that the liquidity floor at i_0 probably is given more by commercial-bank demand rather than that of the non-bank public; the elasticity of LL emanating from the latter may be less than perfect at i_0.

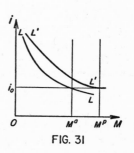

FIG. 31

As one instance of the failure of the common liquidity-preference theory to perceive the effects of open-market operations, consider the central-bank purchases of securities from commercial banks. According to the money definition of currency and bank deposits, the money supply would not be altered, so that the conclusion would have to be—erroneous though it is—that interest rates would be unaffected. Yet interest rates are likely to be lower as banks disgorge themselves of securities and acquire excess reserves. In terms of the approach developed here, the monetary potential would be increased and, if some inelasticity inhered to the composite LL-curve, interest rates would be shown as lower—the correct inference.[28]

[28] As individuals demanded more money at the lower interest rates, there would be some reshuffle of bondholdings between them and banks, whereby M^a

CONCLUDING REMARKS

By and large, this is as far as we shall carry the analysis of interest theory. However, we ought to attempt to reconcile the theory with the earlier analysis of income determination and point up some avenues for the extension of the argument. In developing a consistent theory of interest determination, we shall observe a more distressing omission of the current liquidity-preference approach; namely, its neglect of price-level phenomena.

INTEREST CHANGES AND THE Z-D-FUNCTIONS. The usual approach to the liquidity-preference theory virtually ignores one of the main sources of money demand; namely, the augmented quantity of money required in response to price-level phenomena and, thus, transactions demand, as employment and proceeds grow. For example, in Fig. 29 (b), the activity level is expressed in real terms, Z_r; in effect, this eliminates price-level changes by assuming implicitly that prices are constant as activity grows. Yet, even with constant-money wages, with diminishing returns prevalent over the economy, prices must rise with an output advance. And as money wages ordinarily will go up, this adds another strong push on the price level. To omit the rising price-level demand for funds from transactions demand is to overlook an important force driving up interest rates during expansion movements. This oversight can be avoided by using the Z-concept, developed earlier, which has price-level phenomena built in its track.

If we assume for the moment that rising interest charges, as variable costs, leave the Z-function wholly unaffected but reduce investment and aggregate demand, we have a curve system such as that displayed in Fig. 32. As interest rate goes higher, from $i_1 <$ $i_2 < i_3$, etc., the demand curves fall. Thus, each higher i-level is associated with smaller Z,N-totals: the transactions demand falls with higher interest rates so that the demand curve for money runs downward to the right.[29] Implicit in each point of the latter would be

---

would be enlarged, so that customary ideas become validated in part. But the process can be depicted only with the fuller definitions employed here.

[29] Taking account of interest as a variable cost would tend to elevate the Z-curves as the D-curve falls. Together, both spell an employment fall, though Z is better maintained with the Z-rise. If, however, variable-interest charges are very small, as seems to be the case, we can neglect this effect.

lower income levels associated with higher interest levels. In this way, we could "build in," within an LL-curve, such as that shown in Fig. 30, the effect of varying Z,N-levels.[30]

Equationally, taking the money wage as a parameter, we would have

$$N = N_1(Z,i) \tag{89}$$

$$N = N_2(D,i) \tag{90}$$

$$M^p = L(Z,i) \tag{91}$$

As written, employment is a function of aggregate supply and aggregate demand; this system becomes easier to use in connection with the liquidity equation. From eq. 89 and eq. 90 the relation of $Z(= D)$ and i can be ascertained. With eq. 91 a solution for Z and i can be found (as M^p is a constant sum given by monetary policy). From eq. 89 the N-total can then be found. In principle, therefore, with unknowns $N,Z(= D)$, and i, and the three equations, the system is determinate (given the further mathematical restrictions, involving mainly the shape of the functions).

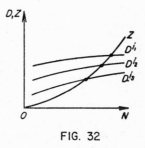

FIG. 32

THE EXPECTATIONAL HORIZON. Among the aspects of liquidity theory that would repay more extended study is the proposition that the L_s-portion of the L-function depends on expectations of future interest changes, and that expected higher rates will lead to increased current cash holdings, until this belief becomes absolute at the liquidity floor at which L_s becomes perfectly elastic. Still, to speak of a future interest rise is vague in the extreme; everything depends on the date of the rise. If it is regarded as imminent, then the analysis holds firm; if it is regarded as being off in the "future,"

[30] Compare A. P. Lerner, *Economics of Employment*, pp. 265–266. Professor Hansen prefers the apparatus of Fig. 29 (b) and seems to be unhappy about using a function such as that referred to, where transactions demand varies at each interest rate, on the grounds that "*concealed* behind it are the investment-demand function and the consumption function"—*A Guide to Keynes* (New York, McGraw-Hill, 1953), p. 150. But all plane diagrams "conceal" something when several variables are involved; Hansen's own curve "conceals" price-level variations. There ought to be no confusion or objection to the technique so long as the premises of the curve are made explicit.

some time remains before a decision in favor of cash and against bonds needs to be implemented. Thus the "expectational horizon" must carry dates; clock time must appear explicitly in the argument. Doing so, we might discern some strange patterns, of trends, of expected oscillations, of longer and shorter intervals between various movements, etc. To compound the difficulties, different individuals will hold different expectational vistas. Further, there is always the question of the assurance with which the forecast is held. Despite these complications, it does seem reasonably clear that L_s will fall to the right; but the expectational horizon and the degree of subjective assurance will contribute to both its position and its slope.

THE STRUCTURE OF INTEREST RATES. The most obvious simplification of current liquidity-preference theory is its concentration on a single interest rate, rather than the interest structure. When one takes account of the existence of loan obligations of almost any maturity, and of stock-market equities, the theory is inevitably modified, though certain of the fundamental propositions can be transposed rather bodily. The essential problem in the fuller statement consists of deriving the equilibrium structure of prices that must prevail in all maturities in order to induce individuals to hold the diversified asset total, including money. Any change in the money supply or in the volume of paper assets must press on the ruling yield structure, edging it to the level at which the new money-claim combination will be held without impelling further equilibrating transactions. In general, an increase in any one maturity (or security) must lower its price (raise its yield). Obviously, substitute relationships abound in the yield structure. It is possible, however, as in the case of equities, that there may be a simultaneous rise in preferences for such issues along with a growth in their volume, with both the new issues and newly found favor a resultant of a common cause; namely, the profit outlook. On this basis, it is conceivable that equity yields may show a yield pattern different from other assets. But this is a vast subject which invites detailed and separate exploration.[31]

---

[31] Joan Robinson almost alone has endeavored to fill this gap in the liquidity analysis. See her "The Rate of Interest," *Econometrica* (April 1951), p. 94. Also, her little volume, *The Rate of Interest and Other Essays*, p. 7. See also, for a particularly illuminating analysis, R. F. Kahn, "Some Notes on Liquidity Preference," *The Manchester School of Economic and Social Studies* (September 1954).

Chapter 9

Rent and Quasi-Rent

The rent concept and its Marshallian offspring, quasi-rent, will occupy us here. While heretofore the income of fixed factors has been described as of a contractual order, it is time to analyze what might be the underlying bases of these commitments in a world of clearer foresight and correct estimates of the productivity of resources. Economic rents will be defined as the *imputed* earnings of fixed factors; the mere allusion to imputation suggests that the full economic rent need not actually be recouped by the resource owner. Hence, as in our elaboration of interest theory, the ensuing pages do not purport to explain fixed payments which have a contractual base and involve an agreed-upon legal transfer whose provisions may be of infinite variety. Contractual income rights complement an enterprise economy in which ownership and property use are separated. Still, whatever the nature of ownership and income claims, fixed factors engaged by the firm have value and possess economic significance, and it is this aspect of economic importance rather than the magnitude of payments which invites study. Value imputations undoubtedly are connected to contractual commitments, but in a dynamic economy the link must often be loose. Only *ex post* or with correct prevision could the economic rents be detected and provide exact mandates for contractual relations.

Following the common license in economics, we shall sometimes slur these obvious facts and speak as if the payments and the values coincide. But we are amply forewarned that to isolate the determinants of economic rent is not equivalent to explaining the total of rent *payments* which are a relic of elapsed contractual history.

THE FIXITY ASPECT

A major confusion in the classical scheme consisted in binding the rent concept to land as such rather than to the fact of fixity, although, as a practical matter, land is the concrete exhibit of a fixed resource, being (largely) nonaugmentable to the economy despite conscious productive activity and (often) immune to any depletion over time. Certain types of capital equipment may be equally fixed in the same essential respects and their earnings wholly equivalent in character. Empirically, within firms and in the economy some factors remain fixed in hire amounts as proceeds and employment vary; it is this fact which separates fixed and variable factors.[1] Essentially there are two causes of fixity. Obviously there may be natural limits, as in the case of land; it is apparent, too, that the fixity aspect here is more germane to the economy than to the firm. Economic forces can be an equally persuasive cause of fixity, for, so long as firms estimate that a further unit of an agent would not be profitable, then the factor is effectively fixed. Unless this relation holds over a wide range of output and demand growth, however, the fixity is merely temporary. Indivisible capital equipment provides a common illustration, for, while it can be augmented, it is the unfavorable cost-revenue ratio that is the deterrent. Even "naturally fixed" factors are in a way susceptible to some variation; swamps can be drained and oceans have been pushed back by dikes. Excesses of cost relative to returns generally have limited the scope for such feats.

Even these brief remarks convey the Ricardian overtones that the analysis will bear.[2] Some purpose might be served by parading a few alternate rent explanations that in degree vie with and at some points cross that to be offered here. A thesis currently popular stresses the excess earnings of a factor in its particular use compared with its next best alternative as composing rent: rent is ex-

[1] Observe that the fixity is defined relative to aggregate proceeds. On any other definition it is hard to maintain the fixity property, for, as viewed by the firm, all factors are variable, including land. But if there are factors whose use remains unchanged, in a global outlook over the period in which the Z-function is relevant, then they comprise the fixed category. Thus labor, whose hire is responsive to proceeds, is a variable agent. For those who prefer their definition in real, rather than money-aggregate, terms, the fixed factors are those whose amount in use is invariant relative to aggregate output. It is this usage which commended itself to the classicists.

[2] This is an anomaly of its own in view of the Keynesian influence and his open hostility to the Ricardian heritage. Yet the Ricardian analysis seems to be the only consistent rent appendage of the Keynesian theory of employment, most apparent in his treatment of the effect of diminishing returns on the price level. (*General Theory,* Chapter 21.)

plained not in terms of the imputed income but rather in respect of the discrepancy between it and alternative earnings. Unfortunately, this concept seems particularly futile in a model in which the growth of aggregate demand affects income and begs a comparison of the new income imputation with the old, rather than with an alternate *current* earnings. The opportunity-cost doctrine thus seems inapplicable to macroeconomic analyses, however perceptive it is in stable stationary circumstances. As the earnings of fixed factors in *all* activities swell during an N-Z-advance, the explanation of their income changes cannot stem from a concept born in a stationary soil.

Too, there is this quixotic aspect to the opportunity-cost scheme: rent, so defined, is taken to refer not to all of the factor's imputed or actual income, but only to part of it—unless the alternate use value is zero. What name is to be given to the remainder of the factor's income? A wage? Interest? Profits?[3] In short, however useful and illuminating the concept of displacement costs is in explaining the principles of economical resource management, the doctrine fails to explain the phenomenon that we have chosen to isolate; namely, the earnings of factors which remain fixed in amount while proceeds vary.

Akin to the displacement-cost concept is the argument that rents accrue only to factors in imperfectly elastic supply, with pure rents assigned to those agents fixed in amount and incapable of being altered—the case of perfectly inelastic supply—while partial rents are imputed to all factors whose supply curve departed from the horizontal. This approach, too, is less than satisfactory: so long as supply curves reflect the volition of those who own productive sources, this argument ultimately involves the idea of rents as constituting a psychic surplus over and above the earnings that a factor owner would find acceptable as a minimum compensation, with the latter based partly on alternate use values. At the latter turn, the explanation tends to merge with opportunity cost doctrine and, applied on the income side, it is strongly reminiscent of Marshall's consumers' surplus.[4] In the latter sense, all factors receive

[3] Usually, the term "transfer earnings" or "opportunity cost" is used. But this is also a nondescript concept in terms of conventional income types.

[4] Boulding, who proffers this rent version, was led to just such investigations. See his "The Concept of Economic Surplus," *American Economic Review* (December 1945). Also his *Economic Analysis* (New York, Harper, 1955, 3rd ed.), pp. 211–214, 724–725, 819–826.

rent, whether variable or not. While for some purposes this may be an interesting conjecture, it nevertheless falls short of an explanation of the earnings of the factor category under scrutiny; namely, those agents whose amount in use fails to fluctuate with changes in proceeds and output despite variations in the use of other agents.

Rent is also associated at times with the indivisibility or lumpiness of the factor.[5] Indivisibility is manifestly a matter of degree: a laborer is an indivisible whole, as is an item of equipment. In contrast, agricultural land can be subdivided into tiny particles. If rent is to be attributed to an agent such as land, it must, therefore, be assigned to its fixity—in the sense of the supply quantity in use—rather than to its indivisibility. The indivisibility attribute is related to rent only by virtue of the fact that additional lumpy agents are unlikely to be hired because their cost outweighs their revenue productivity: *it is the uneconomic aspect of variation,* not their inability to withstand fragmentation, which limits their hire.[6]

RENT DETERMINATION

To launch the rent inquiry under the simplest circumstances, let us stipulate that the volume of proceeds and its allocation among firms is settled, so that employment and output are determinate; also, that the prices and the productivity of variable factors are known and that purely competitive sales markets prevail. Arguing diagrammatically, in Fig. 33 (a) the market price is represented at P_1 and, according to profit-maximization criteria, output is Q_1. Aver-

---

[5] See B. S. Keirstead, *An Essay in the Theory of Profits and Income Distribution* (Oxford, Blackwell, 1953), pp. 7, 8. He writes: "I regard fixity or complete inelasticity of supply as a special case of indivisibility" (p. 7n).

[6] Sometimes it is alleged that, because the supply quantity of land is permanently fixed, then marginal-productivity analysis is automatically suspended, for "it is impossible to talk about its marginal product"—J. K. Eastham, *An Introduction to Economic Analysis* (London, English Univ. Press, 1953), pp. 173, 177. Surely, marginal-productivity analysis can be applied to land in the only way that the doctrine is ever relevant; namely, to examine the incremental change in physical output and revenue product of a further piece of land *in any given output.* To contend that marginal-productivity doctrine cannot be applied because the supply quantity is fixed becomes tangled with the odd idea that the elucidation of the forces prevailing on the demand side must await an analysis of supply phenomena.

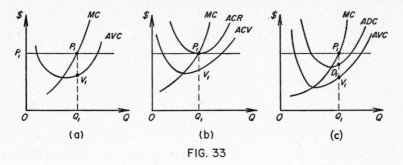

FIG. 33

age variable costs amount to V_1Q_1, total variable costs are $OQ_1 \cdot Q_1V_1$, while total proceeds are $P_1Q_1 \cdot OQ_1$. Subtracting total variable costs from receipts leaves $P_1V_1 \cdot OQ_1$ as a residual. Where there is only one fixed factor, presumably the entrepreneur himself, this remainder must constitute his income, his *rent*.

An important inference to be drawn from this is that, if average costs are written to include rent, in amount P_1V_1 in Fig. 33 (a), then at the output of maximum profits it is inevitable that average costs (including rent) are at a minimum. At the production volume at which marginal costs equal price, an average cost curve which includes rent, ACR, will sit tangential to the horizontal price line of pure competition.[7] Further, it follows that if the several firms in a competitive industry have different AVC experience, with some curves lodged higher than others, then the phenomenon of rent performs the subsidiary function of equalizing the "full-average costs" among firms. Rents thereby come to equalize average production costs whatever the assortment of variable agents used by the individual firms in producing the specified product. Hence, it becomes peculiarly tautologous to assert that in competitive equilibrium price is equal to average costs. For if the latter total includes rent, the proposition merely alleges that the volume of rents is so chosen as to insure the equality, while, if rents are excluded, the statement loses its validity.[8] Discussions of optimal output which run in terms of the minimum AC-position are, therefore, ambiguous unless they articulate the implicit rent hypotheses.[9]

[7] For the original diagram and analysis, see Joan Robinson, *Imperfect Competition*, p. 125.

[8] See p. 176, discussion of Fig. 33 (c).

[9] Misuse of these ideas is common in elementary texts. Sometimes it is

What is always prerequisite to optimal organization, on the other hand, is the intimacy of price and marginal costs or, in some contexts, of average variable costs.

To conclude, with one fixed agent its income consists of the residual sum after all variable payments are allocated. Exhaustion of income proceeds is automatically guaranteed.

MULTIPLE FIXED FACTORS. Assume now that the fixed factors are members of a homogeneous class—acres of land of identical fertility and economically equivalent location constitute an appropriate image—and that each firm engages single units of fixed factors belonging to the diverse factor classes A, B, $C \cdots$ This analysis deserves to be worked out.

Each firm using each type of agent can bid for each of the fixed factors, at most, the maximum residual sum at the $P = MC > AVC$ output position; implicit in a maximum bid for any one factor A, say, is a zero income for the remaining fixed agents. Nonetheless, for every possible price of the latter agents a (particular equilibrium) market-demand curve can be derived for the fixed factor A, which, with its supply curve, can yield its price. With the factor in perfectly inelastic supply, its price must match its availability with the demand quantity.

All this, of course, is a grafting of particular equilibrium analysis onto a general equilibrium problem through assuming that the other factors were initially priced (and allocated) quite arbitrarily. The process can be envisaged instead as completed in a series of tentative steps, with each firm estimating the importance to it of particular agents, literally working out innumerable hypothetical factor combinations.[10] In settling the value of factor A there will inevitably be repercussions upon the demand for, and the price of, factor B,

argued that the minimum AC-point is valid, for "in the long run" all factors are variable to the firm. This argument is not much better; so long as there are some fixed factors to the economy, as is the case with land, the problem of rent determination remains. Of course, with time the array of variable factors widens, but even this limited acceptance of the argument must be hedged until the many question-begging hypotheses implicit in "long-run" analysis are revealed.

[10] Compare Leon Walras, *op. cit.*, Lesson 22, pp. 261–263, especially. Interestingly, Walras employs a "sequence" type of analysis where an additional factor is introduced into an existing equilibrium structure. For a new commodity, see Lesson 15. Compare my *Price Theory*, pp. 127–128.

etc. Each factor in final equilibrium will ultimately gravitate to that firm which promises maximum payment for its use. The price paid by a firm for one factor, however, will not exceed the sum at which substitute factors can be obtained. Residuals that still remain after all fixed factors are compensated comprise entrepreneurial rents, which may dwindle through new entry over time.

Multiple fixed agents that must be used in unvarying proportions, precluding a meaningful separable marginal-productivity valuation, constitute a special case. Nevertheless, so long as the factors are used in different proportions by different firms, *and there are as many products as there are factors,* it is possible to arrive at a determinable market value for each. To illustrate, if one unit of product X, selling for P_x, is turned out with a_1 units of labor and b_1 units of land, while one unit of Y, selling for P_y, uses a_2 of labor and b_2 of land, writing w for the wage rate and r for the rent per acre, the determining equations are:

$$a_1 w + b_1 r = P_x \qquad (92)$$

$$a_2 w + b_2 r = P_y \qquad (93)$$

Knowing the a- and the b-coefficients and the P's, solving the simultaneous equations yields w and r.[11] Although this method of resolution breaks down where the number of products exceeds the number of factor classes, the general theory would resemble that already developed in the wage analysis with equilibrium income conditioning the earnings potential while the factor inelasticity would dominate on the supply side.

VERSATILITY AND HETEROGENEITY. Once homogeneous fixed factors are priced through market-wide demand for their services, their prices will constitute costs that the firm will have to cover in production. Figure 33 (c) reproduces the MC- and the AVC-curves. Added onto AVC are the costs entailed through the use of the homogeneous fixed agents, and shown by ADC; the latter denotes the inclusion of the full displacement costs of all variable and homogeneous fixed factors along its course. As the curve is drawn, the total cost outlays at OQ_1 made for the variable and homogeneous fixed-factor

[11] Compare G. J. Stigler, *Production and Distribution Theories,* pp. 166–167; G. Tintner, *Mathematics and Statistics for Economists* (New York, Rinehart, 1953), p. 33; P. A. Samuelson, "Prices of Factors and Goods in General Equilibrium," *Review of Economic Studies* (1953–1954, No. 54), p. 6.

groupings fail to exhaust all of the proceeds. Heterogeneous agents are thus in position to recoup the remainder.

The very notion of homogeneous factors, fixed or otherwise, suggests that the factor is versatile, with multiple uses within the economy. Typically, analyses conclude that the use of versatile factors involves opportunity costs which must be met; further, it is often contended that versatile factors are not rent agents, and that their costs are economic, with special influence over price and output decisions. Nonetheless, as the fact of fixity conveys special income-determining implications, we shall continue to regard them as rent goods, for, while payments to the variable agents are intertwined inextricably with decisions on employment and output, payments to versatile fixed agents rest partly on an appraisal of the magnitude of the residual proceeds: only if these prove ample will the factor be hired. But the separable residual earnings may well fluctuate disproportionately compared to variable factors as proceeds, employment, and aggregate output vary.

A heterogeneous fixed agent, comprising the full factor class, might also be employed alongside both variable and homogeneous fixed factors within the firm. Examining Fig. 33 (c), a residual, $P_1D_1 \cdot OQ_1$, still remains for distribution which, in principle, can be imputed to the heterogeneous agent and pocketed by its owner. If the heterogeneous agent is the entrepreneur himself, "profits"— more appropriately, entrepreneurial rent—comprise the obvious outlet. If the entrepreneurial abilities are reasonably common, with many others of commensurate ability, the entrepreneurial displacement income will be embodied in ADC and competitive bidding by other equally adept entrepreneurs for the use of the remaining heterogeneous factor would deflect the sum $P_1D_1 \cdot OQ_1$ to the source owner. Hence, whenever there is an undistributed residual, the equilibrium is incomplete, with the vacuum filled through price bids for the heterogeneous agents by firms contemplating *different* uses for them if they are versatile, or by bids from firms eyeing the factor for the same use, if they are specific: intra-industry as well as inter-industry demands for the factor's services exist.[12] Thus, in product B, the factor may be valued by all firms as worth $100, while in product A by firm X it is regarded as worth $200, and by

---

[12] When intra-industry demands are recognized, the alternate-use aspects of versatility loom as of considerably less significance

firm Y, a competitor of X in A, it is regarded as worth \$450. Ordinarily, the factor will be commandeered by firm Y. Where there are several firms equally visioned and qualified as the Y-firm, the full \$450 will be amassed by the factor owner, otherwise its income will exceed \$200 but fall short of \$450. Actual payment will fall between these limits as given by the theory of bilateral monopoly.

PRICE-DETERMINED INCOMES AND NONECONOMIC COSTS. Non-rent agents whose costs influence marginal cost, and thus price, are often described as price-determining costs, while rents are alleged to be price-determined. The principle goes back at least to Ricardo.[13]

In the past, it has not been difficult to debunk this argument on the ground that versatile fixed factors carry an opportunity cost that must be covered by price proceeds, and hence, it was contended, price had to be high enough to meet the opportunity options. This was conceded by Mill, and carried further by Jevons, to the effect that the price of wheat had to be high enough to cover the value of the same acreage when devoted to corn production.[14]

The proposition would seem to be irrefutable, for it simply avers that all displacement charges must be met. Still, to accept it is not to admit that the costs of versatile fixed factors are price determining, for what is entailed is simply the theorem that, *after output is once determined,* then prices must be adequate to cover the displacement cost of the versatile fixed agents. Ordinarily, the fact of displacement costs *merely limits the range of output* over which the factor may be used, rather than determining a unique volume. Necessary payments to the versatile fixed agents may also limit the number of firms in the field and the volume of fixed factors that are utilized

[13] As Marshall, in a moment of pique, declared, in supporting the Ricardian scheme: "It is *wisest not* to say that rent does not enter into cost of production, for that will confuse many people. But it is wicked to say that rent does enter into cost of production, because that is *sure* to be applied in such a way as to lead to the denial of subtle truths which, in spite of their being subtle, are of the very highest importance scientifically . . ." *Memorials of Alfred Marshall* (London, Macmillan, 1925), A. C. Pigou, editor, p. 436.

In his *Principles* (p. 437n), his reproof is only a little softened: "It is . . . inexpedient to say that the rent of land does not enter into . . . price. But it is worse than inexpedient to say that the rent of the land does enter into . . . price: that is false."

[14] For a comprehensive review of the issue, see Daniel H. Buchanan, "The Historical Approach to Rent and Price Theory," *Economica* (June 1929). Reprinted in *Readings in the Theory of Income Distribution.*

there, but it does not influence the precise output volume once the factors are brought in the fold. Otherwise, the argument would lead to the erroneous proposition that fixed costs are output, and thus price, determining. On this interpretation, variable costs remain the sole output determining costs and thereby constitute the price-determining outlays. Earnings of versatile fixed factors continue basically to be price-determined *rent* incomes.[15]

RENTS AND VARYING ACTIVITY

Rent movements with varying activity remain to be examined; on the constant-income (or employment) hypothesis, logic and convenience might well support the versatile-specific dichotomization. It is with varying activity levels that the fixity attribute becomes the structural pillar of the rent concept. Money-wage rates constant, it was noted earlier that the Z/W-ratio would grow under the impetus of diminishing returns, connoting a rise in rents. At the industry level it would involve rising market-demand curves; for the firm there would be the uplift in the perfectly elastic price bar under pure competition. Let us elaborate on this.

[15] Similarly, the prices that need to be paid to acquire control over the use of specific factors are often termed a "noneconomic" cost on the ground that alternative use values need not be sacrificed in engaging them. In a way, this argument magnifies differences of degree into matters of kind, for agents without alternatives fill a rather mythical class; the most specialized machinery holds a scrap value. Even when the gap in layers of alternate uses is proposed as the criterion, it still follows that a tight rule cannot be maintained as a principle of income determination: the alternative use at best sets a border on the value of the factor; it need not be a vital element in income determination when there are several entrepreneurs covetous of the agent's service in that use in which its value superiority is manifest.

Adherence to the specificity concept is often premised on the belief that versatile factors must be economized, while the same deliberate forethought need not be practiced with specific agents. But this is a confusion of ideas. Just as releasing versatile factors can augment alternate outputs, so the assigning of specific factors to their unique use accomplishes the same end. For if a specific factor were held idle, then certain alternate outputs would diminish as versatile factors were rushed in to replace the specific agents. Specific factors thus perform the vital function of conserving versatile factors for alternate outputs; the only real distinction between versatile and specific agents is that the allocative problem is simpler with respect to the latter—if ever purely specific agents were found.

With a rise in proceeds and industry demand under pure competition, and under conditions of diminishing marginal products for variable factors, the effect will be to raise prices and widen the breach between total receipts and total variable costs. In a fluid economy devoid of contracts and fixed payments, competitive bidding would divert the residual sums to the fixed-resource owners. Rents thus become a creature of diminishing returns and the legacy of agents which happen to be constant in amount in use as production varies: they could not appear with constant marginal products —for this implies an absence of fixity—and they would be negative with increasing returns.[16] Paradoxically, in imputation analysis fixed factors will merit a *variable* (rent) and rising real income as production expands while individual variable factors may, on our hypotheses, receive fixed money sums and declining real earnings. Even if the latter earnings rise in money terms per unit, the relative share of fixed factors will be proportionately higher and, in real terms, rent good owners ought to benefit from the income shift— barring the existence of rigid contractual stipulations.

As an interesting side issue which underscores the importance of supply phenomena in deciding earnings even of naturally invariable factors, we can suppose that their owners place a minimum income stipulation on their use, so that, at a given level of activity, less than the full factor set (in physical units) is engaged.[17] As employment and proceeds expand and rents are enlarged, more of such factors enter the production circle. The effect must be to restrain the rise in earnings of the volume of fixed agents used previously though the aggregate and per unit earnings of the group must be enlarged. The case envisaged borders on that of augmentability and quasi-rents; *pure rents thus arise only if all units of a factor class are already utilized* in conditions where other resources evidence some flexibility in the amount available and in use as proceeds vary.

If all rent-goods were homogeneous and their supply price zero, so that phenomena akin to reproducibility and augmentability were not involved, there could never be any unemployment of these agents: all units would always be in use or those not in use would share the zero earnings of those being utilized. As proceeds and labor employment contracted, their total and unit earnings would fall,

---

[16] See Chapter 3.
[17] Walras seems to approach the problem in this way (*op. cit.*, p. 223).

but unemployment of the rent goods, in a sense analogous to involuntary labor unemployment, as idle (homogeneous) acres to match idle (homogeneous) men, could not develop: the intensity of use of each acre would fall, however, with each acre used to the same degree of diminishing returns. Only if some owners of technically identical acres stipulated for definite earnings sums, preferring idleness and a null income to lower earnings, could unemployment of the "fixed" factors develop. But, as intimated, this problem is closely wrapped up with that of augmentability and quasi-rents.

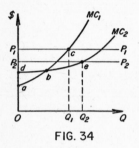

FIG. 34

With heterogeneous fixed factors, such as the differential land of classical theory and empirical fact, unemployment and the vanishing of rent on these instruments is possible even as labor is unemployed. The availability of inferior agents as production expands tends to mitigate the diminishing-returns tendencies of fixed agents currently utilized, and limit the enhancement of the income of the latter resource owners. But the same end is served by all substitutable factors; inferior units, themselves fixed in amount, constitute effective substitutes which partly augment the supply of existing heterogeneous fixed agents.

Turning from the effect of rising activity on rents, we consider briefly the influence of invention and improved technology on agricultural ground rents. The huge build-up in population over the last century has been accompanied by technological change in agriculture and growing scarcity of fertile land, reflected in rising rents even after correcting for the upsweep attributable to price-level upheavals. With constant variable-factor prices, we can write MC_1 as the relevant marginal-cost curve (neglecting AVC_1) in Fig. 34. On the simplest view, therefore, the rent total is given by the area $abcP_1$ when market price is OP_1. Supposing an improvement in agricultural technology which requires the use of heavy equipment, with variable-factor prices remaining as before, then MC_2 is assumed to depict the course of marginal costs. With market price taken as lower despite the extension of demand accompanying the population growth, the new rent total is $dbeP_2$ when the price is OP_2. Rents, therefore, are conceived to fall with the price fall, according to the illustration. This is, of course, a possibility—a sufficiently important technological advance which if not over-compensated by a demand growth would lower rents.

MONOPOLY AND RENTS

Rents in monopoly-pricing structures, where the firm equates marginal cost to marginal revenue while price exceeds both, deserves some examination, although the main point, that bids for fixed factors are governed by marginal revenue rather than marginal-value product considerations, is clear.

If the monopoly-pricing prospect is open to many entrepreneurs when once in possession of a given resource, whether it be fixed equipment, a patent, a location, etc., the result must be that the full residual sum above variable charges, including the excess earnings under monopoly pricing compared to a $MC = P$ arrangement, would accrue as rents not to the particular entrepreneur who happened to be using the resource, but rather to the resource owner. This is an interesting result: the ultimate beneficiaries of the monopoly-pricing tactics are the property owners while the entrepreneurial co-ordinators perpetrating the pricing exactions fail to retain any of the income excesses. This proposition is valid whenever the prospect of monopoly pricing is attached to the fixed resources rather than to any special competence or latent qualities of entrepreneurial origin. Thus, in a particular location which permits monopoly pricing by virtue of its access and convenience to a transient passerby trade, it is the site owner rather than the operator who will be relatively enriched by the monopoly pricing practice.[18] The rewards to holders of patent rights will be determined similarly.

Monopoly profits are thereby transformed into economic rents. If various entrepreneurs contemplating the use of the same fixed resources perceive distinct and disparate demand and cost experience attached to them, then the income and rent outcome is ordered somewhat differently. The successful bidder for the fixed agent would have to pay enough to deny its services to other aspirants and any residual would constitute an entrepreneurial rent, imputable to the superior organizing and selling talents of the highest bidder.

[18] This conclusion is due to Chamberlin. Its understanding ought be more widespread. (*Op. cit.*, Appendix D.)

Whether the excess earnings stemming from monopoly pricing accrue to the owners of inanimate fixed factors or to discernible entrepreneurial talents, they can be described effectively as a rent rather than as a profit, for the monopoly income harvest belongs to the stationary world and has nothing to do with change, the genesis of profits, as we shall argue; if it is preferred to reserve the term rent for the fixity attribute, then monopoly "revenue" can be utilized as an accurate and colorless term conveying none of the dynamism of profits.

While increasing marginal products are incompatible with competitive pricing, for they would involve negative rents and thus either subsidies or the abandonment of $P = MC$ pricing, the contradiction vanishes with monopoly pricing: monopoly revenue can be imputed to fixed agents even at output levels where variable factors exhibit rising marginal products, for monopoly requires only that price, at the output of maximum revenue, exceed average variable cost, and the residual can be assigned as a monopoly rent.[19]

The effects on rents in oligopoly cases, which by virtue of their realism and intricacy have fascinated economists, ought to be apparent; oligopolists can offer fixed-factor owners the difference between sales receipts and total variable costs, or the full residual as a maximum. As these sums cannot exceed monopoly exactions, and may well be below, the general effect of oligopoly is to compress the rent volume, though ordinarily these earnings will surpass those extracted in pricing according to $P = MC$ criteria. Where the oligopoly power rests on the possession of some exclusive external factor rather than in personal attributes, the resources may be bid away by a competing oligopolist at a price which even exceeds the residual earnings. This, of course, is an illustration of the extremes to which oligopoly warfare may go.[20]

MONOPOLY PRICING AND SALES OUTLAYS. Possibilities of monopoly pricing are often contingent on the special sales efforts by way of advertising; even if monopoly revenue would appear without promotional endeavors there is no doubt but that selling outlays do enhance the profit outcome—there is the obvious fact that firms buy advertising as they do other product ingredients. Selling out-

---

[19] Perhaps this case is rarer than the one in which average product is still rising while marginal products are turning down.

[20] *Price Theory*, pp. 173–177.

lays undoubtedly constitute a cost. The excess of income over and above production costs—which at the border are often indistinguishable from selling costs—can be envisaged as constituting the whole of monopoly revenue, as a gross concept, inasmuch as this income magnitude would not be part of a purely competitive adaptation. Gross monopoly revenue could then be subdivided between payments for selling activities and the remainder would comprise monopoly revenue proper: for some purposes we might want to use the gross concept, for other uses, merely the residual revenue. Thus there are activities performed and incomes earned in monopolistic economies which would not appear in competitive systems, although the compensation for their performance, in the advertising industry generally, would emerge as ordinary wage, rent, or profit incomes perhaps even determined in fully competitive factor markets; while only the residual adhering to the firm buying the selling activity would come to be seen as a purely monopoly revenue. The payments for selling activities might, in a way, be regarded as a transfer of profits or a diversion of monopoly income. This is to say ultimately that the composition of output, the diversion of resources, and the distribution of income under monopoly differ from that of a model of thoroughgoing competition, making hazardous any simple comparisons of competition and monopoly. Sales outlays necessary to perpetuate the monopoly-pricing prospects become costs in the ordinary sense, and may be of either the fixed or the variable variety.

CAPITALIZATION OF MONOPOLY REVENUE. Whatever the asset, its expected earnings stream can always be reduced to a present value. Rent goods, insofar as they are external and inanimate, are thus subject to the capitalization process whereby their current market values can be ascertained and the property right sold in the market place. The same capitalization process will mark intangible assets such as patents, trade marks, and copyrights—the "income-factor" category[21]—as well as tangible productive instruments. Only human factors are excluded from the capitalization process in a non-slave economy.[22]

[21] See my *Price Theory*, p. 53, where I distinguish "income" factors from "output" factors, with the former having only a revenue product while the latter have both a revenue and a physical product.

[22] Although in a free economy individuals are not sold, the valuation of

The congruence of price and average cost after the rents are capitalized and included in average cost has created some confusion among economists. For in a stationary framework those who acquire possession of a market in which a very high degree of monopoly power prevails could still protest with an air of injured innocence that their resulting earnings merely equaled market rates, even after exploiting their position to the utmost through $P > MR = MC$ pricing. This, in fact, would be true so long as the monopoly revenue was capitalized at market interest rates on transference of ownership. Monopoly "profits" would be pocketed permanently by the original monopolists; subsequent purchasers of the income source would earn only the normal rate of return.[23] Abolishing monopoly-pricing procedures would thus wreak income havoc only on those who chanced to be the owners of the source of monopoly power at the time when the pricing practices were abandoned.[24] Pondering this point, it ought to become clear that the test of economic efficiency cannot rest on some calculation of "normal"

---

their services (according to marginal-productivity analysis) proceeds from an estimation of their expected future revenue stream over the period covered by the wage or salary contract. The sale of contractual rights, as in the case of baseball players or movie stars, involves considerations not vastly different than those which appear in the valuation and transfer of physical properties. The differences lie in the fact that the individual has the option of refusing the employment under the new auspices (often at a tremendous financial sacrifice): the temperament which influences performances may impart a difference to these transactions compared, say, to a dealing in land or equipment.

The parallel of these cases to what would be common practice in a slave economy is by no means a condemnation of these practices: it happens that in the areas mentioned incomes are among the highest in the economic order, and it is a moot question of whether baseball, for example, as an organized business activity, could endure in a desired form without the unique arrangements. Compare the interesting article, rather long overdue in economic analysis, by Simon Rottenberg, "The Baseball Players' Labor Market," *Journal of Political Economy* (June 1956). I think, however, he is too sanguine as to the accomplishments of a "free market" and fails to analyze sufficiently the place and implications of contracts in a free economy. (Compare Chapter 10.)

[23] See R. F. Harrod, "Theory of Profit," in *Economic Essays* (New York, Harcourt, 1952), pp. 202–203.

[24] Compare R. T. Triffin, *Monopolistic Competition and General Equilibrium Theory* (Cambridge, Harvard, 1940), Chapter V.

profits, or "normal" rates of return on capital investment, or on the identity of price and average cost, including rent. Mischief along these lines constantly is being perpetrated in the guise of a "rule of reason" in rate making in the public utility field.[25]

AUGMENTABILITY AND QUASI-RENTS

It is time to relax the hypothesis of a fixed stock of rent goods, for some factors fixed in quantity as output varies over a given time interval are capable of being augmented at later dates if economic conditions warrant it. Equipment provides an obvious illustration. It was on this category that Marshall hung the felicitous term "quasi-rents."

Reproducibility in response to economic motives primarily distinguishes capital goods from other productive agents. Land, in physical dimensions, is nonaugmentable; population changes are responsive to noneconomic forces besides showing an endogenous response to income.

In the Marshallian long run, an increase in the demand for final output and a rise in the economic importance of equipment which raised the going "quasi-rents" would lead to the construction of new items of capital. Augmentation would continue until the prospective earnings of the new agents, discounted for uncertainty and interest, equaled the construction cost. The analysis is predicated on the belief that the new demand level is expected to be permanent, with the adaptation of the stock of equipment to the new income and swelling quasi-rent circumstances proceeding slowly because of the cost obstacles hindering more instantaneous adjustment. Conversely, on a dynamic view, a rise in demand that is not expected to endure will be ineffective in promoting capital construction. Further, even with an unchanged current proceeds and employment level, whenever income is *expected* to rise new equipment is likely to be erected. There is no need to undertake an elaborate analysis at this point; all of it has been well worked over in modern discussions of the

[25] Alternate procedures undoubtedly would be difficult to introduce. Present practices, however, insofar as they attempt to appeal to economic analysis for sanction, become ridiculous. Legalistic arguments, shorn of economic trappings appealing to mistaken optima, are more defensible *until the objective of rate regulation as a pricing rather than a profit vehicle is recognized.*

marginal efficiency of capital. The point that needs to be underscored for our purposes is that equipment will be ordered almost regardless of current earnings of existing assets of the same type: immediate earnings are ephemeral and ineffective unless they are envisaged as foreshadowing the future trend.

There is some family resemblance between augmentable capital goods and nonreproducible agents insofar as the owners of the latter stipulate a minimum income before permitting their property to be utilized: the difference is one of reserve prices rather than cost data. Analytically, however, this is more than a difference in degree, for, insofar as more units of the agent can be utilized as production and employment expand, this can be taken into account in deriving the Z-function; the "widening" use of fixed agents can be built into Z, while, with augmentability through production, time must elapse before the new equipment makes its appearance: the new equipment belongs to a Z-function for a later period.[26]

Ordinarily, the availability of more fixed factors as N grows must operate to taper the climb in Z. Insofar as it bestows a variable attribute on the factor class, it will serve to check the latter's earnings and place the factor in the variable category even though it may not enter into the variable costs of any individual firm; despite its heretical overtones, the argument is just as pertinent to land as to man-made agents. It is a fault of traditional analysis to have fostered the belief that landowners assent to a zero reserve price, so that even with nil earnings all of the area would be let to private productive use. It is at least conceivable that, at some rent levels, landowners might prefer keeping their holdings fallow, prohibiting their cultivation in the expectation of higher income in the future.[27]

Insofar as a factor is capable of being augmented, either through capital construction or from reserve holdings, a query arises as to whether they ought to be termed rent goods. Quasi-rents mark the reproducible variety whose expansion is limited to a later period; factors withheld from use until earnings attain acceptable levels appear to be in the twilight zone between fixed and variable agents.

[26] The case is thus analogous to that of continuous capital variations. (See Chapter 4.)

[27] User-cost aspects ought also to be recognized when current use affects, say, the future fertility of the land.

If a small boost in earnings leads to substantial changes in their availability, it might be preferable to denote them as variable agents, otherwise as fixed agents. This is a matter of classificatory ease rather than rooted principle, with the main test being one or normality.

DESTRUCTIBILITY OF RENT GOODS. Compared to augmentability phenomena, the analysis of the wasting away of fixed assets through depreciation and depletion involves a negative impact on the capital stock. For the population of fixed factors at any given time, like all populations, is subject to change through the dual tugs of birth and death, by construction and depreciation. Classical land was held immune to either process.

Economic analysis has been preoccupied mainly with the decay of the productive powers of nonhuman agents, although the same withering process affects human agents. Individually, their "depreciation reserve" is believed to reside in saving in years of high earning vitality to counterbalance the lean years when abilities dim and energies wane. Old-age pensions constitute an outside endeavor to cope with the failure of earning powers. Much more might be said; still, having paid deference to the existence of the principle in the human factor, let us, as is the fashion, proceed to the problem involved in the case of external objects of wealth.

So far as the economic attrition of fixed agents occurs merely from the passage of time, little more remains to be said: owners must allocate sums from earnings in order to protect their equity if they desire to preserve their individual wealth position intact. Factor services will go to the highest bidder; deductions by the owner (or his corporate agent) for capital loss are a personal matter in an enterprise economy where capital consumption is a legitimate objective. The far more interesting case concerns depreciation through use, where user-cost phenomena arise. Here, too, it is presumed that, in any given period, owners will let the factors to those able to maximize their earnings. User-cost estimates establish, in a sense, a reserve price; unless earnings outweigh the user-cost computations, the immediate exploitation of the factor will be checked.[28] Interestingly, where the agent is let out to be used, user-cost phenomena extending to periods beyond those covered by the

[28] Some problems of computing user cost remains. (See my *Price Theory*, pp. 378–381.)

payment agreement vanish from marginal-cost computations when the factor is not controlled by its owner, so that the agreed rental payments become in effect a fixed charge.[29] Utilization in any period will thus be pushed farther than if equipment (or land subject to soil depletion) is under the direct control of the owner. This is an important result, for it condemns some modes of tenancy as uneconomic for they foster a divergence between private and social costs.[30]

[29] This is especially true when the rental agreement covers only a single year. When it encompasses a longer interval, the user is an effective owner for this period, and calculations of user cost have some meaning for him.

These questions have tended to be overlooked in recent years. See A. C. Pigou, *Economics of Welfare*, Part II, Chapter IX, Section 7. W. Baumol, *Welfare Economics and the Theory of the State* (Cambridge, Harvard, 1952) has revived arguments for state intervention based on the discrepancies of private and social product, which Pigou developed in his earlier volume.

[30] Historically, economists have often criticized various modes of land tenure, particularly those involving absenteeism or the separation of ownership and use. The evils of the separation could be averted through rental agreements which cover a considerable period of time, for then it will be to the tenant's interest to calculate user cost with care. (See Marshall, *Principles*, p. 775. Also, Book VI, Chapter X.) For some recent studies, see D. Gale Johnson, "Resource Allocation Under Share Contracts," *Journal of Political Economy* (April 1950) and Roland R. Renne, "Land Tenure Reform as an Aspect of Economic Development in Asia," in *Economics and the Public Interest* (New Brunswick, New Jersey, Rutgers, 1955), Robert A. Solo, ed.

Chapter 10

Profits

If hypotheses constitute an invalid portrayal of reality, the deductions from them will betray the same defects. In economics this is never more apparent than when the profit share is examined. Marginal-productivity analysis commonly concluded that wages, rent, and interest would exhaust the total income of the firm, with the profit share conspicuous by its omission. Silence reigned not because of any deprecation of the importance of the entrepreneur but rather as a logical inference from the premises of a model in which entrepreneurial functions had vanished. In a world in which today is a replica of yesterday and an exact image of tomorrow, then with activity and resource organization invariant entrepreneurial energies are stilled, with neither scope nor space for maneuver. Routine eliminates the need for decisions; risk taking, organization, and co-ordination, usually pictured as the entrepreneurial burden, atrophy in this environment and the entrepreneur is at best transformed into a special type of wage earner or capitalist. Stationariness is thus a stultifying hypothesis, for it excludes the characteristic managerial actions and also precludes the emergence of a profit share.[1]

Opinion has consequently veered to the belief that profits are the handiwork of uncertainty and unexpected change. Stress has been laid on the unpredictability of the development, with profits viewed as a fortuitous return to entrepreneurs favored by a happy fortune with losses associated with unhappier outcomes. This conception of profit, generally tied to the name of Professor Knight, will largely be embraced here although at a few points some new accents can be imparted.[2]

[1] Compare Nicholas Kaldor, "The Equilibrium of the Firm," *Economic Journal* (1934).

[2] See F. H. Knight's *Risk, Uncertainty, and Profit* (New York, Houghton Mifflin, 1921). Schumpeter's views place firmer emphasis on "innovators" and "innovations" as the source of change and the well-spring of uncertainty.

Sometimes a conception of "normal" profits as an amount of earnings necessary to sustain an industry at "normal size" is proffered as an explanation of the persistence of the profit category even in relatively stable conditions. Snares have always been recognized in the content of "normality."[3] Yet the concept has been regarded as indispensable for depicting the flow of productive agents from fields of low potential earnings to areas of high income until the incentives to shift were eliminated. Profit is thus depicted as a functional share, with the entrepreneurs entitled to an income bite even under circular-flow conditions in order to assure the continuance of a normal batch of output and stabilize the existing number of firms within the particular industry. Confusion and inconsistency abounded whenever the actual entrepreneurial functions were described, for devoid of function neither the origin of profit nor the entrepreneur could be isolated.

Differences of ability among entrepreneurial agents have usually been recognized and often such disparities have been seized on as the source of "profits," with ordinary ability limited to a managerial wage. Considering the human source of such earnings, they ought well to be characterized as a differential wage accruing to heterogeneous labor of special skill or ability. Alternately, the earnings may be envisaged as a rent, for, though the sums redound to individuals for their personal services, the payments themselves go to heterogeneous fixed, albeit human, factors in each firm, with the magnitude drained out of the total revenue minus total variable-cost residual. The differential aspect is thus fully analogous to the Ricardian differential return to land of superior fertility, so that a separate profit category for this concept of earnings appears rather superflous.[4]

Sometimes the "normal" profit conception is presented as having a measurable objective counterpart, so that several well-meaning attempts to depict their normal size have ensued.[5] More recently, the

[3] See Joan Robinson, "What is Perfect Competition?," *Quarterly Journal of Economics* (November 1934), pp. 106–111.

[4] For an excellent recent appraisal of profit concepts, see J. Fred Weston, "The Profit Concept and Theory: A Restatement," *Journal of Political Economy* (April 1954). Arrived at independently, I am gratified to find that his treatment of profits as resulting from contractual phenomena conforms generally to the arguments of this chapter.

[5] The best known is that of Ralph Epstein, *Individual Profits in the United States* (National Bureau of Economic Research, 1934).

ideas have been construed as essentially subjective; profits are high if individuals consider them so and thereby implement entry decisions; they are low when exit is planned and departures are undertaken.[6] Normal profit concepts thus become as brittle or as rigid as the mental attitudes of those who hold them. Although this analysis becomes consistent with the theory of value, unless the argument is carefully drawn it will border on the tautological.

The term "pure" profits, concocted to describe entrepreneurial earnings in excess of wages of management and a return on "own-investment," becomes in a way the most barren pill of all, for such income vanishes after the factor flux so that its magnitude is always pressing toward zero as resource adaptations are executed. Where real wages or quasi-rents are inordinately high and induce new entry of labor or the construction of equipment, it has not been necessary to introduce a concept of "pure" wages or "pure" quasi-rent; yet the adaptive process pertains to all factors and is neither more valid nor more fascinating when applied to profits.

The thought can be put in another way: the theory of displacement costs is general enough to encompass all factors. It suggests resource reallocation whenever alternate use values surpass earnings in present outlets; hence the profit category is either universal, true of all factors and their adaptation, or superfluous for describing the readjustment. Where profits are associated with unexpected outcomes, even this concept is not in any way confined to a special entrepreneurial sect. Wage or salary recipients also face the smiles of fortune or the sorrows of disaster under the turn of imponderable events. Counting economic blessings or reciting woes is universal, applicable to all agents.

PROFITS AND CONTRACTS

Briefly, the functional concept of profits fails to perceive the crucial significance of contracts, the entrepreneurial pledges which bind all other income groups to him in his task of organizing and directing productive agents. It is this phenomenon of the economic

[6] Compare F. Machlup, *The Economics of Sellers' Competition* (Baltimore 1952), p. 258, for some illuminating remarks on "profits as seen by outsiders." Also see my *Price Theory*, pp. 117–118.

world which must be appraised, for, despite intermittent and casual mention, it has been virtually ignored in the profit literature.[7]

Contracts usually provide for a rigid temporal-payment plan, regardless of economic changes; bankruptcy courts, mutual consent, or expiry dates provide the only escape routes. It is in this fact, therefore, of the rigidity of the payment sequence despite economic change, which permits a profit concept to be forged. For the issue must be faced: on an instantaneous resource and payment adaptation, profits will be transformed into either rent or wage elements[8]; admitting lags in the adaptive-process profits are at best an ephemeral rather than a permanent income. It is the fact of "profit persistence" which constitutes the entrepreneurial goal and which invites analysis.

Business activity requires the contractual base in order to cope with the uncertainty attendant on economic change. Agreements fixed in time with compensations over an unknown, unchartered future are embraced so eagerly under private enterprise because, for one thing, without contracts the mere use of fixed instruments would compel their ownership. There is little doubt that this would impair the functioning of the economy by making it more cumbrous; financing would be confined almost wholly to the issuance of common stock—bonded indebtedness, for example, would be outlawed. As each change in the market value of instruments would create capital gains or inflict capital losses upon entrepreneurs, the latter

---

[7] As recent a study as that by Keirstead, who regards himself as a follower of Knight, fails, so far as I can see, even to mention the word "contract" in his 110 pages, much less assign to it the importance it deserves. (See his *Essay.*) Knight, however, does point up the use of contracts and the implications for profits. Early in his development, Knight argues that uncertainty creates entrepreneurial specialists who are willing to accept the burdens of uninsurable risks, placing nonentrepreneurial agents "under his sole direction for a fixed contract price." (*Op. cit.*, p. 245.) At several places the distinction between contractual and noncontractual income is made. (See pp. 271–272, 277, 284–285, 344. See also, the Bibliographical Note at the end of this chapter.)

[8] In a dynamic model without rigid contracts there will be a revaluation of resources with every supply-demand shift, affecting some incomes favorably and others adversely. Each favorable revaluation—a capital gain, really, for nonhuman agents—could be denoted as a profit, if we must cling to the term. But wage, interest, and rent categories would seem to exhaust the income types, with any earnings enhancement appearing more in the nature of a "producer's surplus" rather than a profit.

undoubtedly would face greater risks than under lease forms which spread the income participation more widely and localize the burdens with those most willing to shoulder them.

Consider the main types of contracts which are of practical significance: (1) rental agreements for use of land, buildings, and equipment, (2) interest and amortization schedules on financial borrowing, and, in a nonintegrated economy, (3) price agreements covering purchases of materials from other firms. Wage contracts may be omitted from this list, for, although the wage rate may be fixed for a year or longer through collective-bargaining agreements, the hire contract itself normally is subject to quick abrogation, within a week or two, so that labor hire is tied effectively to the firm's current output.[9] Rental contracts covering land or buildings generally run for a lengthy time interval.[10]

Contracts for use, rather than outright purchase of necessary equipment, are consummated, for one reason, partly as a matter of liquidity, in the event that those using the factor should want to divest themselves of it at a foreseen cost. Speculative valuations attached to an asset by virtue of long-run forecasts may also render purchase agreements prohibitive; loft space in centrally located urban slum areas provides a case in point: differences in capital valuations may thus impede ownership transfer while rental agreements become a feasible and equitable solution. A parallel argument applies to borrowed funds; deprived of managerial responsibility, lenders prefer the assurance of agreed interest and principal repayment to the uncertain quasi-rent pattern evolving out of ownership and alternating market fortunes.

Diversity of forecasts and risk aversion thus account for con-

[9] Severance pay introduces a minor complication.

[10] Thus, if labor were to obtain a guaranteed annual wage, labor costs would be more in the nature of fixed costs. As it would increase the size of the firm's commitments, it would introduce a new rigidity, particularly formidable for new firms. Its chief merit would appear to be one of insuring a greater degree of income stability within the economy—an advantage of only indirect benefit to the firm and meaningful to it only if the practice were fairly universal. See the analysis of Alvin Hansen and Paul Samuelson, "Economic Analysis of Guaranteed Wages," in *Guaranteed Wages* (Report to the President, Office of War Mobilization and Reconversion, January 31, 1947), Murray Latimer, Director, Appendix F. Also, W. Leontief, "The Pure Theory of the Guaranteed Annual Wage Contract," *Journal of Political Economy* (February 1946).

tractual modes of hire; simple reasons to explain the duration of contracts also come to mind. For one thing, the contractual time interval must at least permit revenue plans to ripen after overcoming initial costs and, perhaps, losses. For example, a farmer plowing and seeding a field will require tenancy at least through most of the harvest season. A firm constructing a building will require a ground lease sufficiently long to insure recovery of principal as well as interest on the capital cost. Beyond this, duration will hinge on a complex of forces, representing the divergent pulls of the optimism and the pessimism of the participants as they bargain and compromise on what is reconcilable in the light of alternatives.

Once contracts appear in the economy, a profit trail is almost inevitable. Any change in economic conditions from the expectations on which the contracts were based will establish some deviation between imputed values and contractual earnings, and it is this discrepancy which creates profits—or losses. For if a firm has agreed to pay an annual rental of $10,000 for a building whose imputed value is now estimated at $15,000, a profit of $5,000 is imminent. And these profits will endure over the life of the agreement unless contractual and market values coincide. Simultaneously with the profit flurry there will be offsetting losses: principals favorably affected have their counterparts in adversity, of the opposite contractual party whose income will be deflated because the economic value of the factor exceeds its contractual price.[11] In this interpretation profits breed a mutual litter of losses: whether the outcome is viewed benignly or as a subject of reproach depends in part on where we stand in the economic process. Conventionally, the focus is on the entrepreneur rather than on his contractual adversary, so that their fortunes are disregarded.[12]

[11] This seems to suggest an "exploitation" aspect of profits in the difference between contractual and imputed values. Losses would then have to be interpreted as an exploitation of the entrepreneur by the other contractual parties.

Exploitation theories of the past will not be discussed in this chapter, which largely aims at a positive statement of profit theory rather than a critical evaluation of the existing literature. The Marxian exploitation argument is, in my view, unpromising for explaining the profit magnitudes in a dynamic economy, where equilibrium adaptations are uncommon.

[12] The same principle could be extended to loan agreements where the pledged interest commitments exceed or fall short of the ensuing quasi-rents

Profits, to conclude, represent the unexpected surpluses ascribable to unforeseen demand-cost changes which, in degree, contradict the premises on which the agreements have been based.[13] Coterminous with the profits resulting from this ex post divergence of imputations from ex ante contractual income splits, there are losses: if landlords earn too little, entrepreneurs earn too much, and vice versa. This difference between contractual payment and imputed value as the profit-source fits the ordinary conceptions rather neatly, for usually it is assumed that businessmen as a group are shrewder in judgment and in bargaining than are those with whom they deal, so that profits, as defined, accrue to them. Against the functional view that profits abound only in the interstices of transition and adaptation, the contractual profit base may be temporally enduring well beyond any Marshallian long-period adaptations. Many real world firms undoubtedly owe their felicitous position, despite antiquated equipment and techniques, to favorable rent bargains which enable them to survive competition from firms with more favorable variable cost experience: profits due to this cause thus need not be "annihilated" by new entry.[14]

A MACROECONOMIC VIEW OF PROFITS

Major economic change, if money-wage rates especially never changed and full employment were always maintained, would be attributable largely to innovations, whose importance Schumpeter was to underscore for modern economics. Even if activity did not show precipitate variations in time, a record for accurate prevision would be unlikely to be sustained. Mistakes place a premium on devices to cope with the uncertainty and contracts become an obvious medium. Profits inevitably emerge thereafter as an institu-

---

out of which contractual stipulations are met. (This presumes that the funds are borrowed to finance the acquisition and the control of identifiable items of equipment.)

[13] Profits of innovation, to be discussed shortly, might appear to contradict this proposition. Yet if all participants who enter into contracts with the innovator did foresee the demand-cost changes, "profits" would vanish. The successful innovator foresees more clearly than others, or is more fortunate than they. Contracts which on a retrospective view are prized by one party must be regarded as unwitting by the other.

[14] To use Schumpeter's vivid word.

tional phenomenon when the developments embodied in the contracts follow an imperfectly predicted course.[15]

Once change is conceded, it is improbable that its dimensions can be precisely plotted ex ante, and the result must be a proliferation of profits and their inner shadow, losses, through the economy. Explanation of profits as a logical imperative leads to an examination of the causes of economic change first in the simplest circumstances when unemployment and fluctuating activity are assumed away. We need not labor the obvious: fluctuating activity imperfectly foreseen can generate profits and losses as results turn out worse, in an output sense, or better than anticipated. With perpetual full employment, changes can be reflected only in the structure or the composition of total output—never in its magnitude, unless economic growth is envisaged with a mounting labor force always occupied.

In Schumpeter's view, which was simultaneously the implicit argument of those who fashioned long-period analyses, a profit annihilation characterized the stationary economy.[16] Innovations in either products or techniques would disrupt the circular flow until new firms organized resources and emulated the successful entrepreneurs, challenging their monopoly position and supplanting the old stationary circuit with a new one. Meanwhile, profits would redound to the innovator; being first on the scene, he would reap the income harvest. Profit, for Schumpeter, thus comported itself as a sort of guardian angel of progress, inspiring entrepreneurial efforts and adding new dimensions to the course of economic development. Once novelty waned, with innovation transformed into routine, the inflow of resources would destroy profit pockets. This was the essence of the process: the chronic quest of greater, more imaginative souls inspired innovation, monopoly, and profits, while the tireless mimicry of lesser men soon whittled the profit excess away.

In terms of our conceptual scheme, this signifies that, at a fixed N-level and W-magnitude (with some slight reservations for in-

---

[15] Conceivably, the actual world might be stationary while forecasts were of change; this, too, could create disappointments, though it is unlikely that the outlook will continually anticipate change while phenomena continue stationary.

[16] *The Theory of Economic Development*, R. Opie, translator, Chapter IV.

terest and user cost), innovation might modify Z, though an important share of the decisive income shifts would come out of the new partitioning of the Z-W-discrepancy. Contractual obligations of decaying industries now supplanted would tend to become worthless, while innovating firms could enjoy surpluses surpassing even the optimistic contractual foundations on which the innovating dreams were based.

The analysis need not be pushed further. It is clear that, if the N-level is fixed and the Z-W-functions are unchanged, innovations create profits only by altering the composition of output and the structure of rentier-entrepreneurial claims. Similarly, besides the innovations in products and productive techniques, changes in tax laws, or statutory provisions circumscribing production, have the same typical offshoots, impairing some income positions and promoting others. And these changes, when they redound to the income benefit or detriment of the entrepreneur, implant either profits or losses. Changes in the degree of competition belong to the same family of phenomena.

All of these changes can be included under the embracing, if not always revealing, garb of "innovations." So long as total output (in employment terms) is constant, innovation alone, by definition, can enhance profit, for all change then is described as innovation. And when monopoly is part of the initial scene, innovations can be construed as covering sales as well as production techniques. Prospective innovations in all these dimensions thicken the uncertainty curtain covering ex ante contractual negotiations.

Although the residual noncontractual sum R is regarded by entrepreneurs as the gross profit category which they must be intent on maximizing, the concept ought to be partially distilled to envelop the case of "own-factors." For insofar as the entrepreneurs' own-plant, land, personal managerial services, and capital funds are used, the provisional solution would be to impute to each of the separable agents their going market value in interest, wages, and rent, so that, barring any contracts whatsoever, only if the full proceeds are not absorbed by imputation could any remainder be labeled as "differential" profits. Compartmentalizing income in this case, however, is a rather empty sport; if it must be done, the residual profit sum can be resolved ordinarily into differential wages, rent, or monopoly revenue.

ACTIVITY AND PROFITS. Zero profits would entail that all firms, lenders, and resource owners generally, correctly perceive the employment level and the Z-W-gap. Contracts consequently would stipulate for the full economic rent of fixed agents, eliminating profits as an income source. Long-period equilibrium thus would require that, for each time interval comprising the contract span, the level of activity is prognosticated accurately by all participants and the full-value imputations of factors is allotted properly by contract.[17]

Merely to state the problem in this way is to acknowledge the inevitability of the profit residual. For it is virtually impossible for all firms and factor owners to gauge activity precisely even when a trend is discernible, let alone the oscillations, surges, and relapses of actual phenomena. Each interlude would have to be foreseen and embodied in the document of income understanding. The severity of this condition—and it is severe when we examine the common forecasts of economic activity—is enough to shatter the image of "long-period equilibrium" in an economy subject to income and employment vicissitudes and circumscribed in its operation by the need for lengthy contractual obligations. In an economic system which instantaneously adapted itself to change, profits, it is true, would be erased, surviving only the temporal moments when the adjustment was incomplete, being ground out as the adaptations were consummated. As a persistent share, profits then would appear only if the economy remained forever in the grip of autonomous demand-cost changes and lagging adaptations. On the other hand, with contracts as the pervasive fact of private enterprise, and change a ubiquitous element of economic life, profits are never absent or obliterated except in the illusory régime of stationary fantasy or own-product organization.

Thus the contractual stress relies much less on chronic change as the generator of perpetual profits than the uncertainty factors underlying agreements. Whether change is continuous or merely intermittent and occasional, so long as agreements are written with change imperfectly foreseen, then profits will always be interspersed among firms in the economy and will constitute one of the enduring income categories of reality. Even the dismantlement of all barriers

[17] An appropriate time interval would consist of the clock time during which the Z,N-level and the underlying demand and cost data were constant.

to entry would thus not eradicate all profits, according to this view.[18] To argue otherwise involves some misreading of the accounts of businessmen and the calculations of accountants which, on this topic, have been too much ignored by economists.

It will serve some purpose, in rounding out this discussion, to enumerate the causes of profits on a macroeconomic view of the economy. Reverting to the diagram of Fig. 15 in Chapter 3, with given Z- and W-functions and the associated aggregate-demand relations, any force which leads to a rewriting of FF' will alter the profit sum; new and clearer prevision by resource owners and entrepreneurs can lie at the bottom of this. Further, with given fixed-payment relations, any cause which leads to a shift in Z relative to W will have the same result: this can be ascribed to innovation or to the endogenous installation of new equipment in view of interest phenomena (relative to wages) or to a revised degree of monopoly power. Apart from shifts in the functions relative to one another, a change in the level of activity will lead to the same outcome. A rise in D_i, say, or in government expenditure, or an autonomous variation in the consumption-expenditure curve or in the entrepreneurial pay-out function of undistributed profits, kR, can create greater profits through modifying the activity level. Further, an alteration in the level of money wages, diverting income from rentiers, can also have the same result. In terms of systematic treatment of the functions, this appears to be all that needs to be said. By refining the Z-W-discrepancy further, isolating changes in the corporate tax bill, in variable-interest charges, in depreciation and depletion allowances, etc., the profit aggregate can be shown to be affected further through these variations. In sum, the level of employment, the level of proceeds, the nature of fixed contracts, the money-wage level, the amount of fixed capital, the productivity of labor, and the degree of monopoly power all have some influence on and govern the profit level. Variations in any of these elements are capable of modifying the profit aggregate available for disbursement among the individual firms comprising the economy.

PROFITS, OPTIMISM, AND RESOURCE ALLOCATION. Although it is often merely a vivid embellishment, not always consistent with the

[18] Compare the emphasis on entry as a competitive force reducing profits by Machlup, *op. cit.*, Parts III–IV.

body of economic doctrine, profits are often portrayed as the chariot which drives the economic process and guides the flow of resources.[19] Indisputably, profits furnish ex post evidence of bargaining shrewdness, good fortune, or both, for those who emerge with the tangible rewards of pecuniary success in the uncertain, unpredictable economic development.[20] They are a visible reflection of a process now completed and imperfectly foreseen originally when the binding agreements were reached.

It is a caricature of economic analysis to insist that profits are the key to resource use: with full certainty, with prices and costs known, profits are simply nonexistent so that rents comprise the residual-income category whose earnings are maximized. In the certain world it would be the owners of all valuable agents, rather than entrepreneurs as such, who would seek out the avenues of highest income so that entrepreneurial action is superfluous.[21] The theory of displacement costs amply describes the equilibrating resource shuffle. Thus it is the price-cost mechanism and the search for maximum wages, rent, and interest which establishes equilibrium in the stationary flow economy.

In the uncertain and changing economy, all resource owners, by the very nature of contracts and earnings potential, must adopt an ex ante forward-looking attitude toward the future outcome; current profits, on any of the common definitions, provide at best only evidence of past structural distortion and scant hint to the future. It would be an unwise—and rare?—entrepreneur who would examine the higher earnings presently ruling in line A and implement a decision to enter without appraising the likelihood of future changes.[22]

[19] Compare the criticisms of this view by Weston, *op. cit.*, p. 158. Also, his article, "A Generalized Uncertainty Theory of Profit," *American Economic Review* (March 1950), pp. 57–60, and the comments by A. Murad and J. A. Stockfisch in the March 1951 issue.

[20] Compare A. Alchian, "Uncertainty, Evolution, and Economic Theory," *Journal of Political Economy* (June 1950).

[21] Compare Wicksell, *Lectures on Political Economy*, E. Classen, translator, Volume I, p. 109, where he explains that either the laborer or the landlord may be the entrepreneur. This is the only view consistent with the stationary setting.

[22] To explore the decision-making process would entail a study beyond our immediate needs. A full investigation would have to appraise entrepreneurial

In the uncertain world, the economic value of machinery, building and land sites, or even of salaried personnel, would accrue to factor owners only if they had correct prevision of economic events and bargained successfully. Alternately, income payments could be assigned on an ex post glance, after the facts were known. Unfortunately, the ex post resolution evades the issue; it could never arbitrate the initial competing and conflicting claims for the use of economic agents while anticipatory omniscience, in the nature of things, is sheerly a mythical solution.

This has some profound and disturbing implications, for it does suggest that the entrepreneurs who are most optimistic—or oligopolists who are willing to face temporary losses with equanimity to deny factors to potential competitors—and willing to bid highest for factors will ordinarily secure the use of the resoures. Victory in the race for organization and production may belong not to the most efficient and most prescient but rather to the most sanguine or even, occasionally, the most prodigal.

It might be contended that, when resources revert to the control of the more optimistic, the effect is only on income division, so that results do not really matter much from an allocative standpoint. This would err on two counts: the argument would be valid only if those most cheerful in anticipation, and willing to bid highest, are those with the best foresight. This need not follow; resource uses which are shut out by virtue of a low bid may still prove most desirable on an ex post view. Secondly, once the income division is molded, this in itself influences final demand, so that, on the interdependent roundabout, the resource allocation and output composition will be affected.

Contractual ties and commitments in resource use thus furnish

stimuli in the form of product-price and factor cost-productivity anticipations, of probability estimates, and of the conviction with which the surmises are held. Further, it would have to inquire whether decision-making is in nature more subjective and amenable to techniques such as that of focus gains and losses described by G. L. S. Shackle, in his *Expectation in Economics* (Cambridge Univ. Press, 1949). The whole topic borders on the psychological and the philosophical, and bristles with difficulties. It is doubtful whether economists alone can provide the answer except for a fully rational—and artificial—man. Rational man probably would use all the known techniques—plus some still undiscovered—with the disquieting prospect that all action would probably be stifled in the mere contemplation of rational behavior!

another illustration of the importance of subjective attitudes in deciding the nature and the extent of want-satisfaction. It is part of the argument which stresses the judgment of planners—entrepreneurs under capitalism—in resolving the great debate on the efficiency of capitalism and socialism as instruments of economic welfare.[23] Resource use must be fixed up in advance, upon some estimate of future demand and productivity. Mistakes are inevitable; the need to gauge the future on the basis of imperfect current information is the lot of worldly man and the bane of economic plans: it is bound to generate some resource waste.

The one salvageable conclusion from the typical approach to the problem of resource allocation is that only under reasonably stationary conditions are factors likely to be used efficiently in accordance with the models of pure competition and welfare theories. In a changing economy, efficient resource use can never be known—only guessed at in advance—with infallible advice given only ex post. As matters stand, in an enterprise economy resources will flow to, and their use will be guided by, those most optimistic about the outlook and in a financial position to support their ideas with factor-price bids: in cases of economic warfare, even the optimism vanishes and financial strength and strategy take over.[24] Resources thus tend to entrepreneurs whose wealth position permits them to support ventures of more or less promise without fear of ruin in the event of miscalculation. In this light, perhaps the most surprising fact of all is that the economy does work as well as observation indicates; the reason probably is that even "wrong" guesses of sales possibilities are not "too wrong" but are kept within reasonable bounds. The better the prevision, however, the closer the economy will come to the images of formal theory.

THE SHARING OF PROFITS

A final topic concerns the sharing of profits which, in the orthodox view, accrue to the entrepreneur. The very reference to the entrepreneur requires his identification—and he has proved an elusive figure to track down.

The entrepreneurial function embraces the planning of the sphere,

[23] Compare Hicks, *Value and Capital*, pp. 139–140.
[24] See my *Price Theory*, pp. 173–178.

the scope, the site, and the work flow within the firm—it includes the amassing of funds; the choice of products; the design and the layout of the plant; the production, hire, and marketing policy; and, not least awesome, the formulation of price policy. In the repetitive stationary model, these matters do not create any hardship; once the dynamics of change are pondered, the entrepreneurial functions loom as indeed formidable, with issues and the need for decisions at almost every turn.

Merely to list the entrepreneurial functions in a realistic way serves to confirm the impossibility of confining them to any one individual. Obviously, in the typical firm, the tasks must be delegated and dispersed. Sometimes it is argued that the common stockholder who elects the directorate of the firm shoulders the final enterpreneurial burden and authority. But this is like charging each individual citizen with the ultimate conduct of foreign policy; because of the imperfections of democracy in general, and the democracy of corporate control in particular, this attempt to personify the entrepreneur seems highly insecure. It seems safest to conclude that everyone who contributes to corporate policy exercises some entrepreneurial authority. The group thus has several centers, and several overlaps, with power sometimes concentrated in one and at other times passing to other hands. Yet this is not to say that everyone who makes decisions becomes a profit beneficiary. The entrepreneurial function is directed and executed with an eye toward profit making; *the sharing of profits is an entirely separate issue*. Usually those responsible for the major entrepreneurial decisions will participate in the cutting of the profit pie, although still others who are but remotely connected with the policy actions may become heir apparent to the earnings accumulations. In short, the performance of the function does not insure a profit correlative, just as workers and wage recipients could differ in a slave economy. Entrepreneurial actions result in profits; profit-sharing presents some transfer aspects.[25]

Under small-scale single proprietorship, both ownership and decision-making are centralized and combined, so that the simple picture is apt. To imagine one person performing all the necessary tasks in a large corporation is to prescribe a herculean task that

[25] Compare Joseph Schumpeter, *Business Cycles* (New York, McGraw, 1939), Volume I, p. 106.

cannot be fulfilled even remotely. The divergence between the proprietorship conception and the corporate facts has sometimes elicited the opinion that there are two profit theories.[26] This seems to place an undue stress on the identification of the entrepreneurial function and the derivation of a simultaneous profit reward. Corporate- and personal-income taxes have by now validated the proposition that the rendering of service can be separated in part from the amassing of earnings.

In the division of profits, it is tempting to argue that there are haphazard and erratic factors rather than general and immutable forces at work. In the typical corporation, after depreciation charges, about one half of the earnings are siphoned off to meet tax claims, with about half of the remainder devoted to dividends. Most of the withholdings, sooner or later, are diverted to plant expansion, undertaken indirectly in the interests of owners—though they might protest the solicitude of management in their behalf, if given the opportunity. Other sums, which are also properly identifiable as profits, will go to swell managerial salaries and endow generous pension and welfare programs, while still other sums will go in much the same way as employee bonuses and welfare payments. Still other amounts, as by a monopolist, may be disbursed to compensate labor above market rates to avoid the embarrassment of riches. With excess-profits taxation in effect, this is even more likely, for the cost involved, for the greater part, is at the expense of the Treasury tax-take rather than dividends or retained earnings. Through some of these channels, variable costs will be inflated compared to strict efficiency criteria.

The analysis need not be pursued further. The essential point is that, even after profits are identified properly, it is implausible and inaccurate to suggest that they will be amassed by a single and separable person or group performing a unique and unitary function. This can happen only under the tautology of definition. This resolution, to be sure, imparted a beautiful simplicity to the traditional classification which distinguished the four productive agents and then bent and fitted income to each, even though the separa-

[26] Latest in this line is Peter Bernstein, "Profit Theory—Where Do We Go from Here?", in *Quarterly Journal of Economics* (August 1953). Bernstein also adds a third category, the rentier, "to whom profit is interchangeable with interest" (p. 408).

tion of labor and entrepreneur, or capital and land, was often forced and false, and the imputation of identifiable income was mistaken, even in the stationary picture ordinarily drawn.

CONCLUSION. If the traditional conception of profits cannot be the driving force for resource adaptation, the contractual conception, which makes no such claims, does at least fare better in conforming to popular views, including those of the businessman, the accountant, and, not least, the tax collector. That profits on either view constitute the residual, exhausting the distributive total, is of academic rather than of practical significance.

More important than the determinateness aspect is the relation of realized profits, resource organization, and innovation. In other than stationary circumstances, resource organization is the consequence of invention and the evidence of innovation, and so need not be examined separately. Indubitably, the pursuit of profits serves to promote interruptions in the stationary flow while their realization contributes to the furtherance of the dynamic ways. That the expectation rather than the realization of profits evokes investment is also undeniable: all that is required is that profits be permitted to be earned freely as a result of activity, not that they be of any particular size over any given time interval. Once profits are amassed, they are available to finance new ventures by the firm, for it is new ventures, new paths that *may* be profitable; well-worn ones are likely to yield only standard earnings, of rent, wages, and interest, and do not excite entrepreneurial talent. Creating new and untried products or techniques is something else again, for here cleverness and good fortune can yield a rich harvest.[27] It is thus that profits constitute a mechanism for change, which is—may be—the road to progress, where the changes are viewed as desirable. In the stationary scheme, on the other hand, the function of profits cannot be a serious matter. Too, without a contractual base, profits would be highly ephemeral and unable to animate the grandiose plans which literally move mountains and drain oceans.

The main bar in the way of the profit theory outlined, as the difference between the outcome of enterprise activity and the contractual income-payment base on which the activity has been pred-

[27] Compare Schumpeter's penetrating discussion of "creative destruction" in his *Capitalism, Socialism and Democracy* (New York, Harper, 1950, 3rd ed.), Chapter VII.

icated, is likely to reside in its rejection of a "long-run" income norm as the motivating quantity. Yet this ought not prove to be an insuperable barrier. Decision-making is the indispensable and vital function, as inexorable in a collectivistic régime as in a capitalistic society. In an enterprise economy, so long as those charged with economic power possess confidence that their actions will cover the layers of equity and debenture claims and satisfy the prestige vanities and the income aspirations of managerial groups, then there is every reason to expect the display of entrepreneurial prowess and the flash of its dynamics. But note, the field and its prospects must be favorable. Equity claimants must find promise of income fulfillment that is at least equal to alternative opportunities. Managerial (= entrepreneurial) agents must see the glimmer of returns, in income advantage and social position, sufficient to preclude alternative actions even though the ultimate outcome does not wholly coincide with these expectations.[28] Hope and promise must remain, and be realized often enough to instill enthusiasm and induce action.

APPENDIX: A BIBLIOGRAPHICAL NOTE

Aside from the several references to contracts in his earlier volume, in his much later article on "Profit" (reprinted in *Readings in the Theory of Income Distribution,* from which the following quotation is taken) Professor Knight observes that: "Any study of profits must recognize discrepancies between contractual costs and income in both directions . . ." (p. 541; see also p. 538). Yet, despite Knight's clear awareness of the part played by contracts, the tradition following him has perpetuated the belief that unexpected change constitutes the source of profits, and that they are eroded through rather rapid equilibrium adaptations. Hence, contractual commitments have often not even been deemed worthy of mention. Professor Knight's exposition is partly to blame for this, for

[28] It is here that I find some difficulty with Weston's definition of profits. He suggests, I think, that if ex ante forecasts are confirmed by ex post results, then profits do not arise. This would involve the fantastic conclusion that, if the owner of a newsstand anticipates earnings of $1 billion per annum, and the outcome is less, then by definition profits have not been realized. What alone seems necessary, I think, is that the outcome is different from the sums necessary to satisfy contractual commitments and any alternative use value for "own-factors." Profits then appear, though they may differ from the original hopes and fears.

he remarks that contractual residuals are apt to be ephemeral "aberrations" or "imperfections," rather than more enduring profit sources, as argued here. (See, for example, p. 539.)

As a sample of the neglect of contractual aspects, L. M. Fraser, in his fine and detailed exposition of *Economic Thought and Language* (London, Black, 1937) fails even to mention them in his pages dealing with the subject. On the textbook level, taking a generally excellent representative, Boulding states that "normal profit . . . can best be defined as the least sum which must be paid to the capitalist to persuade him to allow his capital to be used in the process" (*Economic Analysis*, p. 531). It would seem that this income is more properly a rent rather than a profit. In contrast, Weston consistently brings the contractual aspect to the fore, after defining profit as "the difference between the bases upon which the decision-makers choose between alternative courses of action to enter into contractual commitments and the actual outcomes which are experienced" (*op. cit.*, p. 158). Although this particular definition has been criticized in the closing footnote to this chapter, there is no dispute over the fundamental part played by contracts. Compare also some remarks in Triffin (*op. cit.*, pp. 178–179). Raymond T. Bowman, in undertaking a largely statistical study, adopted the contract view as the basic concept, declaring that "all individuals who receive income the amount of which was not definitely contracted for in advance may be said to receive profits"—*A Statistical Study of Profits* (Philadelphia, Univ. of Pa. Press, 1934), p. 4n. A view of profits similar to Keirstead's, as the difference between ex ante estimates and ex post results, is expressed by G. L. S. Shackle, *Uncertainty in Economics*, Chapter VIII.

Index